GET RID OF HIM

JOYCE L. VEDRAL, Ph.D.

WARNER BOOKS

A Time Warner Company

Warner Books, Inc., 1271 Avenue of the Americas, New York, NY 10020
w A Time Warner Company

Printed in the United States of America
First printing: January 1993
10 9 8 7 6 5 4 3 2 1

Library of Congress Cataloging-in-Publication Data

Vedral, Joyce L.
  Get rid of him / Joyce L. Vedral.
     p.   cm.
  Includes bibliographical references.
  ISBN 0-446-51668-6
  1. Interpersonal relations.   2. Self-actualization (Psychology)
3. Relationship addiction. I. Title.
HM132.V39   1993
302—dc20   91-51168
                                     CIP

Book design by Giorgetta Bell McRee

To the women of the nineties, who insist that a relationship, in order to be worthwhile, must be nourishing, and who have the self-esteem to "get rid of him" if it is not. And to all the men we've loved before—and left. From the bottom of our hearts, we wish you well.

ACKNOWLEDGMENTS

To Joann Davis, for your endless enthusiasm and astute editing.

To Jeanmarie LeMense for your cheerful, good-natured assistance.

To Julia Kushnirsky and Jackie Merri Meyer for your willingness to go the extra mile in working on the cover art.

To Larry Kirshbaum, Nanscy Neiman, and Ellen Herrick, for your continual enthusiasm and support.

To Edna Farley, for your talented handling of the publicity.

To the hundreds of women from all over the United States, who have shared their stories with me for this book.

To Don Banks for your sensitive photography.

To Jodi Pollutro for helping me—by your skillful hair and make-up work—to look like the way I feel.

To Liz Williams, a woman who runs with the wolves—you are the meaning of this book!!

To family and friends for your continual love and support.

To the men—all of them—the wonderful men, and the not so wonderful men—for teaching me some important lessons about myself.

CONTENTS

PREFACE

I was married at the age of twenty-three—a product of the fabulous fifties. By the standards of the time, I was a rebel—or so I thought. After all, I was practically the only girl in the senior class who didn't get married upon high school graduation. And protesting the trend, I attended college, insisting that I wanted to be somebody, not just somebody's wife.

But it wasn't too long after college graduation that I got nervous and got married. Looking back, I realize I felt exactly the way I did as a child when we used to play musical chairs. When it got down to one chair, and the music was started up again, I would eye my competitor with malevolence and say to myself, "It's either you or me, and it isn't going to be me," and I would lunge for the chair.

That's why I got married at twenty-three, to a wonderful man—but a man who was completely wrong for me. All my friends were getting married, and I felt in danger of being an old maid. So I grabbed for what I perceived to be that last chair.

Unable to admit my mistake (although I knew it a week after the honeymoon), I remained in that marriage for ten years—because I believed that divorce was morally wrong and an admission of failure.

During my married years, I limped along, trying to sublimate my frustration and emptiness—but I was failing in my efforts. I had gained over thirty pounds (I went from ninety-eight to one hundred and twenty-nine pounds) and looked more matronly at twenty-nine than I do now, at forty-eight. I was unhappy and unfulfilled, but I felt too guilty and too insecure to leave a marriage that was comfortable and safe. After all, my husband was stable—and, what's more, he was a religious man, a minister. What could be more ignominious than to divorce a man of the cloth?

Did it matter that even my meager schoolteacher's salary was more than double his? Did it matter that his stern, authoritarian demeanor was a daily dose of cold water upon my mischievous free spirit? Did it matter that I married him for all the wrong reasons— among them that I was looking for someone to take care of me—a fatherlike figure?

Divorcing my husband was truly one of the most difficult things I've ever done. Even now, looking back on my life and thinking of all my accomplishments since the divorce—achieving a Ph.D. in English Literature from New York University; working two jobs (high school English teacher and adjunct professor of English at Pace University); making the decision to refuse to go over the hill, and embarking on a physical-fitness program that eventually transformed my cellulite-ridden body and led me to write best-selling fitness books, plus self-help books for teens—none of this—no—none of this was as difficult as finding the courage to leave my husband, to walk away from my marriage and dare to make it on my own.

How do I know this? The answer comes to me loud and clear, every time someone looks at me with admiration and says, "Joyce, you've led such an interesting life. You've taken so many chances and accomplished so much. Tell me, what is the most courageous thing you've ever done?" And each time, my mind, like a high-speed computer, scans my life, and each time, the answer is the same: divorce. Nothing can compare to the inner strength it took to walk away from my marriage.

It is very difficult to leave a man whom you've come to depend upon—a husband or a long-term lover—to pull yourself out of a relationship that has been fused by time and routine, one that you may have allowed to become the basis of your security. It is difficult—but not impossible. Although the price is high, you may well discover in the following pages that it's well worth it.

For many women, it is also difficult to leave relationships of short duration—those which have lasted only weeks or months. But in many cases it is necessary, because several of these brief negative liaisons, when added up, tend to steal your time, your energy, and indeed your life.

I myself have had to walk away from a variety of wrong relationships. It took practice. I realized that I must not marry the doctor to whom I became engaged on the rebound—a critical, judgmental man whom I was determined to marry to prove to the imaginary audience I perceived to be judging me that I could indeed get a substantial husband. I also wanted someone to lean on—someone to help me take care of my child. In the end, I opted not to sell my soul to the devil—not to give up my freedom and potential destiny for the comfort of immediate security.

After making other mistakes and wasting more precious time and energy, I have learned to be discriminating. I have discovered ways to more quickly identify the kinds of men described in chapters two through thirteen of this book, and I have learned, when appropriate, to walk away from them after days or weeks rather than years.

Please don't misunderstand. I have a great deal of affection for men. I've been involved with many people I've liked and am open to perhaps one day meeting a man who would compliment my life—and I his. But if I don't, I know that I can make it on my own. It's a lot more fun being alone and adventurous than being stuck in the mire with the wrong man.

Get Rid of Him is intended as a lifeline to women of all ages. I offer it as a message to my sisters—women of every race, culture, and philosophy. Stop wasting your time with a relationship that is draining your life rather than enhancing it. Get rid of him: Life is too short for it not to be special.

Too late, you say? Not as late as it will be ten years from now. Even if you've wasted two-thirds of your life, why not experience a quality last third? It's not just the beginning that counts, but the end too. Take inspiration from the women in this book, some of them still in college, others in their sixties, who listened to the voice inside that said, "Get rid of him."

In closing this preface, I quote from my favorite psychologist, Carl G. Jung, in whom I feel a kindred spirit. I quote this passage from his autobiography because it expresses a truth about the way I have tried to live my life:

> I have offended many people, for as soon as I saw that they did not understand me, that was the end of the matter as far as I was concerned. I had to move on. . . . I had to obey an inner law which was imposed on me.[1]

You too may find that some of your choices will be offensive to some or even many people. But for the sake of your life, I am rooting for you to make them. I am hoping that you will be able to get in contact with that inner law that guides each and every one of us—that patient, gentle voice which persists in whispering, again and again, until we hear its message. And I'm hoping that you too will find the courage to move on when the time comes.

NOTES

1. Carl G. Jung, *Memories, Dreams, Reflections,* ed. Anelia Jaffe (New York: Vintage Books, 1965), pp. 356–357.

1

Get Rid of Him

You've read all the books. By now you're an expert. You know how to get a man, how to keep a man, and how to please a man. What you don't know, however, may be the most important advice you'll ever need: how to get rid of a man—a man who is bad for you—one who in a big or even small way is stealing your time, your energy, and, in effect, your life.

Who Should Read This Book?

I've written this book for both unmarried and married women. It is for those of you who are in or have been in relationships or marriages of weeks, months, or years. By reading this book you will be able to:

1. Comfort yourself that you are not alone in your situation;
2. Learn from the experiences of those women who stayed in dead relationships and take inspiration from other happier women who walked out of negative ones;
3. Take a hard look at a relationship that is good but could be better (keep this book on the side, just in case he gets stupid);
4. And determine the basic requirements for a man who can be right for you.

What This Book Is Not and What This Book Is

This is not a book about codependency. There are plenty of twelve-step books out there, books that can walk you through every phase of addiction. Nor is this a workbook filled with time-consuming, tedious self-evaluation quizzes and exercises. Perhaps you already know that you want to get rid of him. All you need is a little push in the right direction—and that is what this book is going to give you.

Believe it or not, this is not a man-bashing book. Instead, it is a book that asks you to stop wasting your time blaming *him* for what is wrong and, instead, do what you have the power to do about it—walk out.

This book will also expose the myth that women go over the hill as they age, while men get sexier. I'll make the case that, in many ways, the opposite is true—that women are the catch.

This book will help you to feel that you can control what happens to you—and it will do this by sparking you to take action. Once you take it, you will have power to make other changes. Your self-esteem will rise as you dare to do the things that you are afraid of, and a chain reaction will begin. Soon you will feel a lot better about your whole life.

Finally, this is a book that will help you to determine what traits and qualities a man must have in order to form a positive relationship with you.

I *Will* Arise

In the following pages, I'm going to ask you to use something that men and women have had since the beginning of time—the human will.

I'm going to ask you to locate that place inside you that is strong—that has dignity, is sure, and that you do not want to permanently compromise. In short, I'm going to ask you to call upon your inner strength and by an act of will change your life for the better.

Perhaps you have made a mistake—you've used poor judgment. You saw something that glittered, but now you see it is not gold. Like the prodigal or lost son in the biblical tale, you can change your mind.

In the Bible story, the young son of a wealthy man demanded that his father give him his inheritance, so that he could seek what he perceived to be the good life. As the story goes, the father complied, and the boy went out and, in short order, spent all the money and found himself in extreme poverty. He ended up tending swine and being forced to compete with them for a few measly husks of corn in order to prevent starvation. Then one day the boy came to himself. He realized that it would be better to go home, even as a servant, than to remain in this condition. At this juncture—and these are the key words of the parable—the boy said to himself, "I will arise and go to my father."[1]

What is the message of this time-honored parable? The most salient point for me is that only after he had sunk to a certain level did the boy realize he would be better off back home, as bad as home had once seemed—even with less than he had before. In fact, he was willing now to accept the same deal as the servants, but with dignity.

You may have made a bad judgment in your relationship or marriage. Perhaps, like the prodigal son, you were looking for a fantasy relationship—a miracle, something to save you—and you have been sorely disappointed and are now losing or have lost your dignity. You, like the prodigal son, can find yourself, turn back, and refuse to be compromised any further.

You Can't Work It Out If There's Nothing to Work With

But why not try to hang on to a man, give him a chance? After all, maybe a good relationship will emerge if you work on it. No.

A relationship can only be good if it has a base upon which something more solid can be built—then and only then can it possibly be altered or refined. If two people have come together for all the wrong reasons—if there is no mutual respect, no willingness to develop and pursue some common goals, and no joint desire to love and be loved, there is no base—and indeed nothing to work with.

Stop Blaming Him

Many women blame their partners for their unhappiness, but who is really to blame? Despite the countless books on codependency and enabling, too many women still refuse to heed the time-honored words of former President Harry Truman: "The buck stops here." Why is it that so many women would rather rail at their partners than come to grips with the real culprit—themselves?

Consider the life of the renowned singer-actress Cher. What would have happened if she did not have the courage to ask herself whose fault it was that she was not satisfied with her life? Instead of leaving Sonny and moving on to become one of the most successful entertainers of all time, she might now be a mere memory of the sixties.

Willing to face her responsibility for her own destiny, she separated herself from Sonny and set out on her own. Had she remained with Sonny, despite what I believe must surely have been her inner voice telling her that she must leave that relationship, perhaps she, like so many women today, would be wasting the best years of her life blaming a man for her unhappiness.

You Can Be Alone

Most people don't want to be alone. In fact, if they were completely honest about it, most people would admit that, deep down inside, they are outright terrified of being alone. Why is this so?

Psychologists generally agree that the fear starts in infancy, when we are totally dependent upon others for our survival. If our mother or caretaker should suddenly disappear or abandon us, we would in fact die.

When we were infants, even the best parents didn't always get there the moment we cried. In fact, in the early days of child psychology, some experts believed that it was a bad idea to come to a child the moment it cried. They thought it would spoil the child. So, many well-meaning parents allowed their infants to cry for some time before they attended to the child's needs.

But even if your parents did come the moment you cried, chances are there were times when, for one reason or another, they didn't come as soon as you thought they should. The end result? To some extent, most of us fear being left alone. It brings back old, unconscious fears of abandonment or death. Even so, you don't have to let this irrational fear now rule your life.

When you think of ending your relationship, and you get that almost physical pain—that dreaded feeling in the core of your being—identify it and tell yourself the truth: If I need to, I can make it alone. When I was an infant, I would have died if I were left alone. Now I can survive and thrive. In this book, we will talk about how.

No More Excuses

Had you been born in the era of the caveman, you would have had to depend upon a man to protect you and your young and to gather food for you, especially while you were in your most vulnerable state—pregnant. In fact, even if you were born a hundred years ago, when women were largely limited to being housewives and mothers, you would indeed have had something big to dread if you had no man to take care of you—poverty, destitution for yourself and your children.

Hello. That is undoubtedly not your situation. You live in a civilized country where you can support yourself. You can survive. You don't have to compromise your needs for the wrong man. And, the fact is, in this great big wonderful civilization, there are many delightful, civilized men, and with a little luck and a lot of self-esteem, you just might be able to find one anyway—even though you don't need one for survival.

Stay with the Wrong Man, and You'll Never Meet the Right Man

I might as well stay with Joe. After all, he's a steady date, and I hate to be alone on Saturday nights—and, anyway, with all the diseases going around...

How many times have you heard a woman say something like this? But staying with Joe means her time is tied up with him, when she could be meeting new people. If you stay with Tom, Dick, Harry, or Joe, then for sure nothing will change. You may not get AIDS, but you won't get much of anything else either. Should someone wonderful cross your path, you may not notice, because your energy will be tied up dealing with your current man. When you are available, however, your energy is more free-flowing, and new people sense this.

Another reason to end an old relationship before seeking a new one is that an old relationship can color the one you haven't even begun. You might wrongly be tempted to look at it as a trade-off, asking yourself, "Is this new man worth giving up my old relationship?" This comparative approach falsely raises the stakes of what might come next. You say to yourself, "This new man had better work out. I'm really taking a chance giving up what I already have for him." The right way to meet new men is from a starting point of strength—not weakness.

Run for Your Life

Get rid of him. It's easier said than done. If you have gotten used to depending upon a man—for emotional, physical, or financial reasons, or a combination of all three—letting go of him will be painful but something you must do.

If you had to either amputate an arm or die from the poison it would soon discharge through your body, what would you do? You'd bite the bullet and amputate the arm—right? Well, staying with the wrong man is just as serious as having a gangrenous arm—that relationship will cause you to lose your time and energy which, day by day, add up to your life.

First the Darkness, Then the Light

When a seed is planted in the ground, it remains buried deep in the dark earth for weeks, even months, before it can break through to see the light of day. When you do something strong and right and beautiful for yourself, there may be a time of darkness, when it seems as if nothing is happening—a time of sorrow and aloneness—but it is really a time of growth.

Your unconscious mind needs this time to readjust, to help you find yourself. Without this sometimes painful time of aloneness, there can be no change—no growth. And there is liberation in the pain because, once you experience it and realize that you have not died but have in fact survived to find new doors opened up to you, you will see that it was worth the price of the initial fear. If you do not panic, but allow yourself to go through this time of fertilization, the day will come when new life bursts through.

Are You on the Beam?

I've always felt, along with Joseph Campbell, that there is something deep inside of us that knows when we are off center, off the path, or not on the beam.[2] If you are in a wrong relationship, there's a still, small voice whispering to you, tugging at you, asking you to get back on course.

Chances are your wrong relationship has, up until now, stopped you from achieving your full potential. It's time to get back on the beam. It's time to pick up your life and put it back on track, and to make the most of the time you have.

You Don't Want "Any Man"

Some women are so lonely, they foolishly wish for a man, any man—and almost as if wishing could make it so, sure enough, "any man" comes into their lives—and, sure enough, "any man" is usually the wrong man, who does them more harm than good.

You don't want any man; you want the right man—the man who will encourage you to stay on the beam—to be true to yourself, to fulfill your potential. If you can't find the right man, I believe it's better to be alone. Your aloneness won't last forever but, during that time, at least you will have yourself. With the wrong man, you'll lose your self, or your soul, which is your most prized possession.

The Sisters Are Not Taking It Anymore

Up until now, women were willing to settle for very little—even crumbs in a relationship—whereas men were not. In fact, if a woman had ten vital needs, even if only one or two of those needs were being met, that woman would stay with that man. On the other hand, if a man had ten vital needs, and as few as one or two of those needs were *not* being met, he would leave that woman. But there seems to be a new wave of understanding among women, a growing realization that this situation cannot go on.

One indication of such a change in women's thinking can be found in popular music. I am reminded of the song by Gladys Knight, Patti LaBelle, and Dionne Warwick, "I'm Not Your Superwoman." As the lyrics indicate, women expect a full, well-balanced meal, and if they don't get it, they're going to go to a different restaurant.

How to Read This Book

Chances are, what's wrong with your man will be discussed in not one, but two, three, or more chapters of this book. There's no need to read the chapters in order. You can look at the Contents and turn directly to the applicable sections and read them first. Then make sure to read the last four chapters—for reinforcement and inspiration.

The Women in This Book

I love to listen to women talk because, sooner or later, they get around to talking about men—and I learn a lot. Sooner or later, in conversation, one woman will tell another how she's been hurt or is being burned in a relationship, and how she'd like to "wash that man right out of her hair and send him on his way."

For the last few years, I've listened to these women—and I've recorded their stories. They live in every part of the United States and range in age from eighteen to sixty-eight. They are black, white, Hispanic, Asian, and of mixed race. They've told me their stories—some of them victories, some of them failures. But they have one thing in common: They've either gotten rid of that man or want to do so, and they have a story worth sharing.

The names and details in the stories have been changed to protect privacy—but the essence of each story has been retained in the pages that follow.

What Do You Deserve?

As Nathanial Branden so aptly put it in his book *Honoring the Self*, "Of all the judgments that we pass in life, none is as important as the one we pass on ourselves."[3] You are the one who will decide whether you're going to take it anymore. You are the one who will decide whether you deserve better than this. You are the one who will make this most important judgment about what you want and deserve. It is my goal to help you decide that you deserve the best.

NOTES

1. Luke 15:11–19.

2. Joseph Campbell, with Bill Moyers, *The Power of Myth* ed. Betty Sue Flowers (New York: Doubleday, 1988), p. 229.

3. Nathanial Branden, *Honoring the Self* (New York: Bantam, 1983), p. xi.

Reminders

1. You can't work it out if there's nothing to work *with!*

2. Stop blaming him. Bury the dead and move on.

3. Free yourself from the wrong man, and all kinds of good things can happen.

4. We women no longer have to settle for crumbs.

5. Even if you're happy with your man, keep this book on the side in case he gets stupid.

2

Get Rid of Him
If You Are on
the Begging End

You make embarrassed apologies and excuses when, in a moment of joy, you slip and say, "I love you" (he has not yet uttered those words to you). You try to get into deep conversations about feelings, but he says he is emotionally unavailable, and you feel as if you're trying to drain blood from a stone.

You have been together a while now. You are still excited about the relationship—in fact you can't wait to see him—but when you're together, he says, "Don't bother me, I'm reading the paper," or he turns on the TV and shuts you out.

While many other aspects of the relationship are fine, he doesn't want to get married. You wait your time, because you believe that if you play your cards right, he'll be unable to function without you and will be forced to ask you to marry him.

Even though you're mad about him, he sometimes chooses to see you only on the weekend, or sometimes every other week, when you would love to see him every day. You think of him constantly and want to talk to him more often, but when you call

him, he's either not home or he says he'll get back to you, and you
vow never to call him again. You stay home all evening when you
could have been having dinner with a friend, because you think
this might be the night he calls.

If any of the above applies to you, you are on the begging end of
a relationship—not a very comfortable or pretty place to be.

Perhaps you know other women who have affectionate, attentive men who pursue and treasure them. You bristle with envy
when you observe a man in a restaurant hanging onto every word
his girlfriend says. At first you wonder if there's anything wrong
with you, and then you become angry.

That anger is the beginning of your freedom. It's your inner
voice saying, "I deserve better than this. I'm not going to be on
the begging end of relationships anymore."

In the following paragraphs you will see what has happened to
other women who have allowed themselves to become mendicants
in their relationships. As you think about your own experiences,
and listen to theirs, perhaps you will say, "It's better to have *no*
man than one who doesn't want to be there."

If a man is interested in you, he'll pursue you. Give him a
chance to do so and you'll wonder what you were thinking about
when you were doing all of that silent, and perhaps not-so-silent,
begging.

If You Can't Say I Love You for Fear of His Leaving, Perhaps You Are on the Begging End

If a woman and a man are sharing an intimate relationship, if
there are mutual feelings of warmth and affection, and if the
woman feels love for that man, should she have to bite her tongue
every time the words "I love you" come to her mind and threaten
to exit from her mouth? I think not. If she does, perhaps she
should wonder whether she's on the begging end of a relationship.

Rose and Carl are in the throes of sexual passion, and for Rose, at least, it's romantic love. They have been dating for four months, and Rose has been feeling closer and closer to Carl. Many times, in a moment of joy, Rose has had a strong urge to say the words "I love you." However, she has held them back because an inner voice has been clearly warning her that these words might scare him away.

It has made her sad to have to stifle herself every time a natural and spontaneous emotion has cried for expression, but rather than risk losing him, Rose has controlled herself. One day, however, right after a particularly pleasing lovemaking session, in the glow of feelings of closeness and intimacy, the words "I love you" slipped out. Here's Rose's account of what followed:

> I could feel it at once—the tension so thick you could cut it with a knife. He stiffened and didn't say anything. I felt compelled to apologize and make excuses. I said, "I didn't really mean I love you, Carl. What I meant was, I love the way I feel right now. I love being with you." "I think I know what you mean," he said. But something had changed. I could tell.
>
> And, sure enough, after that he stopped calling as much, until I finally asked him what was wrong and he said he felt that I was getting too serious about the relationship. At first I felt rejected and blamed myself, but then, when I thought about it, I became angry. "Some nerve," I thought. We can share intimate conversations and intimate physical contact, but we shouldn't feel love for each other—and if we do, we dare not say it.

Rose is absolutely right. When it comes to feelings of love, if you've been seeing someone for a while and have become intimate with that person, you should be able to express your feelings freely and let the chips fall where they may. Why should you have to maintain constant vigilance about letting slip those words? If the person can't cope with feelings of intimacy, as Carl couldn't, so be it. You are better off knowing.

How ridiculous to think that you must walk around on tiptoes so as not to let a man with whom you have been sharing your thoughts, your sexuality, and perhaps even your soul know that you feel love for him.

Sex is not enough for most women—in fact, not for most people. Sex gives satisfaction, but love gives comfort. We all deserve the comfort and the joy of shared love. You should never have to apologize for saying "I love you." If you do, take it as a sign that this man is not for you.

Here is some food for thought. Perhaps women who desire intimacy in a relationship would do well to ask themselves these questions before having sex with a man: "Can I say 'I love you' to him freely, without being apologetic? Can he cope with such feelings and respond to them appropriately?"

If the answer is no, depending upon her needs and her goals, a woman might be better off not going to bed with such a man. On the other hand, if the woman wants to enjoy the sheer lust of the experience, and expects nothing more than mutual sexual satisfaction in return, of course there is no need to ask such questions.

If you're worried that by saying "I love you," he will think you are saying "I want to marry you," then you can tell him what it is you mean by saying "I love you." Let him know that if you want to say "I want to marry you," you know how to say exactly that.

Romantic Love versus Lust, Pure and Simple

What is the difference between sheer lust and romantic love? Romantic love of course involves sexual attraction, but it goes much deeper than that. In romantic love, you love the person's soul, the way he speaks, the way he acts, the way he thinks—his very being. The connection that is made in the ecstasy of the sex act serves as a joining of the souls.

On the other hand, when one is merely in lust, sexual satisfaction has a "let me get away from here" effect. It is similar to the feeling one gets after having eaten a full meal and is stuffed. One is not eager to linger at the table. The sight of food becomes temporarily offensive. But, of course, when one gets hungry again, food becomes something very desirable.

If one partner is in lust, he behaves as above. If the other partner is in love, she behaves in the opposite manner. The sexual act has helped her to join souls with her partner, and she now wants to lie next to him for hours—to share his wonderful energy. Sometimes it happens in the reverse, and it is the woman who wants to get away and the man who wants to stay. But this is usually not the case. Why so?

There is a school of psychological thought which argues that sexual involvement in a relationship represents a much larger emotional investment, and a much greater likelihood of romantic involvement, for women than it does for men.[1] If I am to believe the hundreds of woman I've interviewed, I must agree.

What does this mean? Simply put, it means beware. Don't project your feelings onto your partner. Just because you feel bonded to him, that does not mean he feels the same way. As the saying goes, "If you can't see it, it ain't there." The fact is, if your man runs away right after sex, for whatever excuses he provides, it may well be that "it" (love) simply isn't there.

Emotionally Unavailable

Not being able to say "I love you" can be just the tip of the male iceberg. Some men are simply not emotionally available—to anyone, not just you—because they have psychological problems that block them from becoming intimate with a woman.

Relationships need more than superficial conversations and good sex. They need spiritual exchange, otherwise they stagnate. If you don't share your feelings, your emotions, with the one you are going to bed with, it's like having a beautiful automobile that is empty. You can sit in it, look at it, polish it, and adore it—but you cannot move it an inch. A relationship devoid of emotional feelings stagnates.

When June first met Cliff, she was quite impressed. He had been running a local news show for a number of years and was quite a cult figure in their community. June says:

> In the first few weeks of our dating, our conversations were mainly directed toward our mutual careers, and that was just fine because we had more than enough to talk about. But it bothered me that he never wanted to talk about his feelings, his family, or anything of substance, for that matter.
>
> After about five weeks, we ended up in bed. I was sure that after sex we would get closer—that he would open up, but the emotional void was still there. He merely lit up a cigarette and turned on the television.
>
> Time and again, I would talk about my fears, my joys, my goals, my disappointments, but the moment we approached anything about him, he seemed uneasy and changed the subject. How could I share physical love with a man who kept slamming the door on me emotionally?
>
> One evening, I confronted him about his refusal to open up to me. I asked if he was afraid of being hurt. I achieved the opposite of my goal. He became furious and said that he was sick and tired of people being commended for airing their dirty laundry in public. I realized at that moment that he may have been severely hurt as a child, and that his problem was too deep-rooted for me to solve.

After a few more weeks of nonfulfilling conversations and even less fulfilling sex, June ended the relationship. She says: "I felt more alone when I was with him than when I was by myself, and I thought, if that's the case, I might as well *be by myself.*"

Right from the beginning of the relationship, June sensed that something was missing, but she convinced herself that once they had sex, things would change. The fact is, things did change, but only for June, who became more frustrated than ever with Cliff's refusal to share his deeper self with her. Cliff had spent a lifetime constructing a shell around himself to protect his vulnerable parts—and he was not about to relinquish that shell on command, because he simply didn't feel safe enough to do it.

What was June's mistake? She felt that she would be able to melt that shell with the power of her love—that her love would finally be received after sex—but it didn't work because, contrary to the popular belief, love does not conquer all.

Dancing Without a Partner— When He Takes You for Granted

Some men, who may have been there in the beginning, seem to go on a permanent emotional vacation once they get comfortable. At first, they are attentive and considerate—as eager to please you as you are to please them. They are eager to sit for hours and have long, even philosophical conversations. But once the dust settles, they seem to retreat into an old-married-man attitude—to take you and the relationship for granted, to the point where you feel as if you are continually begging for attention.

Dahlia had been going out with Bart for two years. They were practically living together—he either sleeping at her house or she sleeping at his. Although more in love with him than ever, she began to feel that he was taking her for granted, or getting too comfortable. Dahlia gives us an example:

> I get home three hours before he does, so I have time to pretty up, straighten out the house, and get a romantic dinner going. Most nights I set the table with flower buds and candles, take a shower, fix my makeup, redo my hair, and fuss around in the closet to find the most appealing outfit available.

For the last month or two, when he comes in he barely grunts a hello—heads for the bathroom, and then sits on the couch and puts on the TV while, at the same time, he flips through the paper. It depends upon which is more exciting at the moment, but in a matter of minutes, he's either glued to one or the other—the TV or the paper.

Lately, when I call him in to dinner, he asks in a pleading voice, "Can't we eat in the living room? There's a really good show on TV." The one time I said yes he basically ignored me, shushing me every time I tried to talk to him.

When I protested and said, "We have to talk about this," he said, "Oh, my God. Why does everything have to be a big deal? I love you. I just want to relax."

I tell you now, I'm not going to tolerate it. I need more than that. If he doesn't give me the attention I deserve, I'm going to go out and find it somewhere else.

Dahlia is already thinking of cheating on Bart, and they're not even married. Can you imagine how she will feel if they decide to tie the knot? Dahlia will be reading the "bored to death" and "can't stand to go to bed with him" chapters of this book in no time, and trying all those books written for women who want to spice up their relationship. What a life! There's a proverb that applies to Dahlia's situation: "A prudent man [woman] sees danger, and hides himself [herself], but the simple continue on and suffer for it."[2]

What Is Self-Esteem?

Why do women get themselves into situations such as these in the first place? Could it be that they lack the basic self-esteem which is so necessary to stand up for one's rights in a relationship? I dare say it is true, because standing up for one's rights means taking the risk of losing that person, and a woman of low self-esteem cannot afford to take that risk.

What is self-esteem anyway? It is your reputation with yourself—in essence, it is what, over time, you have come to believe about yourself. If you have low self-esteem, you have built up a bad reputation with yourself. If you have high self-esteem, you have built up a good reputation with yourself. If you have built up a bad reputation with yourself, one of the best ways to change that is to begin building a good reputation by starting to do what makes you feel good about yourself. If Dahlia would, in a manner of speaking, put her money where her mouth is and stop spending all of her time with Bart, and if she would begin to date other men, she would begin to change her reputation with herself. Then, the next time she is tempted to tolerate improper treatment from a man, she would be able to refer back to the time when she moved away from an unsatisfactory relationship. In short, she will have changed a bad reputation to a good one and, in effect, will have raised her self-esteem.

Why Should You Have to Beg Him to Marry You?

"Ridiculous," you say. "What woman in her right mind would beg a guy to marry her?" And of course you are right. Women don't get down on their hands and knees and literally say, "I'm desperate. Please marry me." But, in fact, their actions, their manipulations, and their general attitudes often amount to the same thing.

How does this happen to women who seemingly have every other aspect of their lives together? The truth is, some women don't do their homework early enough in the relationship: They don't check out whether the man is open to a commitment, and they foolishly assume that "of course he would marry me." Others choose not to believe a man when he tells them up front, "Read my lips. I don't want to get married. I'm not the marrying kind."

Other women think that they will be able to beguile the man away from his fear. "I'll get him so addicted to me that he won't be able to live without me," they dream. "Then when I've got him hooked, I'll threaten to leave if he doesn't marry me. He'll have no choice but to walk down the aisle," they imagine.

But, sadly, after training the man to bring his laundry over every week, cooking him dinner every night, cleaning up his apartment on a regular basis, or even moving in with him and behaving as a wife and a housekeeper, nothing happens.

Other women believe that they will never find a better catch—that this man is the end-all in potential husbands, and if they let him slip by, they will be missing the chance of a lifetime.

Finally, there are those women who believe that "He just hasn't met the right one, namely me." These women believe that the man will change his mind once he is swept off his feet by their irresistible charm. Unfortunately, such thinking often backfires, and the very man they spent so much time with ends up being swept off his feet by a brand-new woman—perhaps one who listens to who he is and what he thinks—and he marries *her*. Let's look at each style of self-delusion and see what various women learned or did not learn from their mistakes.

Anne, an English teacher, met Blake, a successful lawyer, when she was thirty-five. In her own words, it was "love at first sight," but unfortunately that's all it would remain—love that would not lead to marriage. Anne says:

> The beginning stages of our romance could not be duplicated, even by the most imaginative movie director. Starry nights of champagne and love. Dreamy, lazy days of wine and roses. Long conversations about our hopes and dreams. And the physical—to this day, I cannot imagine it being better with anyone else. We were in love.
>
> After about a year, we met each other's families. Thrilled, I began to fantasize about our married life together. In every way, he was my dream come true.

Another year went by, and still no proposal. I didn't want to seem pushy, so I never really brought the subject up. I would talk about other people getting married and try to goad him into talking about it, but he would just avoid it. Finally, after three years, I asked him where our relationship was going. He looked at me dumbly and said, "What do you mean, where is our relationship going?" I told him that I wanted to get married some day and have children—and I was wondering if he ever thought about this.

It was the first time I really laid my cards on the table. He took me in his arms and told me he loved me more than he had ever loved anyone in his life, but he just didn't want the responsibility of marriage.

I knew he wasn't kidding because, remembering back, he had always made negative comments about married couples—but I wasn't listening.

Anne took another year to finally break away from Blake, but she eventually did it and is now pursuing a career in real estate, sharpening her tennis game, and attending women's groups. She is also doing a lot of traveling—and, as she expresses it, spending quality time with herself.

But why did Anne waste so many years with a man who never had any intention of getting married? The simple fact is, she didn't ask. Too afraid to do so, she assumed that romance would win the day, that things would take their natural course, and, in time, he would propose. As it turns out, things did take their natural course, but not the natural course that Anne had in mind.

The long and the short of it is, when it comes to relationships, when you are dealing with another human being you cannot assume anything about what is and what is not a natural course. One person's natural course is another person's disaster course—so the only sensible thing to do is to ask questions early in the relationship (about three to five months seems a good time to me), and if you don't like the answers, move on!

Jeanette's experience is slightly different. She *was* listening to

Norm, a man fourteen years her senior, and a multimillionaire and owner of a fleet of limousines, when he said he never wanted to get married, but she simply didn't believe him. It took her ten years to finally realize that he wasn't kidding. After three years of going out, Jeanette had reached her thirty-first birthday and started to get the itch to get married, so she brought the subject up. Jeanette recalls:

> He stated his position in no uncertain terms, and that's when I started to think he might be serious. I tried every trick in the book. I would break up with him, only to go back after he would promise that we would get married soon. But then, after a few months of being lovey-dovey, when I would pressure him to make good on his promise, he would be evasive and we would break up.
>
> Back and forth we went for ten years. During the last year, I knew I had to get away from him, but I feared that I would just go back to him.
>
> Finally I met someone else—a man closer to my age. I broke up with Norm, and I've been seeing this guy. I don't know if it will work out or not, but two things are for sure: I will not go back with Norm if it doesn't, and I will not wait ten years to try to get another guy to decide to marry me.

It may sound as if she's going with this new guy on the rebound, but, in essence, she's not. Apparently she realizes that whether or not it works out, at least he will have been a vehicle for her to get out of the relationship. Perhaps it's not the ideal way to leave—with a lucky substitute on hand—but it certainly is less painful. Sometimes you have to just bite the bullet and move on.

The moral of Jeanette's story is clear. When a man says he isn't interested in getting married, believe him. True, people do change their minds, but it is a gamble—and if you decide to take that gamble, then please don't rail upon the guy and accuse him of having done you wrong if, in the end, after ten years of your life have gone by, he proves he's been telling the truth.

When Pamela was visiting her sister in San Francisco, she was introduced to Dan and began a bi-coastal romance. Although she believed him when he told her that he didn't want to get married, she assumed that she could change his mind by virtue of her irresistible charms. She says:

> I found myself inventing all sorts of excuses to go to San Francisco—and it seemed to me that he was doing the same about New York. In three months, I knew we were in love, so I started to feel him out about marriage. He became very nervous and changed the subject. That's when I knew I had work to do. I made up my mind to get this man so addicted to me that he would see he couldn't live without me.
>
> Sexually, I went all out of my way. I did things with him that I don't really enjoy doing—but I did them to the hilt and then some. He loved it and, sure enough, he came into town even more often.
>
> Another year went by and I jokingly said, "Well, Dan, isn't this romance getting a bit expensive? Wouldn't it make much more sense to just live together?"
>
> He said he needed time to think about it. Finally, he told me that it wasn't fair to me and that we should break up so that I could be free to meet someone who was interested in marriage. We broke up, but I went back with him because I felt as if I couldn't live without him.
>
> It's over six years now, and nothing has changed. I keep telling myself he just needs more time, but in the meantime, my biological clock is ticking.

Biological clock indeed. And what about her psychological clock? Pamela has painted herself into a corner. Having laid down a challenge to herself, having told herself that she could cause him to become addicted to her by virtue of her irresistible charms, and having failed to do so, she now finds herself in a bind. To face the fact that Dan is not going to come around is, in her own mind, to admit not mere defeat but that she is in fact not irresistible.

The fact is, Pamela, by a combination of magical thinking (in this case, wishing will make it so) and indulgence in an ego trip (that her charms are irresistible), has rendered herself incapable of action.

But what is really behind such behavior? Perhaps her actions are really a reflection of her need for dependency. Perhaps she is really thinking, "I cannot stand to be without a relationship." Or perhaps she is revealing her true feelings about her personal worth. She may be telling herself, "If I do not win, if he leaves me after all this time, it proves that I am not lovable. What hope will I have of ever meeting a man who *will* marry me?"

Life itself may help to move Pamela along in a positive direction. Chances are, Dan himself will eventually end the relationship, and Pamela will be forced to move on with her life, but it would be much better for Pamela's self-esteem, for her reputation with herself, if she would take the initiative and end the relationship herself.

Every Woman's Nightmare

I've saved Theresa for last in this series, because what happened to her is every woman's nightmare. After going out with Gerald for five years and living with him for three, after cooking and cleaning for him and taking care of all of his needs, without much warning he met, fell in love with, and married someone else. Theresa says:

> Our relationship was stable, and I was happy, but it bothered me that he didn't believe in marriage. It also bothered me that he didn't spend as much time with me as I wanted him to, but I put up with it because I loved him, and because at least he was living with me—and at the time, I tried to convince myself that it was almost the same as marriage. After all, I was the one he came home to every night, was I not?
>
> Well, last summer it all came down on my head, just like a landslide, and I'm still not over it. He went on a

fishing trip with his friends—no women allowed, "just the boys." But he managed to meet a girl all right. I knew something was wrong the very night he came back. He acted very strange.

For two weeks I kept quizzing him, but he continued to insist that nothing was wrong. Finally he blurted out that he was in love with someone else. He told me that he and the lady who runs the boat rental at the fishing place had got to talking the day of the fishing trip and had ended up talking until dawn. They had fallen in love that night and had been seeing each other ever since. He said that he would have told me sooner, but he couldn't think of a way because he knew it sounded so crazy. He said he couldn't explain it; that it was true love, that the two of them were like soul mates, and that no one ever understood him this way.

They got married last month, and I am sitting here with an anger that I don't know what to do with. And just to think, all that time, I assumed that if he lived with me and if he paid the bills, he must love me.

Many men stay with a woman because it is comfortable enough, and they don't want to bring on a confrontation. There are still some pleasant things about the relationship, so it isn't a police emergency to end it. Why should they? They are being taken care of, are they not?

Such men continue in the relationship, even if they are not really in love. Then, when the real thing comes along and they are swept off their feet, suddenly they believe in marriage, only not with you! They drop you cold, motivated by the new love. You, of course, are left in the lurch.

Of course, these things can also happen to a woman who is married to a man—but the marriage tie makes a man think not once, not twice, not three times, but a thousand times before he will get a divorce and flit off with someone else.

Are the men who do such things evil, calculating devils? Of course not. They are simply going with the natural flow of their lives—doing what is right and comfortable for them. You are responsible to do what's right for you.

If you see that your relationship with a man is not going in the direction you want it to go, it's up to you to work on changing the direction of that relationship or to change your own direction— and walk out of it. Don't depend on the man to do it, because he won't, until it's convenient for him—and chances are, when he does, it won't be convenient for you.

What can we learn from the experiences of the women who wanted to get married to the above men? They did not stop to face their own goals and match them up with the goals of the men they were seeing. Although the men clearly indicated through behavior, and often words, that they were not interested in marriage, the women chose to ignore it. Believe it or not, there are plenty of men out there who *are* looking for a commitment. It would make a lot more sense to invest time and energy in them.

You May Be Placing Yourself on the Begging End Without Realizing It

If you continually find yourself on the begging end of relationships, it may well be that, without realizing it, you are placing yourself in that position because of your style of dealing with men. Perhaps without consciously planning it, you find yourself doing most of the pursuing, until eventually you are doing *all* of the pursuing. Finally, the man ends the relationship, and you can never figure out why. After all, in calling him when you want to see him, you're just being honest, are you not? Why should you play games if you're interested in a man? The following story adds some food for thought to such a question.

Kristine, who works for a record company, met Jeffrey at a church gathering. He was a popular guy—very involved in church activities, and the leader of a new hiking group. After three weeks of dating, Kristine found herself scheming to get Jeffrey to spend more time with her. No longer satisfied with seeing him only on Saturdays, Kristine confesses:

> I decided to pretend that I had these really neat tickets that would go to waste unless someone took advantage of them at the last minute. I offered them to Jeffrey, knowing he would probably ask me to join him. But after the concert, he didn't ask me out for the upcoming Saturday, and I was disappointed. I had no choice but to invite him to another concert when I saw him in church on Sunday—and, again, we went during the week. But, again, he didn't ask me out for Saturday.
>
> This time, I had a new plan. I decided to show up for his Saturday hiking group—even though I'm the laziest person in the world and think of it as a chore even to walk to my car.

Jeffrey was quite surprised to spot Kristine on the hike, and, in fact, he ended up spending the whole day walking along with her in the beautiful countryside. Kristine mistook this for a signal to continue pursuit—so she did, continually inviting him to concerts and showing up at the hiking group. But after a while, Jeffrey began to decline her invitations, and, in fact, he avoided her on the hikes, walking and socializing with other women. She was deeply hurt. Finally, when she asked him what was wrong, Jeffrey told her that he liked her only as a friend.

Kristine was appalled. "We had gotten physical—very physical. To me, that was at least the beginning of love," she laments. But it was over, plain and simple, and there was nothing Kristine could do about it but face the facts and perhaps learn from her experience; and learn she did.

Kristine joined a women's group where male-female relationships were discussed. There, she says, "I learned that I had been making a major mistake with the men I'd dated, by removing their opportunity to pursue me. The moment I didn't think I was seeing enough of a man, I would start tracking him, and of course he would run; but one thing I don't understand is, if Jeffrey didn't like me, why did it take him three months to end the relationship?"

In answer to Kristine's question, if a woman is pleasant enough, if she provides a man with entertainment and diversion, a laugh or two, or good sex and, in this case, free concert tickets, why wouldn't he be happy enough to continue a relationship with her? He doesn't have to have "feelings" for her—at least not the kind that Kristine was hoping for. He can think of her as just someone who is nice—someone who is little more than a friend. But when the woman invades his comfort zone, when she starts asking for more time or self than he is willing to give, and it becomes annoying, he will pull away, as Jeffrey did.

Why do women put themselves in this position? The obvious reason is they enjoy the man's company and want the satisfaction of having that company, and they wonder why they have to sit and wait for a man to make all the moves. In fact, they feel victimized and resent the idea of having to be the passive recipient rather than being able to take an active role in a developing relationship. While these feelings are very legitimate and understandable, unfortunately, they must frequently not be acted upon.

The fact is, most men still need some masculine roles, and except in the case of a shy man, or one who is afraid of rejection, one of those roles is that of the pursuer. Time and again, men and women have told me of experiences that demonstrate this truth. There are very few exceptions to the rule. The fact is, if a woman starts doing a lot of calling, she will quickly find that she is doing *all* the calling—a role that women don't like either. So women's liberation notwithstanding, there are some things we still have to let most men do—and one of them is the chasing.

Changing Your Style and Begging No More

Kristine found out that the more she pulled on a guy, the more he pulled away, until he finally got away. But she learned her lesson. She made up her mind to win the next time around. Soon, she attended a party where she met a handsome musician. There was an immediate attraction, and they exchanged telephone numbers and left off by saying that they should have lunch some day. Kristine recalls:

> In the past, I would have waited about a week and, if he didn't call by then, I would have called and said, "Hi. Remember me..." But instead, I said to myself, "He knows your number." I fought every rationalization: "Maybe he lost my number," or "Perhaps he's shy," or "Maybe he thinks I'm really popular and wouldn't go out with him if he called." I just kept thinking about falling back into that same trap of doing all the calling.

Two weeks later he called and they went to lunch. They had a wonderful time, and Kristine was excited about the prospects of the relationship. However, two weeks later, Jeffrey called. Finally, they decided to go out on another date and had a great time. This time, it took Jeffrey ten days to call. Kristine remembers with pain:

> I fought every impulse to call or to ask him, when I did see him, when would he next call? I remember how I used to make excuses with men—saying that I'm never home so I need to know when they would call. I later realized that this made me appear needy, so I kept my cool and let him take it at his own speed. After a while, he called more often, and before you know it, we were seeing each other almost every night.

Kristine and Jeffrey have now been happily married for over a year. When asked how it happened, Kristine replied: "He chased me because he valued me—because he felt that I valued myself. Finally, I was able to say to myself, if he's interested in me, he'll call. If he's not, I don't want him anyway."

Many women tell themselves, "He's so busy, I have to remind him that I exist—but once he's with me, we always have such a good time. If I could just get him to spend more and more time with me, I know he'll see how great we are together." This is absurd. If you have to *get* him to spend more time with you, you are resorting to coercion—and therein lies the rub! He is likely to sense this and to resent you for it—and pull even farther away.

The fact is, if a man sees something valuable in you, chances are he will make an effort to get in touch with you. Do you really believe that a man who is already interested in you will not call you? Isn't it true that men have been known to literally go to the ends of the earth to be with someone they love? The point is, give it time. Where there's a will, there's a way; but if there is no will, there is no way.

The next time you think of picking up that phone with some scheme in mind to get that man to spend more time with you, look in the mirror and say, "I love you. You are a treasure. You deserve to be valued." And put the phone down. Cherish yourself enough to believe that you are worthy of being pursued. And then realize that if this man never calls you again, you are a lucky woman, because you don't need a man whom you have to chase all the time—and one who will probably get away in the long run (again, if you're lucky—imagine marrying someone who kept you begging).

There is an exception to this rule. If you have a male friend or a variety of them, you can of course call them any time you please. These are men with whom you have had a friendly and perhaps even physical relationship, and who have remained in your life. You have maintained a connection and are there for each other when either of you feels the need. It's always great to have male friends!

Most People Have Passed on Someone

There's no need to take it as a sign that there is something wrong with you if a variety of men have decided to pass on you. All it means is that those men decided that you were not for them. So what! When you come to think of it, aren't there a number of men who were interested in you—men whom you avoided or passed on? And don't you agree that those very men probably have

women who would be thrilled to have them call? To take it a step
further, some of the men you rejected are now rejecting women
who would love to marry them.

The point is, not everyone is for everyone. In fact, when you
come to think of it, it's a miracle that people find each other at
all. But they do. The magical combination just happens, and
when you least expect it. But it is more likely to happen if you
relax and take the advice of a country-and-western song I once
heard: *If it don't come easy, you'd better let it go. If it don't come
easy, you're better off alone.*

And to take it a step further, if he lets you go—if he dumps you
first, great. You are well rid of him. If you follow this rule, your
energy will be free, and you will be open and available when that
person who will click with you in the right way—for a two-sided
relationship—comes along.

Don't Play Hard to Get—
Be Hard to Get: In Other
Words, Get a Life

One of the biggest mistakes women make when it comes to dating
men is to allow their lives to revolve around a particular man.
When this happens, many women begin to devise tricks in order
to make a man believe that they are unavailable when in fact they
are waiting by the telephone for that life-sustaining call. My
advice to such women is, get a life. Don't play hard to get. Be
hard to get. Here's what happened to Paige.

> When Mitch and I first met, we saw each other at least
> four times a week, and we spoke on the telephone every
> day. I thought we had a pretty solid thing going, and I
> was really content. Slowly, I dropped most of my friends,
> and, in fact, I stopped going to target practice because it
> was getting in the way of our dates. I enjoyed being with

him so much that I wanted to spend most of my time with him—and he seemed to feel the same way about me.

After about three months, however, things slowly changed. We began to see less and less of each other—he was getting busy at his job, family matters, stuff like that, until I was lucky to see him once a week. Also, his calls became more sparse—once every five days or so. So I decided to make him worry about me.

For one week, Paige made sure she wasn't home at the time Mitch usually called. But each day when she arrived home and checked her answering machine, there were no messages, not even a hang-up. She became quite angry, thinking, "How dare he not call me for an entire week." She waited another three days, this time not even picking up the phone when she was home, monitoring her calls, in the hope that he would call and worry that she was not there. But still nothing happened, except that she had to explain to friends and relatives why she was suddenly calling out, "Don't hang up, I'm home," once she realized it was not him. Frustrated and angry, Paige explains:

After three weeks, when I was mixed between thinking he had gotten into an accident or was perhaps dead, and furious that he had the audacity not to call in three weeks, I called him. He acted as if nothing was wrong. When I asked him if he had been trying to get in touch with me, he said no, claiming that he had been busy at work.

That was it. I nipped it in the bud right there. I told him I didn't want to see him anymore, and he said, "Oh, no. Please don't say that." But when I tried to question him again as to why he suddenly stopped calling, he just insisted that he was busy. I could tell he wasn't being honest. I decided that I didn't need him in any case—because even if he didn't meet someone else, and wasn't lying, then he was pretty coldhearted and inconsiderate to just stop calling like that. I told him it was over and asked him not to call me anymore.

The beautiful part, the thing that really gave me great satisfaction was cutting him off cold—saving myself the aggravation of playing the game out to the end and losing my dignity in the process. By the way, he never called me again—and I never really found out what happened.

Instead of playing hard to get, inventing trips away from home to avoid the telephone, or standing by and listening as the machine picked up the messages, Paige would have been a lot better off living her life. She could have called up some friends and socialized with them, worked out at a fitness center, visited relatives, or even taken a minivacation. The point is, she should have gone on about her business, because one thing is for sure, Mitch was surely going about his.

Of course, in a reasonable amount of time she could have called him (as she eventually did) to ask what was going on. The point is, it's ridiculous to build your life around a man—his calls, his plans, his goals, his anything. The fact is, Paige's initial mistake was abandoning her friends and her hobbies for a man. She would have been much wiser to have kept her friends and interests and, instead, woven Mitch into her already existing life.

I once found myself doing what Paige did, and worse. I had fallen in love, and without realizing it, I had begun to build my life around the man, to the exclusion of all else. Small wonder that every time he broke a date or didn't call, it seemed like the end of the world. But after a good number of crying jags that had me nearly in hysterics, I was forced to take stock of my life—and, as it turned out, I didn't have one. I realized then that I was in trouble, and I began to work on filling my life with interests other than being with a man. In fact, I resumed taking courses toward my Ph.D., and I took up the hobby of mountain climbing and eventually conquered Mount Kenya in Africa, even though it meant leaving that man for six weeks. And you know what— when I came back, not only was he waiting for me at the airport with flowers and champagne, but from that moment on, he showered me with so much love and attention that I began to fear that he would smother me. But had he not turned up at the airport, and had he dropped out of my life completely, I would have been okay. Why? Because I had discovered my self. I had found that there were a host of wonderful things for me to do—with or without a man—and I was bound and determined to do them.

As it turned out, for a variety of other reasons we ended up going our separate ways, but I certainly learned from that experience. Dare to have your own life, and everything else will fall into place.

Never Surrender Your Power

The biggest mistake many women make the moment they meet a man they love is to surrender their power, their center, to him. They forget all about their goals, their plans, and their dreams. They think, "Well, I don't need them anymore, now that I have him." Even family and friends take second place to the man. This should not be.

Why do women do this? They fear that the man will disappear if they are not available when he calls. The fact is, however, that the opposite is usually true. The man will become more visible when you demonstrate that you have a life of your own, because he will not be in fear that you will demand he spend every waking moment with you—and in the process, smother him to death.

Isn't it interesting that men rarely, if ever, surrender their power to women? In fact, if a man became like a puppy dog and trailed after you everywhere you went, if he called you first thing in the morning and several times during the day, and if he became upset every time you didn't call or were not home when you said you would be home, wouldn't you want to run the other way? The fact is, we don't respect such men. Well, it works both ways. If you surrender your power to a man, he will at best take advantage of you and fit you in at his total convenience; or, at worst, he will lose respect for you, value you less, or run because you make him nervous. After all, it's a big responsibility to be the center of someone else's life!

We can learn a proper lesson from the way men react. Generally speaking, men keep their centers in themselves, not in the women in their lives. We must begin to do the same. We already know this, but knowledge is only the beginning. It's time to start living it. Once we do, we'll gain the respect we've been seeking.

Other Reasons Why Women Find Themselves Begging

In the examples discussed above, the women who found themselves on the begging end of relationships may have been perfectly secure, well-balanced individuals who simply used bad judgment, or who got carried away with their own agenda and neglected to evaluate the program of their partners.

There are a host of other women, however, who find themselves on the begging end of relationships, not because they don't stop to evaluate their partners' needs, but because their own needs are so great that no matter how much attention their partners pay to them, it is not enough. Let me explain.

Women Who Love Too Much

Those of us who were not fortunate enough to receive a substantial amount of unconditional love, approval, and respect from a parent or a parent figure when we were infants and young children grew up with what seems to be a big empty hole in the center of our being, a hole that can only be filled, we falsely believe, with love from the opposite sex. When we fall in love, we then expect this person to do the job our parents failed to do—but of course we are asking the impossible.

The only person who can supply you with the missing love now is yourself. Either on your own or with the help of a supportive therapist, you must begin to tell yourself that you are lovable and okay. No one else can do the job.

By begging the man in your life (whether with words or clinging deeds) to "love me, love me, please love me," or overloving him to the point where you smother him with too much attention, what you do is alienate him, because if he is a mentally healthy person, he will move away from you for his own survival.

Why Insecure People Get in Trouble When They Fall in Love

When even the most secure people fall in love, they temporarily let down their ego boundaries. In a sense, they merge personalities with their love object and experience the natural high that comes with complete, if temporary, freedom from the self.

As time goes by, and life forces the couple to realize that they are indeed individuals (the first disagreement should do this), the ego boundaries are found again, and the natural high of being madly in love is gone.

When both parties are reasonably secure, the reestablishing of ego boundaries does not destroy the relationship, because neither one will take the seeming withdrawal of the other person as rejection. However, if one person in the relationship is insecure and has suffered severe feelings of rejection in childhood, that person is likely to panic—interpreting the pulling back as a refusal to give unconditional love.

In short, it will bring back unconscious memories of rejection and betrayal. The "rejected" lover will then say to herself, "Why is it that I want to spend every waking moment with him, but he does not feel the same way about me?" In the meantime, the man who is pulling away may be a nearly perfectly balanced man who is seeking a healthy relationship. It is the demanding one who is needy and is looking to merge her identity permanently with h man. Her goal is to become intermeshed in an unhealthy way.

a healthy man will not allow this. He will fight for his integrity.

Without realizing it, a woman may be asking a man to surrender his core or his self—in essence, his very soul. When he insists upon maintaining his boundaries, a woman may interpret this as rejection. In this case, the woman, not the man, is the one with the problem. Interestingly, it is a woman with just such a problem, in the extreme, that we see portrayed in the movie *Fatal Attraction*. In banging on her lover's door, she is actually pounding on the door that her parents slammed in her face when she was a child.[3] Unable to take this kind of rejection again, when the love object refused to see her anymore and despite her pleadings would have nothing to do with her, she felt she had no recourse but to kill his wife.

In a real-life situation, if the wife were out of the picture and the man still refused to see her, she would probably kill him next, and then herself. Why so? When an extremely needy person is deserted, love can quickly turn to hate—even murderous and then self-destructive hate. First the murder of the love object, then the murder of oneself.[4]

You Wouldn't Want Him Anyway

There's a catch-22 in all of this. Even if you were able to find someone who was willing to merge with you, someone who did not fight for his ego boundaries, you wouldn't be happy. In fact, if he let you, in essence, suck out his very soul, you would despise him, even hate him. He would no longer be someone you could look up to—no longer be able to fulfill your idealized fantasy. You would think of him as being as weak and as worthless as you are (as you see yourself).

When to Get Help

If you feel that there is a pattern in your love relationships, and that you have what is sometimes termed a "dire need for love," and believe that without a man in your life you are worthless, you should consider going to a therapist who can help you to establish your identity and build self-esteem. (See pages 299–302 for a discussion of the benefits of therapy, and advice on choosing the right therapist.) With a little professional help, in time, to your great relief, you may find that you no longer need a love transfusion from a man. You will be able to give it to yourself, on a regular basis, and in a very natural way.[5]

The Power of Action

On the other hand, you may be able to build your self-esteem without going to therapy, by simply taking action. The very act of getting rid of the nettlesome man, and then waking up the next morning and seeing that you are still alive and breathing quite normally, and then going through a full day without him, can give you more power than you've ever had before. Then, when thoughts of "I can't make it alone—I need someone to love me" cross your mind, you can counter them with self-talk, such as: "I can make it alone quite well. In fact, I managed quite well before I met —— and, in the bargain, I had peace of mind." You can calm yourself down and realize that you will, in fact, not die without him. Eventually, you may become indignant at the thought of ever feeling that way about a man again.

If you can continue this building of self-esteem through pursuit of your goals, career advancements, hobbies, and a social life, you may be able to start a chain reaction going. Many women have done it. Why not you?

NOTES

1. Carl G. Hindy, J. Conrad Schwartz, and Archie Brodsky, *If This Is Love, Why Do I Feel So Insecure?* (New York: Ballantine Books, 1989), pp. 32–37.

2. Proverbs 22:3.

3. Susan Forward and Craig Buck, *Obsessive Love* (New York: Bantam, 1991). Dr. Forward uses the analogy of "pounding on the door" as she discusses the inability of an obsessive lover to accept that a relationship has ended; p. 190.

4. Franz G. Alexander, *Fundamentals of Psychoanalysis* (New York: Norton, 1963). Alexander discusses murder of the love-object by the rejected lover, as well as suicide, on p. 223.

5. Albert Ellis and Robert A. Harper, *A New Guide to Rational Living* (No. Hollywood, Calif.: Wilshire Book Company, 1961), p. 25.

Reminders

1. If you can't say "I love you" for fear of scaring him away, maybe you *should* scare him away, permanently.

2. If he's emotionally unavailable, who needs him!

3. If he takes you for granted, dump him. Why dance without a partner?

4. Turn things around. Let him worry about whether or not *you* will marry *him*!

5. Never surrender your power—don't abandon your goals, or anything important to you, for any man!!!

3

Get Rid of Him
If He Won't "Let" You

To "let" or give permission to a child is perfectly correct, because due to lack of experience and maturity, children are incapable of making decisions for themselves. In fact, it is the obligation of a parent or guardian to decide what is right and wrong for children. However, the word "let" does not belong in adult relationships. For this reason, it never ceases to amaze me when a woman, a full-grown, otherwise mature adult, tells me: "My husband [boyfriend] would never let me..."

Ridiculous! Fortunately, many women who are in "let" relationships gradually come to realize that the price of living their lives for someone else is too high. Ivana Trump is one of them. On an episode of "20/20," Barbara Walters showed an interesting before-and-after interview with Ivana. When Ivana was still happily married to Donald, Ivana had stated: "I'm a European, and in Europe the man is always boss, and Donald's the boss, and I like it that way."

But in a later interview, after her divorce and after a taste of autonomy, Ivana said: "I was always behind a man. Now people are judging me for me, because of Ivana, of what I do, what I stand for. Donald was expecting me to do, act, dress a certain way, so I think I was really judged as Donald's wife."

In fact, Ivana has learned that to build your life around a man is a sorry proposition, because that man may or may not be there for you as time goes by. The fact is, a man, no matter how devoted he may be, may decide to pick up and go. You need, therefore, to be able to count on yourself. Ivana was asked to share with other women what she had learned. She said: "You have to trust *in yourself*. You have to believe *in yourself*, and if you have that, if you have confidence, you can really do almost anything [italics mine]."[1]

Ivana has come to the realization that it is the self that must be the base from which you operate, not the man. In the words of Sonya Friedman, author of *Men Are Just Desserts:* "Give a man top priority in your life, make him the main course—and chances are you will lose not only your self but your self-esteem."[2]

The loss of self-esteem that you suffer when you surrender your adult responsibility to think for yourself, and to decide what is right and wrong for you, cannot be measured. As you read this chapter, which identifies men who will not let a woman wear, go, do, or even think what she will, allow yourself to become indignant, even angry, and if anything applies to you, angry enough to do something about it.

Mrs. Charles Vedral

Our culture has contributed a great deal to the "let" mentality in male-female relationships. A prime example of this thinking in our society, even to this day, is the convention that a woman must surrender her surname and take on that of her husband once she is married. As if that isn't bad enough, society even tries to rob a married woman of her first name. Here's what happened to me.

I had been married for about a year and had been employed as a teacher during that time, and I decided to apply at a major department store for a credit card. Using my own credit references and my married name, I applied for the card. On the application, they asked if I was married and, if so, for my husband's name. Although I thought the question irrelevant, I surrendered the information.

You can imagine my surprise when I got the card and it said, not Joyce Vedral, but Mrs. Charles Vedral. I was livid. "What? Will they take away my first name too?" I thought. And I cut the card to pieces and applied for another, this time leaving out altogether the fact that I was married.

That society asks women to change their last names and to take on the surname of their husbands—and then dares to call women on certain printed documents by their husband's first name with the preface of "Mrs."—is, I have always believed, a clear way of telling women that once they are married, they are under the control of their husband—and are subject to his will. (Knowing this, I had every intention of keeping my own last name; however, since my husband's name had a much better sound than mine, which was "Yellin," I decided to take his on anyway.)

Whatever the reason, whether it be the fault of society or the fault of the individual man, there are plenty of men who enjoy bossing women around and treating them as if they are children rather than mature adults. Some men even try to control what their girlfriends or wives wear.

He Won't Let You Wear . . .

Clothing is very important to most women. Women like to dress a certain way because it makes them feel sexy, smart, sophisticated, or just comfortable. To take away a woman's right to dress the way she wants is, in a very big way, to deny her the right to be herself. Men who try to do this don't earn many points with me!

Flora became engaged to her dentist, Jordan, when she was

twenty-five and he was thirty-two. She didn't know, however, that he would be wanting to check out a lot more than her teeth once they had made that commitment. Flora explains:

> I'm really big-busted, and although I'm not risqué in my dress, I do like to choose clothing that shows off my assets. In fact, Jordan used to like it when I showed a little cleavage. However, the moment we got engaged, things began to change.
>
> The first blowup occurred when I bought a beautiful, low-cut velvet dress for my cousin's wedding. I couldn't wait to get it home and try it on for him.
>
> After dinner, I told him to close his eyes, and I came sauntering out in the dress. His eyes bugged out of his head. "You're not going out in public in that thing," he said. When I asked why not, he said he wasn't going to have every man in the place picturing himself in bed with me.

After a rather angry exchange, Flora decided to take off the dress, thinking that it was better to give in than to allow the issue to cause a rift in their otherwise smooth relationship. But it bothered her, and in the back of her mind, she wondered if Jordan would make other demands regarding the way she dressed. She soon found out. Flora recalls:

> The next time it happened was when we were invited to a dental picnic. I had bought a scoop-neck blouse and shorts—with beautifully matched sandals. When he picked me up for the picnic and saw the outfit, he refused to leave the house until I put on pants and changed my blouse. "No one else will have on shorts," he said, "and, anyway, you're hanging out of that blouse."
>
> I took it off and threw something on, and we went, but I was furious. When we got home we had it out. I told him I couldn't live this way. I felt as if I was living with my parents again, and I was getting flashbacks of when my father refused to let me leave the house for a

party because my dress was too tight—and I had to wear something I hated, just to get out.

He's not going to change, and neither am I—in my feelings. But so far, I've given in to him on each occasion, because if I don't, I'll be sitting home alone. I don't know what to do. Do you break an engagement because your fiancé won't let you wear what you want to wear? I have a friend whose husband actually shops for her clothing. Is that what Jordan wants?

Nothing is more important than the right to decide what is and what is not right for oneself. I would never allow a man to tell me what to wear. In fact, some of the men I've dated have tried to boss me around in that area, and they haven't lasted very long.

I remember one fellow in particular. It bothered him that I wore sexy workout clothing to the fitness center. "I don't want those men staring at you," he would say. "I know what they're thinking." I had been wearing such clothing for years, and, in fact, wearing it cheered me up. Try as I would, I could not convince him that I was the last thing on the minds of the hard-core body builders who trained in my gym. Most of them were quite preoccupied with getting that last "rep," and would be unaware if a parade of nude Playboy bunnies sashayed across the floor.

But that was not the issue anyway. Looking sexy to me is a part of being fit. If I have to hide my body in baggy sweat pants, what is the point of being in such great shape? I'm not dressing for the men, I'm dressing for myself—and, I guess, for my female friends who also dress sexy. They too like to show off their hard work. True, I also appreciate the compliments from the men. Why not?

If I do decide to wear baggy sweats, it is my decision—and I do so in a certain mood. On those occasions, I'll tie my hair into a ponytail, leave off the makeup, and basically fade into the woodwork. But my reason for dressing that way will have nothing to do with pleasing someone else. No relationship is worth giving up the right to decide what you will and will not wear, say, do, or be!

Why Some Men Like the Women in Their Lives Fat

This entire discussion reminds me of a problem that many women who have been in long-term relationships, usually marriages, experience—that of being sabotaged by their husbands or boyfriends when they try to lose weight and get in shape. Time and again, I have heard stories from women who tell me that instead of being supportive in their efforts to diet or to work out, the man in their lives complains that they are spending too much time in the gym, brings them fattening "surprises," and, if they make any significant progress, tells them that they "looked better the other way."

Why would a man do this? What stock would he have in such a seeming treachery? A lot of stock. Like Peter in the nursery rhyme (Peter, Peter, pumpkin eater, had a wife and couldn't keep her, put her in a pumpkin shell, *and there he kept her very well*), such men feel safe only if their woman is hidden under a pumpkin-like circle of fat, so that she is safe from the eyes of other men—and so that her self-esteem will be so low that she will be sure to stay at home with him, rather than possibly leave him for another man.

Such a man is extremely insecure, and should be confronted with his problem. If he is unwilling to work on it, the best thing a woman can do in such a situation is to walk before she becomes so fat that she will have to some day roll out!

He Won't Let You Go to Work, Go to School, or Pursue Your Career

A high-school valedictorian, Janet graduated with honors; but due to financial considerations, her parents could not afford college tuition, even though Janet had received a scholarship to pay for more than half of the expenses. Undaunted, she began what became a highly successful career in investment banking. After working three years, she met and married a stockbroker, became pregnant with the first of three children, and became a full-time housewife.

Too busy having children to become very philosophical, for the first seven years Janet kept her nose to the grindstone—concentrating on being a good mother and wife. But after her third child was in school, she realized that she wanted to go to college in order to pursue a career in medicine, an old dream that she had put aside but not forgotten. She approached her husband with this idea. I'll let Janet tell the rest of the story:

> He wasn't too keen on it, to say the least, but I insisted that I needed to do this for myself. He grudgingly agreed but he made it very difficult for me, insisting that I have his dinner on the table every night, on time, and that school not get in the way of my household duties. I worked around him very well, managing to get a house-keeper when needed—who also baby-sat my eight-year-old.
>
> I had completed one semester and was halfway into my second, when my little girl became sick and I had a test and couldn't get a baby-sitter. In desperation, I asked Dave to stay with her until I came back. He could easily have done this because we own our own business, and he can come and go as he pleases—and usually does. But he blew up and said, "I don't want you going to school. I don't care a damn about this women's lib. I want *my* wife at home, where she belongs, taking care of me."
>
> That did it. I decided I'd had enough and that it wasn't really worth the fighting and the loss of my marriage. I quit school and now, eight years later, my oldest child is only two years away from leaving for college, and it scares me to death. My husband and I have nothing in common. I'm dreading the empty nest. I have a feeling that somewhere back there, I made a

wrong turn in the road. I'm not about to go back to school now, and I don't think I would divorce him at this point, no matter what he did to me, short of physical abuse. But I keep wondering what would have happened if I had kept going to school way back then— instead of letting him stop me.

What would have happened if Janet had refused to allow her husband's ideas to stop or alter her plans? She may have been able to develop herself to the point where she would not have had to cower in fear every time her husband threatened to leave her, because she would have become self-sufficient and would have realized that she could make it on her own. But instead, she opted for the path of least resistance, and now she is worrying about what she will do once her last child leaves for college, when she will face her empty nest and, what's more, her empty self.

What happened to Janet is bad enough—but it can get worse. If you allow the man in your life to determine whether you pursue your career, in the end you may find yourself with neither your man nor your career. The pièce de résistance may well be that he will leave you in the end—either for another woman, a midlife crisis, or some such thing—or your relationship may break up over other natural causes. Then where will you be?

In the same position was Ali McGraw of *Love Story* fame, who gave it all up at the peak of her career. She says: "Steve had made it clear that he did not want me to act once we were married; it was not in writing, but it was pretty much understood, and my acquiescence to that wish had cut off my career at its very height."[3]

What made Ali McGraw so willing to relinquish stardom and success for a man? Apparently her problems did not begin with Steve McQueen. They began a long time ago. Ali admits: "My first serious boyfriend in college was a football player—the captain. . . . I loved being the girlfriend of a football star. It somehow legitimitized [sic] me."[4]

Small wonder that Ali was willing to throw it all away for a man. She had learned early in life that the only thing that could validate her existence—"legitimitize her"—was a man. Small wonder that when confronted with a choice between her acting career and a man whom she perceived as being her potential savior, successful actor Steve McQueen, she chose the man. After all, what did her small success mean (only a record-breaking blockbuster movie—or two) in comparison to the ability to attract and keep a coveted man. Nothing, of course!

Ali McGraw gave up her career at its peak, and in the end lost her man, who began running around with other women, in spite of her best efforts to please him. However, she has learned her lesson, and has written about it most eloquently in her autobiography, *Moving Pictures*. She no longer builds her life around men. In fact, she has "long healthy periods of no involvement," and allows men into her life as they fit into her goals and aspirations.[5]

If your worth is based upon the man you are going out with, you will surrender just about anything for that relationship.

Shall we dance, ladies? This attitude about men was most prevalent in the fifties, when I was a teenager, and it always sickened me. Somehow, without the benefit of women's liberation, I always shuddered at the idea of building my life around a man. I always thought, "Let him build his life around me." Needless to say, I didn't attract a rich, powerful man—because in those days, the women those men were marrying were the ones who were willing to make them king.

He Won't Let You Spend Your Money the Way You Want to Spend It

Money is power. Take away a woman's right to spend her money the way she wants to spend it, and you take away a great amount of the control that she would otherwise have on her life. Mary tells her story:

> My husband and I both work—and, together, we make a quarter million a year—yet he won't let me spend my

money the way I want to. The fact is, I had more freedom to buy clothing when I was single and living on less money than I do now.

Last week I went to my favorite designer dress shop and charged an expensive suit that I could well afford. I dreaded showing it to him, although I knew he would love the style, because the first thing he would ask is, "How much did it cost?"

By now I know just how to deal with him. It works every time. I butter him up ahead of time.

When he came home from work, I said, "Jack, Mary did something very very naughty today. She bought an expensive suit so she could look pretty for her Jackie on Friday night when we go to the theater. Mary deserves a spanking."

He softened and I quickly tried it on to show him. He said, "How much?" I put my head down and pouted my lips, and he said, "Okay, okay, as long as you are so cute about it, I can't get mad." In a way, I don't mind playing these games with him, because in the end I always get my way.

How absurd. Why should an adult woman have to reduce herself to the level of a manipulative child in order to obtain the right that, unbeknown to her, is already hers—the right to decide how she will spend her money? Even though her machinations work, is it really worth the sacrifice of her dignity?

Traditionally, men have always used money to control women, and up until recently, when many women began earning as much or more than their male counterparts, women have allowed them to do it. The fact is, in situations where women earn a significant amount of money, unlike Mary, they rarely engage in manipulative techniques when it comes to spending. If their partner has a problem about how they are spending money, such women have an adult discussion and eventually resolve the problem.

But what if a woman *is* earning little or nothing? Should she allow herself to be reduced to the role of manipulative child in order to be allowed to spend money? Of course not. If she finds herself having to invent elaborate schemes in order to be allowed to spend money, it would be a good idea for her to sit down with her husband and have a heart-to-heart talk. She can point out that her contribution to the home, if added up in financial terms, may equal more than his earnings. Having had this conversation, the two of them can then come to an accord—that they are each "allowed" to spend an agreed-upon amount of personal money in any manner they choose, and that they will consult with each other about how to spend or not spend household money.

All of this aside, however, the simple truth of the matter cannot be ignored: The more a woman earns, the more powerful and independent she feels, and indeed is; and the less she earns, the more at the mercy and dependent she feels, and indeed is. There is simply no way around this fact.

He Won't Let You Express Your Ideas and Opinions Freely

Some women are living with men who find it difficult to cope with an opposing opinion. In fact, these women are unable to say what's on their mind—even when vital issues are at stake. Hannah tells us of her relationship with her husband:

> Eddie is very strict and conservative, especially when it comes to raising the children. He's much too rigid, and he comes down too hard on the kids. But whenever I try to speak in their behalf, he become furious and we end up having a big fight. He's always saying, "I'm the man of the house; what I say goes." I try to tell him that this is the nineties and women have as much say as men, but he just storms out of the house and stays away for hours. When he comes back, he won't speak to me for days.
> The last ridiculous thing he did was to punish my daughter for a month, just for coming in a half-hour

later than her curfew. I wanted to tell him that he was
going overboard, but I knew it would only cause a big
argument; and in the end he gets his way, so why should
I ruin our peaceful life together. It doesn't happen every
day—just once in a while.

But sometimes at night I cry because I think I'm not
standing up for my children. I don't mind so much when
he shuts me up about something related to me that's
unfair, but when they have to suffer, it really hurts. I feel
as if I'm letting them down.

Hannah may eventually have to make a choice between her
marriage and her conscience. It is her responsibility to defend her
child from mistreatment. By standing by, by watching things
happen that she knows in her heart to be wrong, just to protect
her relationship with her husband, is to do irreparable damage to
her feeling of self. As expressed by Nathanial Branden:

> When a woman believes that her husband is wrong on
> some fundamental issue, and the question arises of
> whether to express her thoughts or to suppress them and
> thus protect the "closeness" of the relationship . . . the
> issue remains the same. Should one honor one's inner
> signals or disown them: autonomy versus conformity;
> self-expression versus self-repudiation; self-creation ver-
> sus self-annihilation.[6]

By continuing to push aside her better judgment, and by
refusing to speak only to save her relationship with her husband,
Hannah risks self-annihilation, or loss of self-esteem. How can she
respect herself when she continually violates her own conscience
in the name of love for her man? Yet so many women do it. Not
only do they watch their children being mistreated by their
husbands—not just emotionally, with unfair punishments, but
with verbal and physical abuse as well—but they watch themselves
being literally erased by a man who refuses to allow them to speak
their minds freely.

But there may be yet another issue in operation here. Perhaps

Hannah, like many women who allow themselves to be continually stifled by others, does not have enough self-trust to state her position firmly. Such women often empower their husbands with superior knowledge, because they are somehow unwilling to assume the responsibility of going by their own better judgment. But this kind of thinking is dangerous to the self, because it encourages continual self-annihilation.

No man is worth the loss of self—because if you lose your self, you have nothing left. Although it may cost you the tranquility of a smooth relationship, you should speak up and face the consequences. It would be much better than sitting silently by and observing the death of your soul.

He Won't Let You Go . . . or Have Friends

There are some men who would not think twice about spending an evening out with the boys, but if their wife or girlfriend tries to do the same, they have a fit. Other men would think nothing of going on a business trip—or even a little vacation with the boys—but would never allow their girlfriend or wife to do the same.

Consider the case of Abby, who has been seeing Bryant for six years. She says:

> My mother was very dependent upon my father, so I guess that's why I'm the way I am. Anyway, I met Bryant right out of high school, and we've been going out ever since. He's an actor, so he has lots of friends, and he travels a lot.
>
> I'm lonely when he's away, so I like to go out to clubs with my girlfriends, but he won't let me do that. When I tell him that he goes out with his friends, he says, "It's not the same. I have to socialize as a part of my business.

Your doing it will get you in trouble." He wants me to sit home and read or watch TV or visit my family.

I'd love to go out with my friends, or even to take a vacation with them. If I did, though, I would have to lie because he would never agree to it. But I can't do it. It's too much of a risk—I can't afford to lose him. I'm hoping we'll get married next year. All I ever wanted to be was a good wife and mother. In the end, it will be worth it—once we are married. Even though it makes me angry that he's so stubborn, I'd rather not take the chance of losing him.

Abby's problem, apparently, is that she is dead set on building her life around others. Her only goal is to be a good wife and a good mother. While no one could argue that these are admirable goals in and of themselves, they are not enough. What about being a full person—someone with a mind and a will of her own? Then she would be able to be a good wife to a man who would respect her, and a mother who could provide an appropriate role model for her children.

Should a Woman Build Her Life Around Her Husband's Career?

It always galls me when I hear talk of a woman building her life around that of her husband. In my opinion, it is one of the worst mistakes a woman can make. I nearly jumped out of my seat on the Long Island Railroad when, in the process of reading Mary Catherine Bateson's insightful book *Composing a Life*, I came across these words regarding the author's life: "But the underlying assumptions of my life have until recently been . . . that family life would be constructed around my husband's decisions about his career."[7]

I was appeased a few lines later when the author of that book spoke of her mother, the renowned anthropologist Margaret Mead: "She constructed her life around professional constancies and made her marriages fit. She left two husbands and was herself rejected by a third, my father, the anthropologist Gregory Bateson."[8]

Here we have it: the two extremes. In one case, a woman is willing to submerge her career under that of her husband; in another, a woman is willing to lose her husband if necessary for the sake of her career.

What is the answer? Is it really an either-or decision? Must a woman either make the supreme sacrifice and give up her career for her husband, or a husband for her career? I think not. Perhaps, somewhere to be found, there is a happy medium. Perhaps two people can get together and agree upon what is best for both of them!

In all fairness to Mary Catherine Bateson, I must say that she makes a good case for the women who were willing to submerge their careers under those of their husbands. Somehow, they seem to have chiseled out admirable professions for themselves anyway. But this may well be because these women happened to be married to very sensitive, intelligent men, who were all the time considering their wives' careers anyway. In any case, I would never be willing to take that chance. Like Margaret Mead, if it came down to it, I would leave (and indeed have left) a man before I would leave my career.

"Let" Relationships: What You Gain, What You Lose

Women who remain in "let" relationships really have a lot to gain by it. Since the man in their lives won't let them make any effort, they are relieved of the pressure and responsibility of having to do anything. It "lets" them off the hook, and in a very neat way. You see, it's simply "not their fault" that they cannot achieve, cannot go, cannot be, cannot do, cannot change. On the other hand, they also have a lot to lose. Let's take a look at each of the women discussed above.

What did Ivana Trump have to gain by letting Donald make her decisions for her? Financial security! But what did she have to lose? She put herself in the position of being dependent upon a man who valued her only as a bauble, and who could, and indeed did, drop her at will. In short, she allowed herself to be treated as an object, rather than as a person. By disallowing her own humanity, her humanity was disallowed.

What did Flora have to gain by letting Jordan tell her how to dress? A companion—someone to share time with and someone to help her feel less lonely. But what did she lose? Her autonomy. She felt like a teenager again, who was under the thumb of a parent.

What did Janet have to gain by staying with Dave? She was able to avoid the difficulty of facing the long, hard road of academic study that would be necessary before she could become a doctor. What did she have to lose? An opportunity to achieve her full potential and an eventual earning capacity that would make financial considerations irrelevant, if she chose to leave him.

What did Ali McGraw have to gain by letting Steve McQueen stop her from pursuing her career? The freedom from the pressure of finding out whether she would be able to continue making successful movies. Perhaps, deep down inside, it was her fear that her success thus far was just luck and that she would be just a flash in the pan. If Steve McQueen, her husband-to-be, would not let her continue her career, of course, she would never have to find out; and, in a sense, that could be quite a relief. But what did she have to lose? Ten years of the potentially most successful and gratifying time of her career—the years that could have propelled her into continual success—had she gone with the momentum and struck while the iron was hot.

What did Mary have to gain by remaining with Jack, for whom she had to act childishly every time she spent her own money? The financial security of a marriage that produced a net income that was greater than she could ever earn by herself. But what did she lose? Her dignity, as she was forced to become a manipulative actress in order to obtain the right to spend her own money.

What did Hannah have to gain by remaining with Eddie, who

would not allow her to express herself freely? Peace and quiet in the home. But what did she have to lose? Her own peace of mind and a sense of integrity, as she regularly violated her own conscience by standing by and watching her children endure unfair treatment.

What did Abby have to gain by remaining with Bryant, who clearly had a double standard when it came to going away and socializing with friends? The hope of a future husband who would be father to the children she always wanted. But what did she have to lose? Her joy of living, as she forced herself to follow rules that she did not believe were fair.

Take Responsibility for Your Own Life

The word "let" is a safe haven for many people. It allows them to believe that the decision is out of their hands. "He won't let me..." means: I have no power, I can't do anything. I must remain in this position.

If you are a woman who is in a "let" relationship, just think for a moment. What would happen if you no longer allowed yourself to be prevented from doing, saying, wearing, and spending? Would it not place an awful lot of responsibility on your shoulders? In some ways, isn't it safer to just continue to hide behind "He won't let me"? It's silly to blame the man.

If you had the courage to begin doing what you really want to do, and let the chips fall where they may, you might find that the man in your life stops treating you as a child and is willing to develop an adult-to-adult relationship; or you might find that he cannot cope with an independent partner and becomes even more controlling. If he does, rather than hate him, realize that it's human nature to take advantage of a good thing; and that, up until now, he was able to have quite a deal—to be the boss, with no challenge. If he's not willing to cope with the change, "let" him go, with your blessing. Perhaps we can refer him to those companies which deal with mail-order brides—women from distant lands who, due to cultural differences, like to obey their husbands' commands.

I'm not implying that we should be insensitive to our partner's feelings, needs, and opinions. However, there's a *big* difference between conferring with a person with whom you are involved (even married to) out of respect for that person's feelings—and asking permission.

In conclusion, I say with Susan Jeffers, in her book *Opening Our Hearts to Men*, "We can't blame men for walking all over us. We can only notice that we are not moving out of the way."[9]

NOTES

1. Interview with Ivana Trump and Barbara Walters, "20/20" 10 May, 1991, Show no. 1119 (New York: Journal Graphics), pp. 4, 5, and 7.

2. Sonya Friedman, *Men Are Just Desserts* (New York: Warner Books, 1983), p. 3.

3. Ali McGraw, *Moving Pictures* (New York: Bantam, 1991), p. 93.

4. Ibid., p. 149.

5. Ibid., p. 146.

6. Nathanial Branden, *The Psychology of Romantic Love* (New York: Bantam, 1980), p. 59.

7. Mary Catherine Bateson, *Composing a Life* (New York: Penguin Books, 1990), p. 12.

8. Ibid., p. 12.

9. Susan Jeffers, *Opening Our Hearts to Men* (New York: Ballantine Books, 1989), p. 57.

Reminders

1. You are not a child. You have the right to decide what you will and will not wear.

2. If you give up your career for a man, you will live to regret it.

3. Spend your own money, express your opinions, and go where you will—and if he doesn't like it, get rid of him.

4. Sometimes women remain in "let" relationships because they are secretly afraid of being allowed to try their wings.

5. Dare to take responsibility for your own life. There's no greater feeling than the power of self-direction.

4

Get Rid of Him If He's Jealous of You or Does Not Empower You

He constantly criticizes you: your speech, your behavior in company of friends, your way of handling yourself in job situations, your manner of dealing with your family, and, if you have them, the way you handle the children. He often compares you unfavorably with others.

You've spent hours with hair, makeup, and wardrobe, but all he notices is the lint on your jacket. He not so jokingly calls you his "old lady," and points out the crow's feet around your eyes.

He does not seem to believe you can succeed, and if you do, he does not celebrate your victories. There's a strange silence when you tell him about your promotion. Mysteriously, you find yourself soft-selling your achievements, not only to him, but in his presence—and searching for ways to blow up his accomplishments.

He is "concerned" about all the long hours you're putting in at your job—but not concerned about his own undue devotion to *his* job. In many ways, he tries to let you know that he is superior to you.

He cannot cope with your being the center of attraction, so when you're with him, you stifle yourself, even though your nature is outgoing and your wit and humor are appreciated elsewhere.

Why does he say or do these things? Is he jealous of you, or does he really believe that you are inferior to him—in fact, inferior to a lot of people? The answer is interesting, and we'll explore it, but does it really matter? In either case, it's his problem, not yours, yet the unfortunate end result is a continual drain on your psychological energy.

His criticisms may take the form of looking out for your best interests—of trying to save you from making a fool of yourself; or they may be indirect, such as, "Isn't it amazing how Doris's house is always so neat. I wonder how some women manage to do that and still have a career?" Or his faultfinding may be more overt, such as, "What a slob you are."

In any case, by now, he's probably either forced you into a retreat position, where your personality has been altered to accommodate his neurosis, and you are no longer able to be spontaneous for fear of offending him, or you are fighting for your rights and there is not a moment of peace. Sometimes you even think you hate him. But whether you are outright angry or, worse, depressed (the result of suppressed anger), the long and the short of it is, you don't need this.

Although both overt jealousy and hidden envy boil down to the same thing, hidden envy is more difficult to deal with, because you constantly think, "Is this my imagination? Am I becoming paranoid?" In the following paragraphs we'll look at all kinds of male jealousy, both covert and overt, and try to learn some lessons from it.

He's Always Correcting You—
For Your "Own Good"

Trish was quietly allowing herself to be undermined on a daily basis. A highly intelligent college graduate and a successful editorial assistant, she was living with Garrison, a successful salesman. She says:

> The moment I walked through the door of our apartment, I could feel myself change. It was almost as if I shed my persona like a coat and left it outside the door—and once inside, I became a vulnerable child in need of constant guidance.
>
> He spent much time correcting my grammar. He would pick on obscure things, such as the use of the subjunctive in speaking. And even though I had majored in English in college, he had me doubting myself.
>
> When we went out with friends, he would compliment the woman in the couple, saying things like, "Genevieve, you really take care of your nails. Maybe you could share your secret with Trish." If we were having dinner at another couple's home, he would say, "Violet, how do you keep your house so immaculate? Ours always looks like a tornado hit it." In the meantime, he's the one who throws his clothing around.
>
> It didn't end there. Whenever I was ready to leave for work, he would have some criticism to make about my hair, the way I put on my makeup, or what I was wearing. Many are the times when I would change my outfit just because of something he had said.
>
> Another thing. At the table, you know, that time when you sit down with someone you love and share your day? well, I learned to be careful not to tell him anything about how I handled various crises at work, because, invariably, instead of complimenting me, he

would tell me how he would have handled it, and of course it was never the way I did. It always felt like a put-down.

When I asked Trish why she stayed with Garrison in spite of all the torture he put her through, she was quick to point out that he was handsome, confident, and sexy, and that he seemed to know it all. "He was one of those people who speak with authority, and you think they're right just because of the way they say it," she explained. "I guess he just overwhelmed me."

One day she ran into an old college friend, a girl whom she had always admired for her independence. As it turned out, this friend had recently gotten divorced and was now attending classes toward her Ph.D. in psychology while holding a full-time job. Almost jealous of her classmate's happiness, Trish related her own misery and found out that her friend had gotten a divorce for similar reasons, that her husband was always putting her down. She told Trish that she was lucky to realize the problem before, and not after, marriage—and in two years, rather than the seven it had taken her.

Inspired by her friend's example, and also because, as Trish expresses it, she had "had it," Trish began looking in the paper in the "apartments for rent" section. Trish recalls:

> I don't know exactly what gave me the courage—I seem to have gone on "automatic"—but one week after my first apartment-hunting excursion, I found a beautiful garden apartment and dared to put a deposit on it. Another week went by and it was the first of the month—the lady said I could move in. I took off from work and, with the help of a few friends, I moved all of my stuff out—while he was at work.
>
> That night, after he already got home and saw that I had moved out, I called. He said, "What the f——." I told him that I had to do it this way. He called me a lot of names and said that when I came crawling back, he might not be there. He was closing a door, and it was scary, and I thought, "He might be right."

But it never happened. In fact, all Trish felt was relief, and the moment she felt tempted to call him, out of loneliness, all she had to do was remember how suffocated she felt with him. With the support of her family and friends, she quickly adjusted to living alone—and began to enjoy the freedom of being her own person.

Trish is now living on the East Coast, having been promoted to the position of full editor. She's dating a variety of men and, as she expresses it, having the time of her life.

Overidentification: Is He Still an Adolescent?

What was in Garrison's mind when he continually corrected Trish's dress, speech, and behavior, and compared her unfavorably to others? Didn't he know that he was hurting her feelings? Apparently not. He was caught up in his own issue, an issue of overidentification that had never been resolved.

Overidentification affects people who have not been able to establish a firm and separate identity of their own and therefore see their love or marriage partner as a reflection of themselves. They also believe that others view it this way. Using Garrison and Trish as an example, here's how the thinking goes:

> GARRISON: If Trish says something stupid, everyone will laugh at me behind my back and say, "Garrison's girlfriend is such a dingbat. I knew he was a loser. This proves it."

Garrison's behavior would be quite normal—if he were a teen-ager! I've worked with adolescents for over twenty-five years, and I've discovered that one of the most common problems teens suffer from in their younger years is that of being embarrassed by parents. In fact, most adolescents are embarrassed by even inno-cent things that parents do, such as when parents tell jokes in front of their friends, dance around, or wear something that appears either too old-fashioned or too hip. They become even more embarrassed by parents who are overly fat, extremely sloppy, or unduly loud.

Why do teens feel this way? Since they are really half child and half adult, they have not yet made the full separation of identity from their parents. "What someone thinks of my parent," he or she imagines, "someone thinks of me." For example, if a teen's father comes to school on open-school night wearing lots of gold jewelry and an open-necked shirt, that teen pictures everyone thinking, "Look at Jared's father. He still thinks it's the seventies. Jared must be just like him."

Interestingly, it is the younger adolescents of eleven through fifteen who have the biggest problem in this area. As adolescents mature, if they have a reasonable amount of self-esteem, they are gradually less and less embarrassed by parents. They begin to realize that what a parent does or wears does not necessarily reflect upon them. For example, a nineteen-year-old may think it's cute when her mother dances wildly at a wedding, whereas a thirteen-year-old would want to dig a hole in the floor and crawl into it.

Overidentification is perfectly normal in developing adolescents, because they are just beginning to find out that they are in fact unique individuals—completely separate from their parents. In fact, a large part of this process can be demonstrated in the outlandish clothing that teens wear. They are really saying, "I am nothing like my parents—or their generation."

If teens make a good adjustment, they turn into adults who are eventually able to live and let live, not only where parents are concerned, but where others are concerned as well. They eventually come to the conclusion that most people are in fact not concentrating on them at all, and are more concerned about a pimple on their own nose than an earthquake that just killed ten thousand people in India!

Unfortunately, not everyone makes a good adjustment from adolescence to adulthood. For a variety of reasons, many people continue to overidentify with a significant other. For these people, what used to be overidentification with a parent becomes overidentification with a girlfriend, a wife, and later with children. (These are the people who become extremely furious if their children do the slightest thing that would bring embarrassment to them.)

Wisely, Trish left Garrison—who was apparently suffering from this problem. Had she remained with him, she would have been so preoccupied with dealing with Garrison's continual corrections that she might not have been able to concentrate on her job enough to earn the promotions she got; and she certainly wouldn't have been able to move to the East Coast to take on that advanced position.

What was it, really, that saved Trish? Evidently, she did not spend years in therapy. She did not read a hundred self-help books. She did not call everyone in her family and ask for their opinion. She "listened" and she "heard" a message from a friend—a message that was an echo of an inner voice, from a friend she just "happened" to meet at the right time.

When the Student Is Ready, the Teacher Arrives

Or was that meeting just a coincidence? I think not. What happened to Trish is an example of synchronicity—a phrase coined by psychologist Carl G. Jung. He was fascinated by the fact that when many of his patients were trying to work out certain problems, they would happen into experiences which seemed like coincidence, but were connected so meaningfully with other experiences in their lives that they could not have been just good luck. Jung concluded that it must be the unconscious which draws these seemingly lucky events into the lives of people.

If we are actively seeking an answer to a problem, it seems as if our unconscious energy sees to it that we are in the right place at the right time, and for some strange, or perhaps not-so-strange, reason, we can also see and hear differently. In fact, our unconscious has put us on the alert.

Carl Jung cites an example of synchronicity in his early practice. He was trying to convince a woman that the phenomenon of
synchronicity really exists. One night, the woman had a dream,
and in the dream she saw a rare beetle, a golden scarab. The
next day she was in a therapy session with Jung and was in the
process of describing the dream. At that moment there was a
strange scratching on the screen of the window, which became
so annoying that Jung had to stop the session to check it out.
He opened the window, and there on the screen was a golden
scarab beetle, which was almost never seen in that part of
the world. Needless to say, the patient was convinced that
synchronicity exists. [1]

I have had many experiences with synchronicity, way before I
knew what the word meant, and I continue to have them. I notice
that these experiences occur to me when I am calling for help, in a
sense, with the silent voice of my soul. The experience seems to
come to assist me—to give me the final nudge I need to make me do
what I know I have to do. Perhaps your reading this book at this
moment in time is an example of synchronicity for you.

When Trish happened to run into her friend at just the right
time, it was an answer to a cry from her soul. It reminds me of the
oft-repeated saying, When the student is ready, the teacher arrives.

Most important to the story, however, is that Trish not only knew
what she had to do, but she did it. She took action. There's an
interesting pattern found in the instructions given to miracle seekers
in the Bible. As noted by author Alan Loy McGinnis in *The Power
of Optimism*, when people came to Jesus for a miracle, he threw the
ball right back to them by asking them to take specific action:

> "Go wash," he said to a blind man. "Stretch out your
> hand," he said to a crippled man. "Take up your bed and
> go home," he commanded the paralyzed man. When we
> rise from our lethargy and take some action, the action
> enhances our confidence. [2]

The way I see it, it was almost as if Jesus were calling their bluff,
asking them, in a manner of speaking, to put their money where

their mouths were, to back up their own request by an investment of energy—both physical and psychological. By getting up and moving from point A to point B, and by risking making fools of themselves, the miracle seekers fulfilled the requirement and, in turn, reaped the reward.

Trish put her knowledge of what was right together with daring action, and the result was a new life for her—in a sense, a miracle. The lesson is clear. If we are tired of the situation we are in, we must do something different. It's crazy to think otherwise. In fact, I recall reading somewhere that the very definition of insanity is doing the same thing again and again and expecting to get different results.

The Shapeless Blob and the Hot Bodies

Ironically—or perhaps it was synchronicity—I observed a real-life demonstration of the kind of male behavior experienced by Trish with Garrison, just as I was about to conclude the writing of this chapter.

I decided to take a break from my writing, and I invited my nineteen-year-old daughter to spend the day at the beach. While we were relaxing in the sun, a couple who looked to be in their early forties passed by, and we overheard their one-way conversation. The man said to his girlfriend or wife, who was quite pretty and in generally good shape, "Look at the hot bodies on some of these girls." The woman looked up and observed the bodies, and then silently bowed her head. She looked sad.

Ironically, the man was a white, shapeless blob with love handles as big as snowballs. Quite used to hearing men speak to women this way, I merely registered it and kept my silence. But my nineteen-year-old daughter reacted differently. "Did you hear that?" she asked, as she rose up on her elbow in indignation. "She should have turned around and commented on the sexy buns of those jocks playing volleyball in their tight shorts." Then she became sad and said, "That poor woman. I would never take that from a man. I would be gone so fast he wouldn't even know what hit him."

But many women are not so willing to leave. And apparently, hundreds of thousands of women, like the woman at the beach, merely bow their heads in silence as they endure the hurtful comments of the man who shares their life.

He Is Indifferent or Threatened
By Your Accomplishments

Rhonda, a criminal lawyer, has been going out with Saul, a Wall Street broker, for ten months. She made it a habit of celebrating her boyfriend's accomplishments, but never got any positive feedback when she achieved something. For example, she says:

> Last week I won a very difficult case and was thrilled. During dinner, I told him about it. When he made no comment, I repeated myself and said, "Saul, didn't you hear me? I just told you about something that is very important to me. I'm so proud of myself." He said, "I'm glad for you." I added that I had been worried all week, and what a relief it was now that I had won. Then he interrupted and said: "Are we going to have to talk about this all night?"
>
> This happens all the time, and I usually put up with it because other things in our relationship are great—for example, we have the same sense of humor, and we have lots of friends in common. We get along sexually, and we like each other's families.
>
> But this time I decided to confront him. I calmly told him that we needed to talk about this. I asked him why he never wants to hear about it when I do well at my job. He got angry and said, "I'm sick and tired of you

thinking that the minute you do something you think is great, the world owes you applause." When I reminded him that I always rejoice when he accomplishes anything, he looked betrayed and said, "And all the time I thought it came from your heart. Now I know you were just a phoney."

I'm still going out with him, but I know I'll drop him once I meet someone more supportive. In fact, if I met a man who was not threatened by my achievements, I would snap him up in a New York minute.

The problem with Saul, as with so many men who underplay their girlfriend's or wife's accomplishments, is he thinks little of himself. For example, when Saul accuses Rhonda of being a phoney when she compliments him, what he's really saying is, "I don't believe anyone could be stupid enough to believe that anything I do is noteworthy. You are just saying nice things to make me feel better." In short, Saul does not believe he is valuable.

As Rhonda learned, one cannot heal such a person by continual ego-boosting and compliments. In the case of an insecure man, sunshine is wasted on rocks. Nothing will grow or change.

We all have a force that gently speaks, driving us to fulfill our potential. If we have someone there to amen that voice, we are that much more likely to achieve it to the fullest and in the shortest time possible. If there is not, or if there is someone sitting on top of our energy like a weighty sandbag, it is that much more difficult to get ahead. Yet so many women plod along, trying to succeed in spite of such a burden—and miraculously, many of them do. Their success reminds me of grass when it manages to grow through concrete—cracking it to break through. It is sad to think that so many women have to work this hard to excel "in spite of" the man in their lives.

He Thinks He's Superior to You—or Does He?

When Enid, a highly intelligent college graduate, met Troy, a successful copywriter, she mistook his arrogance and sarcasm for self-confidence. Hoping that he could provide the missing link to her happiness, and on the rebound from a broken romance, she married him after only six months of dating. Shortly after, she was promoted to the position of head buyer in a major department store and was earning almost as much as he was. She says:

> As soon as I got my promotion he began to complain that I was spending too much time away from home, even though I was usually home before him. I got the feeling that what was really bothering him was my success, because from time to time he would say things like, "Why don't you get a real job?" or "Aren't most of the buyers bitchy women? You'd never see a man become a buyer, would you?"
>
> He made up a series of nonflattering nicknames for me too—like "air brain," "dingbat," and "ditz." He would call me these if we were watching TV and I missed a point that he thought was profound, or when I forgot to do something I was supposed to do.

Even though Troy was a delight to the eye, he became Enid's psychological nightmare. She found herself feeling lonely and depressed and began to wonder if she wouldn't be better off without him—a man who constantly reminded her that she was lucky to have such a superior person for a husband. After four years, and still unable to do what she really wanted to do—divorce Troy—Enid got lucky. As she explains:

> It's almost as if I willed it. He met another woman and started up an affair. When I caught him, rather than

fight to save my marriage, I just said, "What do you want to do?" and when he said he wanted a divorce, I quickly agreed.

He was amazed because he's so egocentric that he thought I would fight for him. But this was my out, and I took it. The divorce was ugly, and there was a lot of name-calling and threats, but there was never a moment when I seriously considered changing my mind and trying to dissuade him, because every time I thought of it, something said, "Let him go."

Enid has been divorced for three years now and loves living alone. "I can walk around the house in rags, if I feel like it, and eat standing at the refrigerator, if I please, and I don't have to worry about working late hours." Coming and going as she pleases, and calling friends when she needs to talk, Enid says that she has every intention of staying single forever.

What went wrong in Enid's marriage? Clearly, Troy believed that he was superior to Enid—or at least it would seem so on the surface. However, if we look a little closer, we see something quite different. Apparently, what Enid mistook for arrogance and self-confidence was something quite different. Alfred Adler, the psychologist who first described the superiority complex, and demonstrated that it is really an inferiority complex, explains: "Behind everyone who behaves as if he were superior to others, we can suspect a feeling of inferiority which calls for a special form of concealment."[3]

Apparently when Troy was growing up, he did not get the feeling that he was lovable enough. In fact, he felt inferior to others. It was this feeling of inferiority that caused him to develop a system that he believed would make him acceptable—a system of building himself up and, at the same time, cutting others down. In fact, this is exactly what he was up to when he protested Enid's spending so much time at her job—once her salary approached his. After all, was it not his unconscious nightmare to have Enid equal to or surpassing him? Would it not prove to the world what unconsciously he believed to be true—that he was indeed inferior? It was also the reason behind his efforts to expose everyone else's stupidity, while at the same time demonstrating his superior intelligence.

Superiority-inferiority complexes do not go away by themselves. Not even success is enough to cure them. In fact, success, to a person with an inferiority-superiority complex, merely serves as a temporary appeasement. It is similar to throwing fresh meat to a mythical lion whose hunger can never be satisfied. The more meat you throw, the more meat the lion demands.

Many women ask me if it is possible to help such a man by giving him the unconditional love that he surely missed growing up. The answer is clear. You are not a trained therapist, and even if you were, you couldn't help him. As you may already know, therapists never attempt to treat their own families; nor do medical doctors. Emotions run too high for success. Personal involvement prevents objectivity. You cannot save him. But you can save yourself by making a decision to leave such a man. In this way, you can at least separate his problems from yours, and deal with the problems you can handle—your own.

He Cannot Cope with *You* Being the Center of Attraction

Jody is a delightful woman. Naturally witty, fun-loving, and intelligent, she is a professional ballet dancer who was engaged to Logan, a cardiologist. Gradually, their relationship started to undergo a shift as Jody came under criticism for her behavior in social settings. A typical example:

> We were at a party with all of his peers, and all sitting around talking. As usual, I ended up exchanging witty repartee with various members of the group. Without making a special effort to do so, I kept everyone laughing.
> The only one *not* laughing was Logan. Later on he

gave me a sullen look and a general "attitude," and I
began to wonder what I had done to offend him, so I
asked him what was wrong. "Wrong?" he asked. "What
could be wrong? You were the center of attention as
usual, so what could be wrong? Why can't you just stay
in the background for a change?"

That hurt! After all, the only thing I was guilty of was
being myself and socializing with his peers on their level.
I would have thought he would appreciate a fiancée who
could be an interesting conversationalist rather than a
social drip.

That weekend, when Logan was away at a convention, Jody did
a lot of thinking and also a lot of talking to friends and relatives.
After telling her cousin what was wrong, she found herself
blurting out, "I don't want to marry him." Relieved to hear her say
those words, her cousin pointed out that she had noticed that,
since the engagement, Jody's whole personality had seemed to
change. In fact, she noted that where Jody used to walk with a
bounce, she was now walking with a shuffle.

That did it for Jody. She decided once and for all to break
her engagement with Logan, but dreaded the reaction of her
family, because, after all, he was a good "catch," a highly
respected cardiologist. But Jody was in for a surprise. She
explains:

I felt so guilty breaking up with him. I thought that
surely something must be wrong with me if I couldn't
find a way to make this relationship work. But I was
relieved when my family told me, "Doctor or no doctor,
what's the use of marrying a man who makes you
miserable?"

I'm now going out with an orchestra conductor who is
sensitive and secure—and we get along just fine. With
him, I don't have to watch anything. Being myself is just
fine. I feel as if someone has let the oxygen into the
room and now I can breathe again.

What was Logan's problem? Was he jealous of Jody, or did her outgoing personality just annoy him? Without knowing more about him, it's difficult to determine exactly what his problem was, but one thing is for sure—he didn't accept Jody for what she was. As a matter of fact, he didn't even seem to like her.

I wonder as I write this, how many women out there are going out with, or are married to, men who don't even seem to like them—and how long will it take for these women to come to the point where they've had enough?

It's His Issue

If you are in a situation where a man is jealous of you, or if you are with a man who does not empower you, for whatever reason, realize that it is in fact his problem, and not yours.

Is he a bad person? Should he be condemned for his attitude? Of course not. He comes to your relationship with a whole set of problems of his own—parents who may not have been the most accepting, experiences that may have caused him to build up phobias, lots of other psychological baggage. In fact, his self-esteem may be so badly damaged that he may be operating in what is called an emergency psychological state. In such a condition, a person cannot afford the luxury of living and letting live. In fact, he will feel compelled to be constantly vigilant, in an effort to guard against being exposed for what he fears he is: a worthless fraud. It is similar to the way one feels when one is in physical danger; the first and only worry is to remove the threat to one's life—whether it be an approaching murderer, a serious disease, or even a high fever. The point is, until the threat to one's physical existence is dealt with, one cannot go on and enjoy life.

All the devices used by the men in this chapter are merely emergency techniques for making things right. As they see it, they

must continually diminish the women with whom they are connected (and others as well) in order to prove to themselves and
the invisible, judging audience that they are not inferior. If, at any
moment, someone else threatens to shine brighter than them,
they feel compelled to throw water on that fire. If they do not,
they fear that they will be exposed for the rotten person that, deep
down inside, they believe they are. Their job, however, is endless—
because there will always be some new threat looming on the
horizon.

Stop Blaming Yourself: You Are Not Omnipotent

It is interesting to note that Jody blamed herself for not being able
to make the relationship work. This is a typical stance taken by
women when relationships begin to fall apart. For some reason,
they seem to believe that it is in their power to make it work; and,
in fact, if the relationship does not work, they take it to mean
that they must have done something wrong or neglected to do
something right.

In psychological parlance, such self-talk is called omnipotent
thinking. Irrationally, the individual who engages in such self-
condemnation when a relationship fails assigns herself supernatu-
ral ability—the power to enter into the mind of another human
being and heal, amend, or at least control that person's mental
problems and personality quirks, which are helping to make the
relationship unworkable.

Needless to say, none of us is omnipotent. No human being
possesses the power to control another person's behavior, and no
person can take full responsibility for a relationship. Two people
are involved. It is at best silly to think that you, and you alone,
have the power to make a relationship work; and at worst it is
dangerous. It can cost you a lifetime of energy wasted in
self-flagellation.

You Can't Choose Your Parents but You Can Choose Your Mate

When we are growing up, our self-esteem is formed largely by the way our parents react toward us. If we are given a heavy dose of unconditional love, we come out with high self-esteem. If we are not, we struggle all our lives to build it. In any case, it's the luck of the draw. Not a one of us has chosen our parents.

While we cannot choose or switch our parents, we can choose or switch our mates. If we did not get proper treatment from our parents, there is no reason to punish ourselves further by selecting men who punish us in kind. We can, by an act of will or, if need be, with the help of a therapist, remove ourselves from the presence of a man who does not empower us.

There are enough people in the world who will pose themselves as enemies to us—people who will come into our lives and make trouble, whether we like it or not. Why should we choose to have the enemy in our own camp—someone who is, in essence, not on our side, for whatever reason? Don't you deserve to have a relationship with someone with whom you can have an it's-you-and-me-against-the-world feeling?

Advice to the Psychologically Battered Woman

Chances are, if the man in your life has been bombarding you with a constant stream of criticisms, whether these attacks have been waged against your mental or physical qualities, you are not feeling very confident right now. In fact, you may be saying to yourself, "If I leave him, who knows? I may not be able to attract another man—and maybe I'll wish I stayed with him."

If you feel this way, do yourself a favor and try a little experiment. Get up a half hour earlier tomorrow morning and put a little more time into getting dressed for work or wherever you are going that day. Do your makeup the way you would if you had a date with a wonderful man you had just met and for whom you wanted to look your best. Take the time to get your hair to look just the way you want it to look. Wear something just a bit sexier than usual. Put on the jewelry that you know completes the outfit—a finishing touch that you wouldn't usually bother with.

Then, as you go about your daily business, adapt a devil-may-care attitude. Put a smile on your face. Let the world know that you are happy to be alive. Fall in love with life itself—even for just one day. It will be fun to see the reaction you get. To your pleasant surprise, you will find that men will pay more attention to you than usual. Why is this so?

It is usually more a woman's attitude than her actual looks that determines whether she will get male attention. A woman who walks around with her head down, or with a scowl on her face and with tight, mean lips (because she is always thinking of her sour relationship), will of course not attract a whole lot of male attention. On the other hand, a woman who is smiling, who has a saucy walk and a sparkle in her eyes, will surely attract men.

This point is made time and again when women ask me, "Why is it that whenever I fall in love, all kinds of men approach me, but when I'm not seeing anyone, I never meet anyone?" The answer is clear. When you are in love, you walk as if you are floating on air. You look around you and appreciate your environment. You exude positive energy. Men respond to it and feel free to speak to you. So if you are having trouble adapting the right attitude, just make believe you are in love. You'll be amazed to see how this works.

NOTES

1. Carl G. Jung, *Synchronicity* (Princeton, N.J.: Princeton University Press, 1973), pp. 21–24.

2. Alan Loy McGinnis, *The Power of Optimism* (New York: Harper & Row, 1990), p. 24.

3. Alfred Adler, *What Life Should Mean to You* (New York: Putnam, Perigree Books, 1958), p. 50.

Reminders

1. Men who continually criticize women may be suffering from adolescent overidentification. If you want a baby, have one—don't go out with one, and whatever you do, don't marry one!!!

2. If he doesn't celebrate your successes, could he be jealous?

3. His superior attitude may be a thin mask to hid a very insecure man.

4. You can't choose your parents, but you *can* choose your mate.

5. Test the waters. I'll bet some other men will know how to treat you.

5

Get Rid of Him If He's Not on the Mainland (He Has Too Many Psychological Problems)

He's a great guy, but he's got problems. He may not be an outright mental case, although your father might have called him that one or two times—but either he is slightly or dramatically off base (not on the mainland) or his personality combined with yours causes problems.

Maybe he lies a lot—much more than the normal "white lie" kind of thing. Or perhaps he's usually depressed, and you have to continually find ways to cheer him up. Maybe he can't cope with even the slightest criticism, and you find yourself having to watch every word you say around him.

Maybe he cannot be alone—is obsessed with you and demands that you spend every waking moment with him—and becomes insecure the moment you are out of his sight. Perhaps he is overly jealous, to the point where you have to watch every innocent move you make, for fear that he will misinterpret your words or actions and think that you're flirting with someone. Maybe he's extremely cruel or sadistic—something that you've gradually come to realize, and now it scares you.

Finally, perhaps the two of you just can't be normal together. People say you have a love-hate relationship. There seems to be no happy medium—either you're furiously fighting or passionately making up.

Not on the mainland. This is a chapter about men in your life who are, to put it bluntly, more trouble than they're worth.

Lies About Who He Is

Heather was very excited when she and Samuel got engaged and set a wedding date. After six months of dating, Samuel had asked Heather to marry him. "I was thrilled," she says, "because, as you can see, I'm no beauty queen and, frankly, I was thirty-five already, and I was beginning to worry that I'd never get married." As the wedding day drew near, Heather began to feel curious about the dry-cleaning store in New York Samuel said he owned— after all, it was the store that she would manage once they got married. She began nagging Samuel to let her see it, but he continually put her off, saying that he wanted to wait until it was completely renovated. Finally, when she put enough pressure on him, he gave her an address, but it looked suspicious, as Heather expresses it. "It was an East Side number for a West Side address."

Unable to control her growing misgivings, Heather decided to go and check out the store, and one evening, with her sister in tow, she drove to the address. Heather recalls:

> Sure enough, there was no such address on the street he gave. As it all came together, my heart beat triple-time and I began to realize: If he lied about this, there must be other lies. I was sick to my stomach.

In a panic, I thought of my wedding. What would my family and friends say if I had to call it off? My mind took every turn: "Maybe I won't let on that I know anything—marry him anyway and then, once we're married, help him with his problem. Then at least I won't have to face the embarrassment of having to tell everyone what happened." But my saner side took over and I started my detective work.

Heather soon discovered a pattern of lies. As it turned out, Samuel had never served in Vietnam, as he had claimed, and he had no children by a former marriage. The only thing true about his story was that his ex-wife was a nurse. She said that she divorced him because he was a pathological liar. Heather was livid.

I called him up and confronted him, and he started to cry and begged me to listen. He said he could explain everything. I didn't want to hear it, because I knew I would just get more lies. It was a creepy feeling, and I felt almost as if I had been raped. He kept calling me, but when I got an unlisted number, I never heard from him again.

Apparently, Heather had no idea at the beginning of the relationship that she was dealing with sociopath—a person who, without conscience, can lie about anything in an effort to manipulate people to suit his own needs. He can do this without worrying about the pain he causes or the consequences, because he functions from a completely "I" point of view. In fact, he can't imagine how others feel. He sees events and people only as they serve him. In this sense, at times he can seem almost inhuman, and in fact his behavior is frequently destructive.

Heather got rid of Samuel with very slight hesitation. For a fleeting moment, she thought of going through with it anyway, but quickly realized that the price of a little embarrassment was nothing in comparison with spending her life with a mental case, and she showed that she meant business when she got an unlisted number.

When women want to end relationships, when they really mean it, they take a final step. In effect, they close the door so that there is no turning back. For Heather, the changing of the number was that step.

Why We Sometimes Ignore the Warning Signs

Could Heather have done anything to save herself from this pathological liar before she became engaged to him? Probably. If she were not so carried away by her desire to get married, if she were not thinking about how unattractive she thought she was and how difficult it would be to get another man at her age, she might have asked more questions—if not about his children or Vietnam, at least about his business activities.

If you think about it, in most situations where someone has lied to you there has been a gut feeling that something was wrong, a sixth sense that you may have brushed aside time and again—either because of your own neediness, the person's charisma, or a combination of them both.

The good news is, you *can* learn from experience. The next time you sense that something is wrong, instead of plunging ahead, you can stop and ask, "What am I thinking?" and then start asking the questions that will help you to arrive at the truth.

Lies About Other Women

When Jackie met Richie at a dance club, she thought she had found the love of her life, but soon realized that he was also the

love of many other women's lives—and that he would never tell
the truth about any of them. Jackie says:

> We both loved Latin music, and we danced so well
> together that we ended up going out at least three times
> a week. Soon we were sleeping together almost every
> night—at my place, even though he also had an apart-
> ment, which I never got to see.
>
> Later I found out the reason—he was living with
> another woman. I was furious when I found out, but he
> said she meant nothing to him—his relationship with
> her was ending. He claimed that she knew all about me
> and that he was only staying there until he could find
> another place. I didn't like it, but I figured, "Oh, well."
> We kept sleeping together almost every night, so I
> thought, "How important could she be in his life?"

But soon, Jackie caught Richie in his first lie. A family wedding
came up, and he said that he wanted to go alone because his
family wasn't ready to meet her. In the meantime, he brought the
woman he was living with. When Jackie confronted him, he
invented a series of excuses that were all but satisfactory. Jackie
told him that she wanted to end the relationship, and that's when
he really threw her a curve. He asked her to marry him. Jackie
says:

> I was shocked and thrilled at the same time, and I said
> yes. I thought, "Once we are married he will change.
> After all, he didn't marry any of these other women, did
> he?"
>
> But it turned out that his offer to marry me was just a
> trick to keep me around, because no matter what I said,
> he refused to set a date. I broke it off with him and
> stayed away for three weeks, but then I ran into him at
> the dance club, and we started up again. We went on
> and off like that for one year. In the meantime, all
> along I was complaining to my best friend, and she had

been nagging me to go to therapy. I finally took her advice.

After a few months of counseling, Jackie built up enough self-esteem to say, in her own words, "I deserve better than that." She cut him out of her life completely. Having learned her lesson well, Jackie wonders:

> When I think of how I used to let that man dominate my life, how I had no peace of mind, how all my thoughts were occupied with worries about what he was up to—what he was really thinking, what he would do next—I don't believe it was really me! You have no idea how a little good therapy can change your whole way of thinking. Now, I would never let a man jerk me around that way.

Jackie was caught up in a whirlpool that would have kept her busy for the rest of her life. Fortunately, she was willing to share her doubts with a friend, who continually warned her that something was wrong and eventually convinced her to see a therapist.

Don't Keep It to Yourself

It is always difficult if not impossible to, as it were, "see the forest for the trees" when you're in a romantic situation, because you are emotionally involved and have too much at stake to look at it objectively. After all, if you did add up the cold, hard facts, you might have to admit that leaving him is your only option.

Find a friend, a relative, a clergyperson, a mental health professional, even an acquaintance—but find someone to talk to. If your doubts are confirmed by these objective parties, you may find the strength to do what you must do—and, in the end, save yourself years of anguish.

If you still have doubts, you can try this little test. Make believe that a dear friend has come to you with the exact problem you have. Picture her giving you all the details and imagine yourself listening carefully to your beloved friend. Now imagine the advice you would give your friend. Then take that advice yourself.

He Is Always Depressed or Down

Although some of us get satisfaction when we succeed in lifting our mate's spirits when they are low, it can be a nightmare to be with a man who needs constant cheering up. Listen to Katrina talk about Oliver, a successful boat dealer who never seemed happy, even on Christmas Eve with his children gathered around, eyes aglow, ready to watch their father open the gifts that they had carefully selected for him:

> With a sour puss on, he sat there and lethargically opened the presents, one after another, making some comment such as, "This will never fit me," or "You really bought this for yourself; you know I'll never wear it." Everything he said was negative. It pained me to see the disappointed look on his children's faces as they watched him speak.

Later, when Katrina was alone in the kitchen with Oliver, she asked what was wrong. "My mother died around the Christmas holidays," he said. Katrina said she was sorry and asked when it happened, thinking that it must have been recently. "Fifteen years ago," he said morosely.

> "Wake up to the world," I thought. "No offense meant to your mother, but bury the dead and move on. You are

still alive, and so are your children." Naturally, I didn't say this to him. I just said, "Well, it's sad that she died, and especially that it happened around the holidays, but I guess we have to thank God for what we do have. Look at those beautiful children you have there and how much they love you."

I made some more positive comments, and he cheered up a little. But that night I did some thinking. It would be one thing if this were an isolated incident. After all, people do get depressed around the holidays, and no matter how long it has been since your mother died, you would still feel pain. But with Oliver, depression and gloom were his middle name. I had spoken to him about seeing a psychologist, and he laughed it off. "I'm not crazy," he said. As I lay there in my bed, I asked myself a question. "Do I need this for the rest of my life?" And the answer was NO.

I felt really bad about doing this, because I pictured how desolate and depressed it would make him. I know how I felt when my last boyfriend broke up with me—I cried for a week. I thought my heart would break. But I had to do it, so I called him and told him it just wasn't working out and I wanted to end it. Morosely, as usual, he accepted it, but I felt very guilty about it, and even now I worry about him.

Overidentification: Inappropriate Pity and Guilt

Katrina has the right to end a relationship that is not meeting her needs, yet she feels guilty about doing this because she imagines how Oliver will suffer, recalling a time when she cried for a week after having been dumped by one of her former boyfriends.

What's wrong with this picture? Katrina is overidentifying with

Oliver. She is imagining that he will feel exactly the way she felt when she was in a similar situation. This, however, is fallacious thinking, because no two human beings experience events in exactly the same manner. People grow up with all sorts of different life experiences—a whole set of unique psychological patterns that cause them to react to events in completely individual ways.

While it is true that no one is going to jump for joy upon hearing the news that he or she is being dumped, it is unrealistic to assume that someone else is going to feel the exact same degree of angst that one perceived in a similar situation. The fact is, Oliver has developed his own way of coping with disappointment and is probably a lot better at it, in his own morose way, than Katrina. She would be wise to stop wasting her energy on feeling guilty and pitying him. He will do just fine. After all, he was a "gloomy gus" but alive and breathing before he met Katrina, and he will probably be the same gloomy gus and still alive and breathing after she leaves him.

But just on the outside chance that he is not going to be okay after Katrina leaves him, is it really her responsibility to remain his keeper, just because he a depressed person? Of course not. Oliver is a fully functioning adult and is responsible for his own life.

To expect oneself to be responsible for the future well-being of another person is to engage in a form of omnipotent thinking. (A different form of this thinking has been discussed on page 76). In such thinking, one falsely believes that, like God, one is responsible for the eternal well-being of another person—and is indeed capable of maintaining the well-being of that individual.

I am particularly eager to make this point, because so many of the women I've interviewed for this book, after finally making the decision to leave a man who is wrong for them, say that they sit and worry about the pain the man must be experiencing and how he must be suffering. They confess that they are tempted to go back with that man because they cannot stand to think of what he must be going through. This kind of thinking can be most dangerous, because it can result in a boomerang pattern, where a woman finds herself being catapulted back into a negative relationship, despite everything within her that tells her to run in the opposite direction.

If you ever feel this way, my advice to you is, the moment you catch yourself contemplating such thoughts, nip them in the bud by telling yourself out loud: "Stop overidentifying. You don't know exactly how he is feeling." And then remind yourself that he's not your responsibility.

Cannot Cope with Criticism: Always on the Defensive

At first, Rachel and Stephen got along just fine. But Stephen soon showed signs of being hypersensitive to any form of criticism. She says:

> One day he was complaining about the high prices on the menu, and I said, "Oh, it's not so bad for an upscale restaurant." He immediately went on the defensive: "Are you trying to say I'm cheap?" he said, in an angry tone. It took a lot of explaining to calm him down. He seemed upset for the entire evening.
>
> The next time it happened was when I asked him why he never finished college. It wasn't really a criticism—I was going to tell him that I thought with his intelligence he could complete his degree in no time. Before I could finish my point, he began defending himself and saying that book knowledge is meaningless, and he's sick and tired of being put down just because he doesn't have a six-figure income.
>
> I could go on and on with incidents where one minute we were laughing and enjoying each other's company, and the next minute he would blow up about some innocent comment I made. Each time it happened, I would have to take great pains to explain myself and

prove that I'm not trying to put him down. It's to the
point now where I'm checking myself every time I open
my mouth.

As far as he's concerned, our relationship is fine. He
doesn't know anything is wrong. But sometimes I feel
like it's work just being with him. Why are some men
like this?

In answer to Rachel's question, some men, and some women for
that matter, are hypersensitive to criticism because they believe
that, in some specific areas, they are inferior. Such people may
have been highly criticized as children; and, unable to defend
themselves, they interpreted the criticisms to mean that they were
flawed. Now, as adults, when a topic comes up that even remotely
relates to an area of sensitivity (and these areas are many, since
critical parents usually cover a lot of ground), they become angry
and immediately defend themselves in the hope of preventing the
speaker from finding out that they are right.

The tragedy here is that the anxiety which is experienced by
the man who is hypersensitive to criticism is based upon weaknesses
he *believes* he has, not ones that actually exist. For example,
Stephen is neither cheap nor stupid, and probably no one,
except himself, is disappointed that he doesn't earn a six-figure
income.

Because of Stephen's imagined flaws he will find it necessary to
be constantly on guard in order to protect his underside. The
moment any comment is made that skirts around his perceived
areas of weakness, he will go on the defensive.

I know that it is said, "If you want a good relationship, you have
to work on it," but fair is fair. Why should you have to expend all
that energy reassuring someone who has mental problems, when
you could be using it to advance in your career, pursue goals, enjoy
hobbies, or develop a relationship with someone who *is* on the
mainland?

He Cannot Be Alone

People who cannot be alone define who they are, not by anything related to themselves, but by others. They depend upon validation from an outside source. When that source is gone, even temporarily, they feel lost, even terrified, because they feel that their self is gone too.

If you ever get involved with a passive-dependent person, you may at first mistake his inordinate attentions for love and assume that he is smitten by your charms. In the meantime, his clinging to you may be born more out of desperation than of passion.

Karen was fooled by Joe. Their relationship began slowly—an occasional lunch, then daily lunches, and finally dinner dates and a blossoming romance. She says:

> Joe and I were not just lovers, we were friends. But as our relationship developed, Joe wanted to be with me constantly. He expected to see me every single night— and if I wanted to do something on my own, like go for a tennis lesson or to a movie with a girlfriend, he would start a fight and say that I was selfish and I didn't love him as much as he loved me.
>
> Next thing you know, he was waiting for me every night when I got off the train, even though his train got in an hour earlier. He was smothering me. When I tried to put my foot down, he took it as an insult.
>
> I wished I could just tell him that we were spending too much time together and that I needed more space, but I knew that, with him, this would never work. It was all or nothing. He was not the type of guy who would settle for an occasional date.
>
> When I told him I didn't want to see him anymore, he threatened to kill himself, saying that he couldn't live without me. That really scared me, so I looked in the directory and got the number of a psychologist at the mental health center. I spoke to a counsellor and made

an appointment. The psychologist listened to my story and asked me to bring him in. He agreed, but only under the condition that I still talk to him on the phone as long as he was going to see her.

As it turned out, he liked the woman, and she was able to help him. Eventually, he stopped calling me. In a way I miss him, but in a bigger way, it's a relief to know that I have my life back again.

Karen was fortunate in that she was able to let Joe down gently. I realize that you may not have the time or the patience to do it that way, but you may have no choice. As Dr. Susan Forward points out in her book *Obsessive Love:* "If healthy lovers are rejected, they generally grieve the loss of the relationship and get on with their lives. But obsessive lovers become flooded with panic, insecurity, fear, and pain which drive them to resist tooth and nail the deterioration of the relationship."[1]

It may cost you time and some money (you will have to pay for at least your initial session with the therapist), but it may be the safest way out.

He Is Overly Jealous and Possessive—You Are a Prisoner

When a man is extremely insecure about his ability to hold onto the woman in his life, he may believe that unless he is constantly vigilant, another man will come along and whisk her away. That's what happened when Kent, the owner of a prospering office equipment company, married thirty-year-old Danielle, who then began working as his secretary. Kent was Danielle's idea of a real catch. He had all the qualities she always admired in a man—drive, control, confidence, and, most of all, success. But shortly after they married, says Danielle, the relationship deteriorated:

He began questioning where I went, what I did, who I saw, and to third-degree my girlfriends when they called. He acted as if I were trying to deceive him, even though I gave him no reason to think that way.

The tension was getting to me, and I feared a nervous breakdown. I convinced him to let me go to a woman's week at a health spa, so I could unwind. But the day after I arrived, so did he, in the form of a dozen roses. The women couldn't understand why I wasn't happy to have such a lovely gift from my romantic husband.

He gave me no peace there, calling every night and gradually bringing the subject around to "Are there any men there?" In the beginning, there weren't, but at the end of the week, a football team arrived for training, and I panicked. I worried that if he came up for a visit he would see them and believe that I was lying, so I left two days before the week ended.

I keep working on the marriage, but things are getting worse, not better. He gave up his office, and I work with him at home now. I can't tell anyone about my situation, because he's always around. The last time I called a friend when he had gone out, he came back while I was on the phone and, in an angry voice, said, "Who are you talking to?" Then he questioned me for an hour.

I keep thinking he'll change—maybe mellow out with age or something, but I don't know. I just don't know.

No one should have to live the way Danielle is living, yet she remains with Kent. Why? She is afraid—afraid of Kent and afraid of life without him as well. Her dilemma has rendered her powerless to act.

I suspect that she is depending upon a mental breakdown to get her out of the situation. But it doesn't have to be that way. She can decide to take her life into her own hands and do something about it.

For example, she could arrange an escape by planning another trip to a spa and, while there, call a women's abuse center and get the help she needs to get out. Whether counselling or immediate exit were advised, at least something would be in the works toward an eventual resolution of her situation.

He Is Cruel or Sadistic

Evelyn met Adam, a seemingly staid bookkeeper, at a party. Although she wasn't really interested in him (he spent most of the evening complaining about how boring his job was and how he was just passed up for a promotion), she gave him her phone number because he was a nice guy and she didn't want to hurt his feelings. The only reason she went out with him was, as she puts it, "He kept calling, and I had nothing better to do." You can imagine her surprise when she found herself enjoying the evening. In a matter of three dates, they were in bed. She was in for another pleasant surprise.

I have never in my life enjoyed sex with anyone more than with Adam. In fact, that's why I fell in love with him. After a few months of going out, I couldn't imagine myself ever sleeping with someone else. It's no wonder I decided to move in with him, even though I had promised myself never to live with a guy unless I married him.

Then he started playing games with me—using sex as a weapon. For example, he would tease me into thinking we were going to make love and then say, "I just remembered I have to go make an important call."

The first time he did it, I thought he was kidding. We were in the middle of it, and suddenly he jumped up and mentioned the call. I said, "Can't it wait?" With a cold and controlling look, he said, "No. It's important." Then when he got back, he said he wasn't in the mood.

The next time he did it was when I started kissing

him, and he was responding, and all of a sudden he said, "I don't like that perfume. Go take a shower and wash it off." It would have been one thing if he said it humbly, or in a normal way, but he was mean and imperious about it. It was humiliating. I didn't want to do it. But I did. Finally, we made love.

Other times, he would refuse to make love if he didn't like his dinner, or what I wore when I met him for lunch to meet his boss, or if I said something that annoyed him.

A sadistic person manipulates his victims into needing him, and when they are too weak to leave (he causes them to become sexually, emotionally, or financially dependent), he tortures them at will. He feels as if he has been defeated by life and is terribly angry, so he feels compelled to spend his time defeating others. He is in fact deadened or desensitized to the pain of others because of the battering he feels he has taken himself. But how was Evelyn to know this about Adam? She met a seemingly boring guy who turned out to be a cruel devil.

Sadistic people do not usually expose themselves at the outset, but wait until they have gained control before they start torturing their victim. Notice that it was not until Evelyn became dependent upon Adam sexually that be showed his true colors.

What makes people into sadists? They imagine that everyone else is living the good life, while they are in torment. They are so caught up in their own misery that they find it impossible to believe that other people have their woes. Apparently, this was true in Adam's case.

He was not happy in his job situation; in fact, it was the first thing he mentioned to Evelyn at the party. His way of dealing with his misery was to continually throw darts at other people's happiness. Like all sadists, he seemed to know intuitively how to zero in on the weak spot. This could be seen in his behavior with Evelyn.

Can people such as Adam be helped? Not unless they are unhappy with their behavior and want to change. As Dr. M. Scott Peck points out in *People of the Lie*, there are those who enjoy hurting others. The last thing such people would want to do would be to allow their thoughts and deeds to be scrutinized—laid out in the open. Why? Because once the light was shed upon the problem, it would put pressure on them to change—and they don't want to change. In fact, the shedding of the light would actually enrage them.[2] Such people are, by their own repeated choice, beyond help.

Women Rescuing Men

Why do so many women try to rescue men—men like Adam and men with every other kind of psychological problem? They believe that they can change such men by the power of their love. This, of course, is a myth, and it always gets women in trouble.

When a woman assumes the job of fix-it artist, she tells herself that it is her responsibility to heal the man because she loves him. But the fact is, not only is it not a woman's responsibility to heal a man she loves, it is not in her power. She simply can't do it. And in fact, in many cases, even the best of therapists can't do it. The person himself must want to change and then assume the responsibility for changing. He must then take action and change himself— with, and in many cases without, the help of a therapist.

In summary, there are certain men who are so far off the mainland that they should be avoided at all costs:

Pathological Pete: He's continually lying. There are discrepancies about major things he's told you.

Gloomy Gus: He's always depressed or down. You find yourself having to constantly hold him up.

Criticized Cal: He cannot deal with the slightest criticism, no matter how constructive in nature or carefully delivered. He perceives criticism where it does not exist.

Smothering Sam:	He wants to spend every waking moment with you. He seems to be unable to breathe without you.
Jealous George:	He stalks you and watches your every move. He monitors calls, interrogates your friends, and is in constant search of evidence that you may be betraying him.
Mean Morton:	He enjoys seeing others suffer, especially you. The moment you let down your guard and begin to enjoy him, he throws a poison dart to burst your balloon.

A Bad Combination

There are other men who may, in and of themselves, be not so psychologically off base, but in combination with you, they make for a very nettlesome relationship, so that in the long run you are better off without them.

There are two kinds of bad combinations. The first is simple incompatibility. This happens when people disagree on too many things. For example, two people may not share each other's values; one person believes in working endlessly to pile up money, the other thinks it's okay to earn just enough to get by; one person believes it's okay to cheat in business, the other believes integrity is more important than personal gain.

Sometimes people are incompatible, not because they differ in values, but because they are simply two different people. They may simply have very different interests and patterns of behavior. For example, one person is a homebody—someone who enjoys a quiet evening by the fireplace and an early bedtime—the other is a gadabout—someone who enjoys dining out every night and tracing around after new adventures. In any case, it just doesn't work.

The second bad combination has to do with psychological dynamics, where each person's psychological weakness, or issue, aggravates or makes worse the other's. For example, if Val has an issue with abandonment, because her mother was sick and could not spend time with her when she most needed nurturing, she may have a tendency to cling to men, and find it difficult to cope with relationship-threatening arguments. If she meets a man like Julius, whose father abandoned the family when he was five, she will have trouble, because he too will be dependent and unable to cope with relationship-threatening arguments. The dynamics of the couple will be extreme anxiety, which increases as the couple interacts. In such a case, every argument takes on a life-and-death tone.

On the other hand, Val may go out with a guy like Lenny, whose parents were there for him but who grew up in extreme poverty and worked his way out of it. Now he needs to pile up money for a future "famine," no matter how much he has, but she may have no problem in getting along with him—money problems and all. He, on the other hand, may have no problem putting up with her insecurity about abandonment. The couple can argue without being afraid or defensive, or experiencing sudden bursts of rage, where they feel as if they want to kill each other, or themselves.

Basic Incompatibility

Beth and Anthony got together for what they thought were all the right reasons. They enjoyed each other's company, shared a similar sense of humor, and were highly attracted to each other physically— Beth called it "electricity plus." But in the end it turned out that they were bad for each other in every other way. Beth says:

> If I said black, he said white. If I said, "I believe in that," he said, "that's ridiculous." If I said, "It's too

expensive," he said, "You're too cheap." If I wanted to go to Hawaii, he said, "What's wrong with the Hamptons." And so it went. But he was still sexy and funny as hell at times. We just couldn't see eye to eye on most anything. What really did it was his refusal to understand the importance of keeping your word. I always keep my word, and I have no respect for a man who does not keep his. For example, he was never on time—no matter how many times he promised that this time it would be different. Also, he would promise to do things—like take my nephews to Playland, or fix my mother's kitchen sink—but he didn't deliver the goods.

He seemed lazy to me. I'm a hard worker. In my spare time, I go to school at night, and when I'm not doing homework, I'm reading self-improvement books. I don't believe in sitting in front of the TV for hours rotting my brain. That's what he did. It bothered me to see him vegetating contentedly—with no goal in life. I actually didn't respect him after a while.

Finally, I got away from him. I had gotten myself so caught up in the turmoil that I actually stopped going for my B.A. in social work. One day I was so depressed, thinking about what my life would be if I stayed with him, that I just told him it was over. He was very hurt. Something in his eyes told me that he knew this time it would be for good—and it was. I moved on.

Beth has now finished her bachelor's degree and is well on her way toward her master's. She has landed a job as a case investigator for child adoption and is dating a psychologist, whom she met at her job. She says of her present relationship, "I never thought it could be exciting without the ups and downs. I thought it would be boring, but it's not. It's just calmer, more peaceful."

What was it that kept Beth and Anthony together for so long? It was the sexual chemistry and the magnetic nature of their mutual sense of humor. Such a combination can be quite alluring. In fact, it can make a woman feel as if she's on a vacation from life. Once a woman gets used to such a feeling with a man, it isn't difficult to imagine how threatened she would be about the thought of ending the relationship. In fact, she would worry that no other man could provide such feelings.

The Approach-Avoidance Conflict

Relationships such as Beth's and Anthony's are difficult to resolve, because they have approach-avoidance elements. People caught in such binds remind me of rats in a cage where a piece of electrified cheese is kept. When the rats approach the cheese, they are filled with delight, as they smell the alluring aroma and anticipate the juicy bites they will soon be taking. However, once they sink their teeth into the cheese, an electrical shock sends them flying to the other end of the cage. After they recuperate, they again smell the cheese and, brushing aside their former negative experience, again approach it, only to be shocked and thrown across the cage again. After a while, the rats learn a lesson and sit quietly at the edge of the cage, viewing the cheese suspiciously. They say to themselves, "This time we're not going for it."

Many women who have been in a bad relationship have learned to say, "I'm not going for it anymore." They have finally realized that the pleasure is not worth the pain. Some women, however, need more jolts than others before they come to their senses.

Every person has a different tolerance level for discomfort in a relationship. Apparently Beth reached hers when she realized that the conflict of staying with Anthony in this love-hate union might eventually cost her her life's goals. She decided to make the break, as painful as it was, and give up what was good about her relationship with Anthony, because what was bad was too costly.

It was just such a sacrifice that Jesus was talking about when he said: "And if thy hand offend thee, cut it off: It is better for thee to enter into life maimed, than having two hands to go to hell."[3]

Unless you or your partner are willing to probe deeply into your value system, and examine the rules by which you have decided that life must be lived, it would be better to give up the relationship—even if, in a host of other ways, that relationship is satisfying. In the end, the drain upon your energy can divert you from your destiny, at worst; and, at least, it can destroy your peace of mind.

Psychologically Incompatible

When some people get together, they fight constantly—and the reason has nothing to do with the particular issues at hand, but everything to do with psychological dynamics. Fran, who met Nathan in high school and continued her relationship with him through college, says:

> I used to blame him for everything that went wrong in our relationship, but now I know it was really both of us. Our combined energies were bad.
> With him, I retreated into the attitude of a dependent baby. I would crack up if he even mentioned going somewhere without me—but in the meantime, if I wanted to go somewhere, I expected him to accept it. Yet, with other people I was never that way. He brought out the worst in me. On the other hand, he was possessive and childlike himself. He would become jealous and petty and overly inquisitive.
> We didn't trust each other. I required constant reassurance that he was telling the truth, and he was always doing detective work to find out if I was really where I said I was. There wasn't a moment's peace in our relationship.
> Finally I realized that I could never be okay with him. We were dealing with conflicting demons, or issues. We broke up over a fight about him not wanting me to go away for a weekend without him.

Now I'm going out with a guy who is incredibly secure. Of course, he has hang-ups too, but they don't seem to bother me. For instance, he's unable to express affection. But that's okay, because I love to leap up and get him in a bear hug and smother him with a hundred kisses. He gets all embarrassed, but I can tell he loves it.

It's obvious to me, now that I'm in this good relationship, that we need to watch out not to get involved with people who bring out the darker side of ourselves.

The negative dynamic, as seen in the relationship of Beth and Anthony, can be observed in couples everywhere. They bring out the worst in each other. Yet, if those same people are lucky enough to find someone else with a whole set of different problems, issues that are complimentary rather than inflammatory to their own, they may get along quite well.

While who we meet is often luck, who we choose to go with and continue to see is not. If a woman has made the mistake of getting involved in a relationship where mutual wrong buttons are continually being pushed, the best thing she can do for herself is to get out—that is, if she thinks she deserves a peaceful, happy life.

As a matter of fact, this truth applies to any "not on the mainland" relationship. Why should you spend your life dealing with someone else's problems? Don't you have enough of your own?

NOTES

1. Susan Forward and Craig Buck, *Obsessive Love* (New York: Bantam, 1991), p. 28.

2. M. Scott Peck, *People of the Lie* (New York: Simon & Schuster, 1983), p. 77. Dr. Peck's fascinating book sheds light on the entire subject of evil versus wrongdoing.

3. Mark 9:43.

Reminders

1. The perpetual liar will keep your life in a permanent spin. Such a man will give you more than vertigo. Dump him before you lose your mind.

2. A depressed man is like a heavy sandbag on your back. Throw him off.

3. An overly jealous or possessive man is like a noose around your neck. Cut him loose before he chokes you.

4. Some couples are just a bad match. If you realize that this is true in your case, cut your losses and move on, before you waste another minute of your life.

5. Women were not put on this earth to rescue men. You could be doing something more productive with your time.

6

Get Rid of Him If He Cheats on You and Has a Double Standard

It's not fair. I know he's seeing someone behind my back. Of course, he denies it. But if he ever caught me cheating, he would kill me. I don't know what to do.

Men believe that sexual fidelity is very important—for women. Study after study shows that most men understand quite well how a man could stray by having a one-night stand, a short-term affair, or even a long-term relationship outside of marriage or outside of a regular relationship, but they could never comprehend how a woman could do the same.

The fact is, most men believe that women could never have a meaningless affair, one that is born of and based upon sheer lust. They believe that, unlike men, women are much too emotional to do this. They reason that because of the emotional component, a sexual encounter outside of the relationship would mean disloyalty because it would involve a bonding that does not take place when men cheat. In other words, most men believe (perhaps because they have experienced just this phenomenon) that women cannot separate sex from love.[1]

No wonder you have men such as the fellow quoted in Shere Hite's *Good Guys, Bad Guys* saying:

> If I had a wife who had sex outside of marriage, I am sure I would be terribly depressed and outraged. This is the worst thing that can happen to the male ego. . . . in my experience with eighty-three women with whom I have had sex outside of marriage, I had several experiences where jealousy nearly killed me. These were occasions when I learned that lovers had had sex with other men when they were ostensibly my women. Each time it was an almost unbearable affront to my belief that I am the greatest thing that ever happened in bed.[2]

Some nerve. Don't you just love that kind of thinking? In the following paragraphs, we will discuss what to do if you are going out with or are married to a man who cheats on you—but who does not believe it's okay for you to do the same.

If your man cheats on you, the way I see it, you have four choices:

1. Be happy that he cheats, because now you can try to convince him that you too have the option of doing the same, should the mood and the opportunity arise.
2. Accept it. Realize that you have no desire to go with anyone else, or you are too afraid to do so, and that you are not ready to give him up. Face the fact that, from time to time, no matter what you do, he will cheat, and learn to live with it.
3. Try a marriage counsellor, and if that doesn't work, spend your life trying to get him to change his wicked ways.
4. Give him an ultimatum, and if he doesn't agree to stop cheating—or if he agrees to stop cheating but doesn't live up to it—get rid of him.

By now you might be able to guess which of the four choices I would recommend, but let's explore the first three before we talk about that.

1. Try to Get Him to Agree to the Same Privileges for You

If your man cheats, it could be lucky for you. After all, now you can have your cake and eat it too—the security of the relationship and the freedom to enjoy an occasional dalliance. No longer do you have to ignore the handsome, sexy men that flirt with you. This could be an ideal situation if...

First of all, it would depend upon your values. If you are a strong believer in fidelity, skip this section right now. What is the good of having a privilege that you know you would never use? Next, even if you are not a strong believer in fidelity, perhaps you are much too possessive and jealous to cope with the idea of his being with another woman, even though you could cope quite well with the idea of your being with another man. If this applies to you, skip to section 2.

But if you love the man, yet you know that he may be compelled to go with another woman once in a while for the sake of variety—and at the same time, you've often been tempted to go with another man for the same reason—this could be an ideal situation. His short-lived, meaningless affair will be much less noxious if you have one or two yourself—with his consent. But will he give it?

DO OPEN MARRIAGES WORK?

Before we get to that, let's discuss the consequences of open marriages or open relationships. The bottom line is, it takes a very unique couple to agree upon and then live happily with such an arrangement. In fact, it has been established by marriage and couples' counsellors that less than one percent of the population is able to do so.

What usually happens in such relationships is that eventually one or both of the parties fall in love with someone else and want to spend more and more time with that person, until it breaks up the relationship; or suppressed jealousy explodes into continual fights, until the couple breaks up.

In the few cases where it does work, these days AIDS and other sexually communicable diseases make such an arrangement a risky proposition. The threat of such plagues adds additional tension to a relationship, since one partner will always wonder, "Is he (she) being as careful as I am?"

Let's say, however, that you are willing to put all these things aside because, in fact, you would love to have the freedom to enjoy a sexual encounter once in a while, without fear of it breaking up your relationship if he found out. The best way to do this is to make a mutual agreement that the two of you can see others on the side, without informing the other. (Couples who inform each other of each date end up fighting too much. It just doesn't work.) Such an arrangement usually involves an agreement that neither partner will get serious with or fall in love with the affair party (and, as mentioned above, herein lies the quirk in the deal—it's easier said than done).

I've often thought of such an arrangement myself. Having been married once, I know how it is to feel trapped—until "death do us part." Half the time, I felt as if I were already dead! In fact, I did propose such an arrangement to my husband just before our divorce, but he turned it down cold. The very thought of my going out with someone else was enough to drive him mad. I can readily understand that, because he was in love with me in a way that I was not in love with him.

When I consider getting married again, I tease myself with the idea of making such an arrangement with a man. But when I really think about it, what I actually want is for him to agree that it's okay for me to have an occasional fling. I would want to be understood and forgiven, but even though I might give him the same permission, I would hope that he would never take advantage of that permission; and if he did, I fear that I would secretly hold it against him—for life.

In fact, when it comes to seeing others in an open-marriage situation, I must admit I have a double standard. I can cope very well with the idea of my going out with someone else once in a while, but I would not be able to deal with the idea of his doing the same thing—especially if I were deeply in love with him. Of course, it would not be fair to the man if I asked for such a one-sided arrangement; so, I guess, unless I become a little more liberal in my thinking, open marriage is not for me.

All this notwithstanding, if you like the idea of an open marriage and can cope with the two-way-street aspect of the deal, the big problem is, where do you find a man who would agree to such an arrangement? If you locate one, let me know. The fact is, it's nearly impossible to find a man who would agree that what is good for the goose is good for the gander. A much more realistic, but in my mind unfortunate, conclusion is to . . .

2. Realize That He Will Cheat, but That You Can't, or Won't, and Learn to Live with It

Abigail and Nicholas are deeply in love; however, Nicholas is honest about his thoughts of infidelity, and Abigail appreciates that. She says:

> Nicholas has admitted to me that he's often tempted on his out-of-town trips to engage in a one-night stand, and that he's afraid that one of these days he might. He says the worst part is the dread that I would find out and it would break up our marriage. He says it is becoming an obsession with him.
>
> I told him not to worry; if he ever did it, I would understand. Yes, I would be jealous—even if it really

didn't mean anything to him. Then I asked him how he would feel if I cheated on him. I told him how the electrician was always giving me the eye, and how I had thought about how it would be to have a fling with him. He became visibly upset and told me that he could never cope with it. "I love you too much for that," he said, and then he added, "Somehow it's different if a woman does it; I know it's not fair, but that's just the way I feel."

Even though, on the one hand I think he has some nerve, on the other hand I am honored. After all, if he cares about me so much that the very thought of another man touching me makes him go out of his mind, he must really love me. I would never cheat on him because I know it would destroy what we have.

What about if he does it? I'll cross that bridge when I come to it, but I know I wouldn't go out and do the same thing, or leave him. I'll just deal with it.

ARE THESE WOMEN FOOLING THEMSELVES?

Abigail has made her peace with the situation. She is, I believe, falsely flattered by the idea that Nicholas would go out of his mind if he found out that she was with another man—and she allows this to influence her thinking. However, when she says that if she did it, it would destroy their marriage, she is probably right. Clearly, Nicholas is one of the men discussed above—a man who believes in fidelity—for women.

If Abigail is happy with this arrangement, what's wrong with it? Isn't she being an understanding wife—every man's dream? Yes. And that's just it. In my opinion, she's too understanding; it seems to place her in an unjust position. She is being faithful to a man who is unfaithful to her. No matter how you cut it, to me, that's just not fair.

Felicia has been living with Andy's cheating for years, and she seems to have come to terms with it. In fact, she rather likes the setup. She says:

At first I was shocked—the literal lipstick on the collar, the perfumed shirts, the late nights, the excuses that didn't fit with the checking up I did. I was going to confront him. After all, how could he insult me this way? But then I thought about it. He's always after me for sex, and to me it is more of a chore than anything else. It isn't that I'm not sexual, but I just don't feel like it most of the time—with three children and all.

What would the advantage be in confronting him? Andy's a good provider. We own several laundromats and are doing really great. I have everything I could ever want as far as material things are concerned. He is also a good father to my three children. He takes them to baseball games, attends school plays, and does not hesitate to shell out the money for their private school tuitions.

I know he's been fooling around for the past fifteen years. He thinks he fools me, but I even know who his latest fling is—one of the girls who works for him. We are both happy with this unspoken arrangement. He would never leave me for another woman. He's too dependent on me. I'm not just his wife and the mother to his children—I practically run the business from behind the scenes. I'm a shoulder to cry on when things go wrong—I'm there when he needs me.

As far as me cheating on him, I could never do it. That's not the way I was brought up. In my religion, it's wrong for men too—but he's not religious. I am. I can't make him be true to my convictions, but I must be true to my own.

Seemingly, Felicia has found a way to be happy in her situation. She reasons that since she's too tired for sex anyway, it's just as well that he gets his satisfaction elsewhere. She says she is happy that he is a good husband in the sense of providing material things, and a good father to the children; and she claims to be content with her role as secretary, sympathetic listener, and friend. She has rationalized that this is as good as it's going to get, so why upset the apple cart?

But the fact is, the man in such an arrangement may some day fall in love with one of his affairs, and himself upset the apple cart. In fact, it is difficult for me to believe that Felicia, and any other woman, for that matter, who knows her husband is cheating, would not be wondering about just such a thing—and perhaps, on some level, even dreading the day when it might happen—a day when the comfortable routine of their lives would be forcibly disturbed and change would happen to them, whether they liked it or not.

But in fact if their husband did leave, such women might be better off. For example, if Andy left Felicia, who is to say that she could not meet a man who would turn her on sexually, three children notwithstanding, and who would be so in love with her that he wouldn't want to have a string of affairs behind her back?

I CAN'T PICTURE LIFE WITHOUT HIM!

In contrast with Felicia, Alice is not at all content with her situation. She says:

> Kenneth and I have been going out for three years. We're not married, or even living together—I wish we were. I just can't picture life without him. When I'm in bed with him, I feel loved and needed. He's the only man who ever made me feel that way. Also, he's my steady date—every Saturday night, it's the two of us. We are together at least three times during the week. He's my strength emotionally. When I feel upset about something, he's always there for me.
>
> The only problem is, I know he cheats on me. Friday night is "boys' night out." He claims that he just needs male companionship once in a while, and that all he does with the guys is go out to have a good time—have a few drinks in a club, play cards other times, you know—just engage in male camaraderie. But I know better. More than once I overheard him on the phone talking to his friends in a sneaky way about some girl. I also

found girls' things in his car—hair clips, a lipstick case, and even underwear.

When I've confronted him, he's gotten angry and accused me of being paranoid. He always has a reasonable explanation. The lipstick is his mother's. The hair clip is his sister's, and the panties are the result of a desperate friend who begged to use his car for a few hours.

Even my best friends have told me that they've seen him around town with other women. Sometimes I think of cheating on him just to get even, but I can't take the chance, because I know that if he ever found out, he'd drop me so fast I wouldn't know what hit me.

I stay with him because I believe that he must love me. After all, it's me he always comes back to after he goes with these other girls.

The first problem Alice must deal with is her self-esteem. If she is willing to let another person become her strength emotionally, and if the only time she feels wanted and needed is when she's in bed with a man, she is in trouble. If she felt better about herself, if she were able to get her center back in herself, where it belongs, she would believe that she could stand on her own two feet, and the thought of life without Kenny would not terrify her.

What can a person like Alice do—short of going to therapy in order to build up enough confidence to take action? She can search deep within herself for the human dignity that each of us is entitled to, a dignity that sometimes transcends insecurity and fear. She can say to herself, "I've had enough of this," and she can leave him. This act, in and of itself, would be a strong step in building self-esteem.

But what if you can't find any dignity when you search deep within yourself, because, in fact, you don't believe that you have any? This is an indication of very low self-esteem. If you feel this way, you are not alone. Many women suffer from low self-esteem, and they may or may not know it. What they do know is, they feel vaguely uncomfortable when confronted with situations where they must stand up for their rights or make any changes in their lives, because they secretly think, "Who am I to dare," and "I'd better stick to what I know. At least it's safe. If I try anything new, I may be destroyed."

You may be wondering if you are suffering from low self-esteem. Here are some characteristics of it:

CHARACTERISTICS OF LOW SELF-ESTEEM

1. When you are mistreated by a man, despite your outward protest, deep down inside a little voice says, "You are not lovable. You are bad—rotten to the core. You're getting exactly what you deserve."

2. When you succeed in something, or when people praise you for an accomplishment, a little nagging voice says: "Wait. It's only a matter of time before you are exposed for the fraud that you are." And instead of feeling unmitigated joy, you feel vaguely uncomfortable.

3. When you do meet a man who treats you well, you run as far away from him as you can. You don't know why, but you continually gravitate toward men who mistreat you. The reason is, you secretly believe that a quality man will soon reject you. You also believe that you don't deserve a quality man, but you cover up all of this by calling every quality man "not your type."

4. When someone else accomplishes something or is blessed with some happiness such as a marriage, a promotion, or other seeming good fortune, you experience a sinking feeling in the pit of your stomach. A nagging voice says: "See. Here's the proof. These things only happen to good people. You are bad. They will never happen for you."

5. You are constantly calling yourself names when you make the slightest mistake, not just in public, but in the privacy of your own mind. "I'm such an idiot. I can't do anything right. That's what I get for being so stupid," you continually think. If you didn't already believe it, by now you've convinced yourself that you are a worthless idiot.

POSITIVE SELF-TALK: HOW TO WIN THE BATTLE OF THE MIND

What can you do about it if you feel this way about yourself? How do you get out of the fix that you're in? You can begin to answer yourself back every time you think the above thoughts—you can challenge those nagging voices with a comeback based upon reality. In other words, you can set yourself straight—once and for all.

For instance, in the first example, when you are mistreated by a man and that voice says, "You're getting exactly what you deserve, you are not lovable, you are rotten to the core," you can come back with the retort: "That's not true. I am lovable. I was born a beautiful, innocent baby. I may not have had perfect parents, but I've made the best of what I've had and, all things considered, for what I've been through, I've done rather well. Other people might have given up by now." Then, list in your mind all the things you've had to overcome in your life. After that, kiss your hand and say—and mean it—"I love you. You're beautiful. You deserve the best. You deserve to have a loving, caring man in your life. You don't have to settle for anything less."

In the second example above, when you've experienced success in some form and are robbed of the full joy of experiencing your triumph because a nagging voice whispers, "You are a fraud. It's only a matter of time until everyone knows what you really are," you can answer it with, "My accomplishment is real. I did it. If anything, it's only a matter of time until I've accomplished even more and people find out about that too. I am a worthwhile, intelligent person, with a lot to offer. If I stop putting myself down, and let myself go free, there's no telling what I will accomplish. And if something I attempt bombs, so what? Everyone experiences failures and temporary setbacks—even the most accomplished people. There's no shame in it. They simply try again, and eventually succeed."

In the third example, when you meet a man who treats you well, and you find yourself making a list of excuses to reject him, stop right there. Ask yourself: "What am I thinking? What is it that I really don't like about him?" You may find that there's nothing you dislike about him, but that you feel uncomfortable with him because (a) you're not used to being treated with respect; (b) it makes you uncomfortable to be treated with respect, because you don't feel worthy of it; and (c) you are afraid that once this good man finds out how bad, how rotten to the core you really are, he will reject you, and in fact he should, because you don't deserve him anyway (this pattern of thinking goes back to examples 1 and 2); and rather than endure this pain, you would do well to nip the relationship in the bud—before you get hurt.

But instead of letting the momentum of such thoughts take you over, refuse to yield to the old pattern. Rather than refuse to go out with him again, force yourself to see him at least three times. When you are out with him, instead of worrying about what he's thinking about you, think about him. Ask questions about his beliefs, his values, his life. Find out what he's really like and decide if you like him. You may surprise yourself and find out that you do—and if you do, continue to see him. Who knows, you may finally allow yourself to fall in love with a wonderful man!

In the fourth example, when you get that sinking feeling when someone accomplishes something or is blessed by good fortune, ask yourself: "What am I thinking?" Soon it will come to you that you are imagining that when good things happen to other people, it is a signal that such things will never happen to you—it is proof that others deserve these things because they are good, and that you don't deserve these things because you are bad.

Challenge these thoughts immediately with a comeback, such as: "I'm sure all the people who experience good fortune and success are not perfect. I'll bet they too have faults. In fact, it's a good sign that others have good fortune. If it happens to other people, it can happen to me too." Then, instead of resenting the person who just experienced a windfall, congratulate him or her and mean it. Make believe it happened to you and put as much enthusiasm into your joyful celebration of that person's boon as you would put into your own celebration. Then tell yourself, "Your day will come."

Finally, in the fourth example, when you catch yourself saying out loud, "I'm so stupid," or some such thing, no matter who you are talking to, stop immediately and say out loud to that person, "What am I saying? I'm not stupid. I made a human mistake. I'm really very hard on myself sometimes." The person will not think you are crazy but will in fact probably think, "Isn't that a wonderful thing to do—to be kind to yourself instead of cruel."

Do the same thing with all negative self-talk. Every time you catch yourself putting yourself down in your own mind, when you don't live up to your own standards, press the stop-eject button. For example: When the clock rang this morning, you didn't get up but thought to stay in bed sleeping for five more minutes; then, the next thing you knew, it was an hour later and you missed an important appointment. When you woke up, the first thing you said to yourself was, "You lazy dog. See what I mean? What a loser you are. You can't do anything right." Stop right there and answer yourself back: "No. I'm not a lazy dog and I'm not a loser. I was very tired because of the hard work I do and the full life I lead. I did a very understandable thing in wanting to give my tired body an extra five minutes' sleep, then my body took over and stole the entire hour. I think I'll buy a clock with a snooze button, one that will ring in five minutes, so that this doesn't happen again. In the meantime, I forgive myself for being human."

Why are we so cruel to ourselves in our self-talk? The fact is, most of us would never talk to an enemy the way we talk to ourselves in the secret of our own minds, much less to a friend. So the next time you catch yourself being harsh and critical of yourself when you make a human mistake, stop and reverse the talk.

Is all of the above just a Band-Aid and antiseptic for a serious wound that really needs a doctor? Perhaps. But if you can't afford a doctor, sometimes a Band-Aid and antiseptic are a lot better than nothing, and, in fact, they might stop an infection. True, the wound might have healed a lot better had a doctor been called in, and there may have been less of a scar. The point is, if you are suffering from low self-esteem and you can afford therapy, great. If you can't, then you can do a lot for *yourself.* An awful lot.

3. Go to a Marriage Counsellor, or Spend Your Life Trying to Get Him to Mend His Wicked Ways

In situations where a wife catches a husband cheating, and the husband admits his guilt and is willing to go to counselling, wonderful. And if that counsellor is able to help that couple resolve the issues that were the cause of the cheating, and bring that couple to an honest relationship, all the more wonderful. In fact, when such resolutions do occur, the man and the woman may feel much closer to each other than they did before the cheating occurred: A new love and understanding may have been reached.

The problem is, all too often it doesn't turn out that way, and even though the man agrees to counselling, and indeed goes through it with his wife, he ends up cheating again—and again, and again, and again. What do you do when this happens? Do you resort to the second part of this alternative—and spend the rest of your life trying to get him to mend his wicked ways?

Obviously, that, in my opinion, would be the very worst of all possible choices, because unless he wants to change, he's very unlikely to do so, even if you spend your life trying to force him. Nevertheless, some women stay in the ring, plugging away, in the hope that they can reform their man. Eve tells her story:

> Clarence and I have been married for twelve years. During that time, I've caught him cheating five times, but I suspect that he's done it more than that. Each time I catch him, he promises never to do it again and insists that it didn't mean anything. Finally, I got him to agree to go to a marriage counsellor.
>
> After about three months of working together, and trying out some of the things the therapist suggested, I thought for sure he was cured. But just last night I found the name of a girl and a telephone number in his wallet

when I was, yes, I'll admit it, snooping for new evidence. When I confronted him, he said it was a joke his friend played on him. I asked why it was in his writing, and he said it wasn't, it just looked like it.

The next day I called a private detective agency and arranged to have him followed. This time, if I catch him, I'm going to make him take me on a three-week couples' retreat run by the church. If that doesn't change him, nothing will.

I'm afraid that Eve is right only in the last part of her statement—nothing will! Some men cheat because they do not have a sense of self-value or self-worth, and rather than deal with the real issue, that of self-esteem, they seek to validate themselves in the arena of sexual conquests. For such men, one woman, no matter how terrific she is, could never be enough. As a matter of fact, no amount of women would be enough to do the impossible job that he is asking these women to do.

Cavorting around with women seems to temporarily fill a gaping void in such a man, so that to give up seeing other women would, in essence, feel like a death sentence. He would feel a void, an emptiness that he could not otherwise fill. As expressed by author Alexandra Penney: "Certain men are—or will be—unfaithful because of unmet needs that no woman can meet. These men are 'The Unreachables,' the womanizers, the sexual addicts, the deeply neurotic men who require extensive psychological repair work."[3]

The question is, why would a woman want to remain with such a man? Does she really believe that she can rehabilitate him? Perhaps not. Perhaps some women enjoy the game of cat-and-mouse. It is something to do to fill up their otherwise empty lives. If the game ever ended, they would be at a loss as to what to do with their time and energy. In addition, such game-playing renders them powerful. They can use the cheating as a weapon with which to threaten their husbands or lovers, and can take full advantage of their partner's guilt as it reaps the reward of extensive apologies, lavish gifts, declarations of love, and honeymoonlike vacations—and even couples' retreats, where a woman can feel like queen for a weekend as she is lavished with attention twenty-four hours a day. In fact, one wonders whether such women would really be happy if their spouses suddenly stopped cheating and became doting husbands. Where would all the excitement go?

What a way to waste a life! My advice to a woman who is spending her life playing this game with a man who will never change is option 4: Get rid of him and get a life!

DECEPTION TAKES ITS TOLL

The worst form of destructive anxiety comes from not knowing the truth about the world you are operating in. When this happens, you cannot realistically orient yourself to that world, and you cannot find a way to fit into it or function in it.

Even children fare better with truth than lies—and even if it involves parental rejection. A study was made wherein it was discovered that children who were rejected by parents who openly admitted to them that they did not want them around, did better than children who were lied to by parents who pretended to want them, but in other ways indicated that they did not want them.[4]

If your husband or lover is continually cheating but does not admit it (and how many men do?), and you know it, you may be in more trouble than you realize. If you fear that, at any moment in time, he may be out with someone else, you will be in a state of constant turmoil. Even your moments of joy can be dampened by the haunting thought, "I wonder if he's seeing someone else?"

This constant state of mental disharmony is dangerous to our health. Dr. Bernie Seigel says: "The state of mind changes the state of the body by working through the central nervous system, the endocrine system, and the immune system. Peace of mind sends the body a 'live' message, while depression, fear, and unresolved conflict give it a 'die' message."[5]

The research is clear. Continual stress can cause high blood pressure and, worse, heart disease and even cancer. It's not worth it.

On the other hand, once you know what you are dealing with,

once it is admitted and out in the open, at least you can take action based upon what you know for sure is solid ground. You are free to move on, if you so choose.

PERHAPS HE CHEATS BECAUSE HE REALLY WANTS TO GET RID OF YOU

There is yet another possibility to consider. Perhaps your man cheats on you because he's hoping you'll find out and end the relationship—because *he* lacks the courage to take the initiative.

Consider the case of Vivian, whose husband owns a multi-million-dollar modeling agency. At sixty-five, this former model says:

> I've put up with his adulteries and, worse, his disrespect and dislike for me for years. He can't speak a civil word to me—not even in the presence of our servants. It's gotten to the point where I'm embarrassed to have dinner guests because of the tension in the air.
>
> Why didn't I leave him ten years ago—even fifteen, when I first became aware of his extramarital affairs? We had met when I was twenty-three and just starting out in the modeling business. He was ten years older than I, and my boss. I looked up to him.
>
> After dating for a year, we became engaged and then married. He was everything to me—not just a husband but a father too. But more important, he was the first and only man I've ever gone to bed with.
>
> I know I'm still attractive, and I look at least ten to fifteen years younger than my age, but I can't leave him. I just don't have the energy. Money would be no problem—in fact, for business reasons, he put everything in my name. I could walk away with the lion's share. But my self-esteem is so damaged. All those young girls he goes with—he even puts them up in apartments and pays their bills. I hear about these things. The gossip gets back to me. I'm so embarrassed. In many ways, I really hate that man.

I tell myself it isn't so bad—and in a way it isn't, because we really do lead separate lives. I go to our winter home in Palm Beach and to our summer home in Vermont, and he remains behind, taking care of his business and his monkey business. I've had plenty of opportunities to cheat—but I've never dared to do it. I'm very lonely because I know he feels no attraction to me. If I hug him, he pulls away. I can tell he can't stand to even think of sex with me.

He's hinted at our getting separated, but I've ignored it. But I ask myself sometimes, what if I just left and started a new life?

What if? Vivian could have a fine finish to her life—even if the start and the middle were not so great. After all, isn't it the long run that counts? Just because up until now she's put up with the disregard and disrespect of a man who would rather be somewhere else does not mean that she must continue to do so. She can opt for a life of self-respect, independence, and fun.

WHY WE PUT UP WITH IT

Women are taught that any man is better than no man. A man can be old, fat, dull, have bad taste and less class, and be burdened by three ex-wives and a slew of children to support, but if he's able to walk on two legs and wears pants rather than a skirt, he's a catch. Why is this so?

Our culture, and most others as well, for that matter, has taught us to believe that a woman is incomplete without a man—that she's a failure. For this reason, many women have come to the mistaken conclusion that any man is better than no man.

While this conclusion may have been true thousands of years ago, when a cavewoman depended upon a man to protect her and then provide for her children, or even a hundred years ago, when substantial means of employment were not available to women, it is no longer tenable. Let's face it, ladies. Times have changed. Sexual drives and biological clocks notwithstanding, a man is no longer a dire necessity. The only reason to keep a man around is if he adds to your life.

We all know that sexual needs can be fulfilled without getting into any kind of a relationship, and these days there are ways to have children without the assistance of a man! I'm not for one moment suggesting that I would prefer these methods over having a relationship with a wonderful man, but if it came down to sacrificing my peace of mind in order to have a relationship with a man, I'd rather use those methods or do without.

4. Give Him an Ultimatum, and If He Doesn't Agree to Stop Cheating, or If He Doesn't Live Up to It, Get Rid of Him

The fourth choice is my preference. If your man cheats on you, and it's unacceptable to you, lay it on the line: either he stops cheating on you or the relationship is over.

If you give him such an ultimatum, he has three possible choices:

1. He can promise to stop cheating, and live up to it (perhaps he was secretly wishing to be placed in this position), in which case, your problem is solved.
2. He can get out, in which case you are rid of your problem.
3. He can lie to you and claim that he will stop cheating, because he does not feel ready to make such a commitment, nor is he ready to leave; so he promises you anything just to buy some time.

If he chooses number 3, and then cheats again, you can probably make the inference that he never will never stop cheating; and unless you change your standards, the best thing you can do is to get rid of him. If you don't, when you catch him cheating *again*, you will probably find yourself twice as angry—angry with him for not keeping his promise, but, more important, angry with yourself for allowing yourself to be duped yet one more time.

A word of caution is in order if you choose to give him an ultimatum. Be ready to face the consequences of his choice. In other words, don't say, "Either stop cheating or leave," when what you really mean is "Stop cheating, but no matter what you do, don't leave me." If your offering him an ultimatum is merely a device to control his behavior, to scare him into behaving in the way you want him to, and he is in fact not intimidated by your threat, he may take you at your word and leave.

Many women make this mistake, and when the man leaves, they feel betrayed and angry because they were not in any way ready to face the possibility that he might leave; in fact, they were not ready to give him up under any circumstances. All I am saying is, know what you're doing before you give him the ultimatum.

It would be very tempting to carry a grudge on the cheating man, to even hate him. It isn't a good idea to waste your energy on such negative emotions. The fact is, he may have lots of wonderful traits and in other ways be a very decent human being. Nobody is all bad. But since his problems are interfering with your life, you may have no choice but to let him go—and count yourself lucky to be free of a bad deal.

I'm not saying that you shouldn't offer your condolences to the next woman he gets involved with him, or forget the law of karma that says, What goes around comes around. I'm just saying, wish him well and let him go. Life will take care of him.

A LAST RESORT: WHY BOTHER?

As for rose petals and X-rated films, I say don't waste your time—or save it for your next lover, the one who brings it out in you naturally. You won't be able to entice your cheating man into being faithful by using a bagful of tricks.

All the advice in the "How to keep your man" books—such as sprinkling the bed with roses, arriving at the door in a trenchcoat with nothing underneath, going out to dinner and forgetting your underwear—will, if you take it, only make you hate yourself when you realize that you are working so hard to save a marriage (a joining together of two people in love, commitment, and mutual accord) that may never have been there in the first place. These things may be partial solutions for couples with temporary sex-relationship problems, but who also have and have had many other positive qualities to their relationship.

If you do resort to such emergency techniques, chances are he will take advantage of the novelty and enjoy a night of not-so-boring sex, which will give you the false impression that everything is all right. But the next day, or the next week, or the next month, he will go his merry way as a man about town.

Don't misunderstand. I'm all for excitement and adventure in the bedroom—with the right man. Why should you waste your time trying to beat a dead horse? Sex should be sincere, spontaneous, and sensual—not a conniving game. The best sex comes from a spiritual connection with someone you trust and love—someone with whom you can totally let yourself go, and he with you. And what hope is there of this happening in a cheating relationship anyway?

NOTES

1. Alexandra Penney, *Why Men Stray and Why Men Stay* (New York: Bantam, 1989), p. 20. Ms. Penney discusses a study done by Robert Sternberg that yields such evidence. She further indicates that two-thirds of married and committed men engage in extrarelationship and extramarital affairs, without the knowledge of their partners. See pp. 1–22.

2. Shere Hite, with Kate Colleran, *Good Guys, Bad Guys* (New York: Carroll & Graf, 1991), p. 73.

3. Penney, *Why Men Stray and Why Men Stay*, pp. 107–108.

4. Rollo May, *The Courage to Create* (New York: Bantam, 1975), pp. 60–61.

5. Bernie S. Seigel, *Love, Medicine & Miracles* (New York: Harper & Row, 1986), p. 3.

Reminders

1. What's good for the goose is good for the gander—or is it?
2. Build your self-esteem, and you will no longer tolerate certain treatment.
3. Use positive self-talk to bolster your power.
4. Living a lie takes a toll. Count the cost and make a decision in your favor.
5. Vedral's Believe It or Not: Any man is *not* better than no man!!

7

Get Rid of Him If You Can't Stand to Go to Bed with Him

It has been said that sex holds only a two-percent importance in a marriage if it is good—but a ninety-eight-percent importance if it is bad—and I suspect the same thing holds true for sex in a long-term relationship outside of marriage. In other words, if it's good, you can put it aside and think of other things—the real issues of your relationship, such as mutual respect, friendship, affection, sharing of common goals, and so forth. If it's bad, in time, all you think about is how to avoid it.

But sometimes bad sex in a relationship or a marriage is not just an indication of physical dissatisfaction or incompatibility, but of something that goes deeper. It can mean that there is no genuine admiration for each other, no shared values, or perhaps that there is deep disappointment and even loss of respect. In the following paragraphs, we'll discuss these possibilities.

Why would a woman want to stay with a man with whom sex has become, at best, work to be done and, at worst, a repulsive experience? In the following pages, we'll meet both married and single women who have been willing to take a hard look at their situations. We'll find out why some have remained and why some have bolted.

Pretending, Just to Get Through It

Many married women have admitted to me that they pretend to enjoy sex with their husbands. Their acting abilities are sharpened as they anticipate the goal of getting it over with quickly. Betty, who has been married to Tim for fifteen years, says:

> I can't give you an exact date as to when I started hating to go to bed with him, but it's for at least the last seven years. That's when I began pretending to have orgasms, just to get him off my back. I would make all kinds of noises because I knew it would excite him. It worked for quite some time, but then it got to the point where I couldn't even pretend. I would just lie there and wait until it was over.
>
> A friend of mine recommended a couples' counsellor, who eventually sent us to a sex therapist. We tried all the suggestions (I hated to, because he really turned me off) and nothing worked. It was a lost cause.
>
> Lucky for me, Tim doesn't have a very high sex drive, so I can get away with having sex with him about once a month. But even those times I dread. I can't stand to hear him breathing heavy, to have his sweaty fat body on top of me. I'm in great shape, and I don't see why he can't at least give me the same respect. If I wasn't married to him, he'd be the last man in the world I would pick to have sex with.
>
> Do you know what the worst thing about this is? He's really a nice person. Other than the physical part, I don't mind being married to him.

Men like to make quite a fuss over women's bodies—and to talk about (and even act upon) trading them in for a younger model. Well, whether they know it or not, many women feel the same way. What woman gets excited about jumping into bed with a man who may, in their own minds, have come to resemble a beached whale?

I wonder what would happen if Tim started working out—and eventually developed a statuesque, muscular physique? Apparently sex was once good with the two of them, so there may be hope. However, working out takes a certain amount of commitment, and one wonders whether a man would resent embarking upon such a program in order to please his wife—in fact, in order to become an acceptable bedfellow.

Possibly so. However, many men would not take such a suggestion in stride. They would resent the fact that they had to "pretty up" just for their wives; however, if the situation were reversed, I dare say, some of these very same men would probably demand that their wives go to the ends of the earth to get in shape.

For the moment, Betty is remaining with Tim, but unless he does something to change the way Betty feels about having sex with him, he may be living on borrowed time.

Here's what happened to Amanda.

She Began to Lust After
The Pool Man

Amanda has been married to Eugene for fourteen years. Sex was never good for the two of them, but then, as Amanda says, sex was not important to her when she first got married, at the age of twenty-two. Now that she is thirty-six, she says:

> It's heartbreaking that I have to try to work on making him romantic. I turn down the lights, put on mood music, sprinkle the bed with musk—I do it all. But he's

the same clod, asking me what I want him to do next. Why can't he just do it?

One day I had a talk with him about our sex life. I told him that we should try new things. He seemed pleased with the idea. The next day, he brought home a sex manual, put it on the bed, and said, "Let's try to get into some of these positions." I thought it was a bizarre idea to have sex à la instruction book, but I went along with it, thinking, "Who knows?" He kept asking me, "Does that get you excited?" or saying things like, "That's it. Do that to me, that really turns me on." The whole thing turned into a job, and I hated it. It contradicted everything I always felt sex should be.

The truth is, Eugene doesn't have a romantic bone in his body. Let's face it. He's not Italian. He can read every sex manual in the world and it won't help him.

Apparently, like most women, Amanda did not hit her sexual peak until her mid-thirties. When sex was not as important to Amanda, she willingly put up with Eugene's practical approach to lovemaking; however, once in her prime, she began to seek real sexual satisfaction, and Eugene was unable to provide it.

Some men are just not romantic, and apparently Eugene is one of them. I'm not so sure that romanticism is limited just to Italians, although I must admit, I've never met a nonromantic Italian man—nor have I met one who is not extremely sensual, and I've heard the same from many other women. (I know there have to be some out there, so if you've met one, please give me the details; otherwise I may be tempted to recruit some of them as tutors to the unromantic, cerebral-in-the-bedroom clods complained about by so many women. But who am I kidding? As Amanda discovered, romance and sensuality cannot be learned. They are innate. Either you have them or you don't.)

Another element may be present here besides lack of sensuality or romanticism, however, and that is spirituality. Perhaps Amanda is able to lose herself in the act of lovemaking, and Eugene is not. As expressed by Sam Keen in *Fire in the Belly*, some men can experience pleasure and joy in sex but are not able to abandon themselves to loving sexuality. He points out that this is usually true to the extent that the man has not yet found his "self" elsewhere. In other words, it takes an extremely secure person to, as he puts it, "surrender to another in love."[1]

Mr. Keen's proposal makes sense. It is one thing to take a logical, analytical approach to sex, where one feels completely in control at all times and can maintain a certain amount of detachment, and quite another to abandon oneself to the spiritual aspect of the sexual experience—to let oneself go completely. To do this, for many people, would be very threatening.

Some couples can save their marriage by finding a way to get closer—first to their own selves, and then to each other. However, in a case where communication in a marriage or a relationship has always been lacking, it's difficult to suddenly find such openness—even with the help of a professional, although it can be done.

Amanda decided to take a different route:

> I began to literally lust after the pool man—his tanned, brawny body, his jaunty, masculine walk, his ready smile, his sun-streaked blond hair. One day, in what I guess was an unconscious effort to seduce him, I offered him a cool drink. We sat by the pool talking for a while. Then one thing led to another, and we ended up in bed!
>
> Our affair continued a month, until he moved away to Florida. After he left, it wasn't so much that I missed him but that I knew I could never again settle for an awful sex life. In fact, after the pool man, I stopped having sex with my husband. I just couldn't bring myself to do it.
>
> At first I thought I'd search for another sexy man to have an affair with—but then I realized that this was no way to live. Why should I have to constantly look over my shoulder? Wouldn't it be better to get divorced and live my life in the open?
>
> I told Eugene the truth—that I loved him, but more as a friend and a person than as a husband. I admitted that I didn't enjoy sex, and had tried to make it right, but it just wasn't working.

He was very upset and wanted to go to counselling, but I refused. I felt as if I didn't want to put myself through that with him. I had made up my mind to get out of the marriage, and that was that.

We got divorced, and I am the happiest woman alive. I don't have to have sex with anyone unless I want to. You cannot put a price on that wonderful freedom, especially if you were captive to a man with whom you dreaded having sex. I will never get myself into that situation again.

As you read this page, there are probably thousands of women who are having sex with men who repulse them. How lucky Amanda is that she dared to take that step and get out. Even though it was late (fourteen years is a long time), it was by no means too late. In fact, Amanda still has the best half of her life to live!

Disappointed and Angry

In many cases, sexual rejection can be traced to growing disappointment in a man—a feeling that he has let you down—and the anger that goes with it. Here's what happened to Dolores and Danny:

When we first started going together, Danny and I couldn't get enough of each other—in bed and out. That was when we were both working in the motor vehicle bureau as inspectors. We got married, and as time went by, I rose to a top position, but Danny remained in the same spot—making less than half what I made. We had lots of arguments about his lack of ambition—he would call me a workaholic, and I would call him a sloth.

I can't give you a daily or weekly record—or a blow-by-blow description as to exactly how my sexual feelings for Danny diminished and then turned negative. I do know that I started getting into car accidents—two that almost took my life. That's when I decided to see a counsellor to find out what was going on.

In just one session, the therapist helped me to see that my problem was anger with Danny, turned against myself, and she showed me that if I didn't do something about it, I could destroy myself. That day, I went home and confronted Danny. I told him that I didn't respect his values—that I could no longer be married to a man who had no ambition. We argued about it a lot. He put his cards on the table, calling me a workaholic, and asked me why I couldn't be like other women he knew, happy with what they have. I asked him why he couldn't be like other men I knew, eager to get ahead. Finally I went to bed, knowing what I was going to do in the morning.

Without further ado, Dolores made an appointment with a divorce lawyer and in a week was legally separated. Dolores is now living with a girlfriend who's also divorced, and says that she has no regrets whatsoever, In her own words, "It was long overdue."

Dolores's therapist wisely pointed out that Dolores's car accidents were not so accidental. Her disappointment in Danny had turned into rage—and because she was unable to admit her anger toward Danny for not being ambitious, she turned it against herself in the form of potentially fatal accidents.

Clearly, Dolores's sexual rejection of Danny had little to do with her physical attraction to him, or sexual compatibility, and everything to do with anger toward him for not living up to her expectations. Such is the case in many marriages where the woman rejects the man (or even vice versa) after having had, at one point in time, a satisfactory or even superb sex life.

What does one do in such a situation? The first thing is to talk about it with one's partner. Apparently, Dolores already did that, but in a combative and accusatory way; and naturally Danny retaliated in kind. If the two of them wanted to work it out, a more productive way to approach the situation would have been to jointly seek the counsel of a wise outside party, such as a clergyman or a marriage therapist. Had Dolores and Danny done this, perhaps they could have saved their marriage.

In any case, the situation had gone too far, and when Dolores finally did seek counsel, it was too late for the relationship, but fortunately not too late for Dolores, who almost destroyed her life by suppressing her feelings of unhappiness with her marriage.

Living against one's inner knowledge is always dangerous. If ignored, warped, and pushed down, sooner or later the truth will out—but in a most inconvenient way. If you are in a situation where you can't stand to go to bed with the man in your life, whatever the reason, I strongly suggest that you don't ignore it. You would be doing yourself a favor if you looked at the situation squarely and either walked away or talked to someone you trust, who could help you to make that decision.

Bad Sex Takes Its Toll

Barbara had been married to Bill for seven years. She didn't realize how much of a drain her negative sexual relationship was until certain events forced her to see things clearly:

> For some time I had been turned off to having sex with Bill. I felt very guilty about this, and every so often I would actually get drunk, just to be able to endure the experience. One summer I was invited to participate in a six-week photography course in another state. We would talk on the phone every other night, and each time he would tell me how much he missed me and how he couldn't wait to see me. But, as usual, he had no interest in the course I was taking, and he didn't want to hear anything about why I was so excited about the new

things I was learning. I got that same "invisible" feeling and small-talked my way to the end of the conversation. Being away from him was good for me. It gave me a chance to clear my mind. For the first time in months, I started getting new ideas for photography projects. I made up lists of people to call—things to do to get started. It seemed as if something that was squeezing my neck was suddenly loosened, and I could breathe again. I couldn't wait to get home to get started.

But no sooner did I see his face at the airport gate than all the energy drained from me. I felt exactly like a balloon deflating. That's when I realized what a toll it was taking to live with a man whom I couldn't stand sexually.

While I was thinking these thoughts, he walked up to me with a big smile and said, "There's a surprise waiting for you at home." When we got there, he had the house decorated with crepe paper and balloons, and he had signs up saying, "Welcome home." He also had champagne and a fine dinner made. After dinner, we sat on the couch and he started kissing and fondling me. I wanted to push him off me, but I didn't have the heart. I forced myself to go through sex with him—out of guilt. After all, he had gone to all that trouble. I felt bad for him. But afterwards, I felt angry and violated.

The next morning, I woke up knowing that I had to do something. I waited for the weekend, when we had time to talk calmly, and I told him I wanted a divorce. He didn't understand why, but I kept explaining that I just didn't feel sexually attracted to him anymore. I didn't tell him that I never really was. He was the *only* man I'd had sex with. What did I know about sex?

Barbara has been divorced for a year now, and she's landed a job as a still-life photographer for a department store. She says she feels so much better now that her energy isn't being drained off—out of guilt *for not* sleeping with him and anger *for* sleeping with him.

Apparently Barbara and Bill lacked the kind of intimacy that could carry over into sex. Clearly, she did not feel "seen" by Bill, as demonstrated in her use of the word "invisible." How could she feel visible when Bill, although professing to miss her and not to be able to stand being without her, virtually ignored her excitement about the course she was taking and the new things she was learning?

Apparently, Bill had no real interest in Barbara the person. His interest in her was more as someone to fill some need of his own. This gives a woman the feeling that she is an object, and when a woman feels this way, clearly it is difficult to open up sexually to a man. Apparently Barbara's rejection of Bill was connected to this blank wall between them.

Feeling psychologically not seen or shut out by a man can also take a toll upon creativity; and, apparently, it had done so in Barbara's case—as she realized once she got away from him for six weeks.

I am reminded of the words of psychologist and thinker Abraham Maslow, who points out that there is a voice within each of us which tries to point out a direction that our lives must take. He points out that if we deny that voice, out of weakness, for advantage, or for any other reason, we will be most miserable and unfulfilled.[2] It was only when Barbara came to terms with that nagging inner voice, the voice that was telling her that she was being stifled by her relationship with Bill, that she began to flourish.

Why is this so? When we are not being true to ourselves, when we are allowing our souls to be stomped upon, the life force (which includes creativity) is temporarily shut down. Nothing can happen when we are in this state. (Notice that Barbara could think clearly only when she was away from her husband. The moment she returned to his presence, it was almost as if a cloud descended upon her.)

Why did Barbara try so hard to make it work? Why was it that only when things became nearly unbearable did she ask for a divorce? Why is it that, once married, so many women feel it is their responsibility to make it work—even if the sex is horrendous? Could it be that, to this day, it is women who feel responsible for the sexual success of their relationships?

Why Married Women Get Turned Off to Their Husbands

In summary, why did the women in the above paragraphs, and why do women in general, get turned off to their husbands?

1. The man is badly out of shape, and he couldn't care less about his appearance, yet he expects his wife to be in shape, to look sexy, and to be turned on to him.
2. The man is no longer romantic; chances are he never was, only now that she has been married for a while, and in addition is coming into her sexual prime, she notices it more readily.
3. The couple is sexually incompatible. The woman may not have noticed it before, but now that she's in her sexual prime, she expects more from sex. She may be a very sensual lover, and he may be a very spartan or intellectual lover.
4. The couple never had spiritual compatibility and, in a sense, never made a soul connection. The woman has tried in vain to reach out to her man, but no matter what she does, he simply does not seem to "see" her. She feels invisible and stifled in his presence.
5. At one time, the sex was great, but now she has lost respect for her husband because she feels that he has disappointed her or let her down. She finds out that she does not, in fact, share his values, so she rejects him sexually.
6. If any of the above are true, and she happens to meet a sensual, spiritual, physically attractive man (or any combination of the three, depending upon her needs), she may have an affair. Once that happens, she can no longer stand to go to bed with her husband—not even once in a while.

If the above examples were limited to the experiences of the women discussed in this chapter, I would not be impressed. However, in my interviews with hundreds of women who told me that they literally couldn't stand to go to bed with their husbands, the above reasons, or a combination of them, were typical. Do any of them sound familiar to you? (Write to me. My post office box is given on page 306.)

He Thought I Looked Like a Prostitute!

Some women are lucky enough to catch the problem before marriage. Crystal, a student of oceanography, was engaged to Chad, a marine biologist, when she realized that he was not tuned in to her sexual preferences. His lack of sensuality and his athletic approach to sex put her off. She tried to get him to come around to her way of thinking. Crystal says:

> At first, because I felt I loved him, I put aside a creeping thought that I wasn't really enjoying sex with him—and it didn't stop me from saying yes when he asked me to marry him.
>
> I guess I thought we just had to get used to each other—to learn each other's ways in bed—and things would work themselves out. I figured I could help him to be more sensitive and gentle in bed—more passionate in a sensual way rather than in an athletic or animal way.
>
> I was thinking that maybe sexy clothing would do it. I decided to surprise him by wearing a red-and-black lacy outfit, garters and all, under my robe. But it backfired. When I took off the robe, the look on his face showed horror, not sexual arousal. "You look like a prostitute," he said. "I like my woman to be innocent and cuddly, not look like a hooker."
>
> My heart sank to my feet. I was hurt and angry at the same time. How many guys would kill to have their future wives dress up this way—to be a little "kinky"? But no. I had to get the only puritanical man left on the planet.

From that day on, I became more and more unhappy about our sexual relationship. I began to be alert to every little thing he did that turned me off. Soon, I found myself avoiding having sex with him. It even got to the point where I didn't want him to kiss me. Who was I kidding? How could I marry this man? I had already rejected him sexually.

I broke off the engagement. I'm seeing a man now who could be called "Mr. Sensuality." When you find someone this compatible, you wonder what you were thinking about before.

Some people believe that sexual compatibility will come automatically, if everything else is right. I disagree. Sexual compatibility can be separate from psychological and emotional compatibility. If this were not true, think of all the wonderful men you could have married. It's a very real possibility that Crystal is a much more sensual person than Chad—and no amount of talking will change that.

As to Chad's overreaction to the garters and sexy outfit, it's probably not so much that Chad is puritanical, but more that he suffers from a madonna complex.

Traditionally, women have been expected to live up to the image of the pure, the untouched—in short, the image of the virgin mother—untainted by human desires. Even though times are changing, some men still hold to the demand that their wives be madonnalike (the biblical Madonna, certainly not like the pop singer, who is the diametrical opposite), even in bed. If the future wife of such a man began to demonstrate lust or sexual desire, such a man would be horrified. He wants to save his wild sex for women he considers to be whores or prostitutes.

Disappointing Sex and the Single Woman

When a married or engaged woman finds herself unhappy with her sexual situation, she thinks not once, but often a hundred times before she leaves the man. Single women seem to make their decisions more quickly. Here's what happened to Stacy, who met Matthew on the bus on the daily commute to work. She's twenty-six, and he's forty-one. Their romance began in small steps, but once it was in full swing and they went to bed together, it became immediately apparent that there was trouble in paradise. Stacy recalls:

> We had both been drinking quite a bit, so when he couldn't get an erection, even though I worked on him forever, I just read it off to the liquor. Anyway, I was already in love with him, so I think it almost wouldn't have mattered what he did in bed. To me, he was a sexy older man who could fulfill my greatest fantasy—sexually, emotionally, and in every other way.
>
> The next time we went to bed, there was no drinking involved. He did finally get hard, but it took him a half hour and a lot of work on my part. I was exhausted, but so much in love that all I felt was relief that he finally made it. Later, I worried that it was my fault—maybe I didn't turn him on enough. He must have sensed this, because after we made love, he said, "You have to understand something, Stacy. I'm an older man. I take a little longer."

Not content to leave it at that, Stacy spoke to a friend who frequently went out with men in their forties and fifties, and was told that she had had no such experience—and it sounded to her as if Matthew had a problem. Rather than let this discourage her, Stacy took it as a challenge. As she expresses it, "I made it my goal to get him to the point where he would get hard just by looking at me." But nothing changed. Each time Stacy and Matthew had sex, Stacy found herself doing an awful lot of work before Matthew could get an erection, and she began to resent it. In the meantime, she was falling more and more deeply in love with him.

Stacy explains:

> His problem only made me want to save him, to care for him; but on the other hand, I wanted to pull away from him. "Do I want to marry this man and have this to look forward to in bed for the rest of my life?" I began to reminisce about my old boyfriend, who got hard as soon as he was within five feet of me and stayed that way for three hours of lovemaking.
>
> I was confused. I realized that I couldn't live that way—even though he had become father, friend, and confidant, as well as a lover.
>
> I started to become critical and grouchy with him, picking fights over minor things. Finally I suggested that we see other people. From there, I petered off the relationship and resumed going out with my girlfriends and meeting other guys.

Now, when Stacy sees Matthew on the bus, flirting with other women, she cannot help but ask herself if those women would run the other way if they knew about Matthew's sexual problem. She also asks herself whether she would have gotten involved with him in the first place had she known—and yet she feels a bit guilty about ending the relationship, "just because of sex," as she puts it.

Should Stacy feel guilty for ending the relationship because the sex was completely unsatisfying? I think not. In fact, I think that she was very smart and indeed showed a lot of self-knowledge and courage in being able to admit to herself that she could never be happy with a man with whom sex had become a chore—a man who, in addition, was busy denying his problem. She could have chosen to make believe that it would go away—but, instead, she took the more courageous path of admitting that things would not work out and then letting the relationship go.

But what was Matthew's problem? Either he really believed that all men in their forties take forever to get an erection or he was trying to fool himself, and Stacy as well.

There are all sorts of reasons why men have difficulty in getting and maintaining an erection—both medical and psychological. The question is, would a woman want to get involved with such a man to whom she is not married? I think not.

Does Size Really Matter?
It Depends

Claudia couldn't get any satisfaction for a different reason—a combination of size and technique. In any case, this sophisticated radio talk-show hostess was forced to give up her dream hunk when it became obvious that with her man, bedtime would be best used for sleeping.

Claudia was delighted when she met John, an intelligent, accomplished man who, in addition, had all the physical traits she loved in a man. A graduate from an Ivy League college, and a former wrestler, John, a Wall Street executive, seemed like a fantasy come to life. From the moment they made eye contact in the coffee shop and began a conversation, they fell in "mind love," as Claudia expresses it. They talked about everything from the state of art to the state of the union to love at first sight. A romance had begun.

It was only, after about five dates, when they found themselves in bed, and after Claudia was already having fantasies of marrying him, that her dreams came crashing to the ground. Claudia explains:

> One evening, after a romantic candlelight dinner at his apartment, we ended up in bed for the first time.

He was so romantic—undressing me slowly, and then removing his clothing, first his shirt, then his shoes and socks, then finally his underwear. I'm a little shy, so I had my eyes partially closed as all of this went on.

But he wasn't shy at all. He stood right in front of me and said, "Look at it. I want you to see what you do to me." Excited by his commanding voice, and anticipating the thrill of seeing what I was in for, I opened my eyes. There in front of me was a six-foot man with a two-inch penis—fully erect. I don't know exactly how I reacted visibly, but I do know that I felt a combination of shock, disbelief, and embarrassment. I thought he was trying to apologize for his size or to get an unpleasant revelation out of the way by saying so boldly, "Look at it."

Not so. The man behaved as if he were showing me Mount Rushmore. Either he had no inkling about his proportions, or he was the greatest actor that ever lived.

I made up my mind to go through with the sex—after all, everyone knows that it isn't size that counts, it's what you do with what you have, right? "I'll bet he's a great lover," I thought. "There are more ways to achieve sexual satisfaction than with the penis." I expected him to follow through with great lover's techniques. But the man did absolutely nothing to me—and in a matter of minutes he ejaculated. Then he had the nerve to say, "Wasn't that great?" I'm sure it was for him, but what made him dream that it was for me?

At first I was so disgusted I didn't even want to talk about it with him. I was planning to make excuses and never see him again. But I had developed a liking for him, and, I thought, maybe I should try one more time. Maybe he was just nervous. The same thing happened.

The next time John called, Claudia told him that she was going back with her ex-husband. "It wasn't so much his size as his attitude," she says. "Here he was, a grown man, underendowed, and, in the bargain, he didn't know the first thing about pleasing a woman. I wasn't about to become his teacher."

What could Claudia have done other than stop seeing him? She could have expressed her dissatisfaction with his lovemaking techniques, hoping that he would be willing to learn. However, I'm wondering why a woman would want to become tutor to a fully mature man who is so completely unaware of his lover—even if he happens to be well-endowed, much less if he has a two-inch penis.

When to Face the Facts: This Just Isn't Going to Work!

The single women discussed in this chapter were very lucky that they were able to face the truth about what they would be willing to live with when it came to sex and the man they would marry.

Crystal was smart to realize that Chad's hang-up about sexy lingerie was more than just a passing fancy, and that his feelings about sex were too deep-rooted to be resolved in a simple conversation. She chose to let him work out his madonna complex in therapy, rather than on her, knowing full well that she would not be able to stifle her sexual freedom while Chad worked out his problems.

Stacy was wise to admit to herself that she resented that sex had become a job and that bringing Matthew to sexual satisfaction was "work" to be done. As much as she loved him, when she pictured her future with this man, she realized that it would be better to let him go now than to spend the rest of her life resenting him for something that he might never be able to resolve (the difficulty in getting and sustaining an erection).

Claudia was quick to realize that John, although a dream hunk physically (small penis notwithstanding), was not a dream lover and never would be; and rather than take it upon herself to teach him how to make love to a woman, she let him go.

I commend these women for their honesty with themselves. It would have been easy for them to push away the facts and to create a fantasy—or to engage in wishful thinking and believe that the problem would mysteriously go away, just because they willed it to go away. Instead of avoiding the facts, these women faced them head on and then asked themselves some hard questions:

1. What is it that I don't like about him sexually?
2. What are the chances of this problem going away or being solved (if so, how long would it take)?
3. If it is not solved or does not go away, how would I feel if I had to live with it for the rest of my life?

Having asked and then answered those questions truthfully, these women were able to save themselves from marrying the wrong man. I hope once you have read this chapter that, if you become involved with a man who has sexual problems, you will ask yourself the same questions and answer then honestly—and then make a wise choice, so that you won't end up having to make a harder choice later, when it will hurt even more.

NOTES

1. Sam Keen, *Fire in the Belly: On Being a Man* (New York: Bantam, 1991), p. 79.

2. Abraham J. Maslow, *Toward a Psychology of Being*, 2nd ed. (New York: Van Nostrand, 1968), p. 7.

Reminders

1. If you have to pretend just to get through it, you're in trouble.

2. Bad sex is a drain on your psychological energy—it can effect your career and every other aspect of your life.

3. Some men have too many sexual hang-ups. Why waste time on them?

4. If you're still single and you see a BIG sexual problem, run for your life!!

5. Let's face it, ladies, some couples are simply not sexually compatible—no matter how many rosebuds you sprinkle over the bed, and no matter how many red lights you turn on in the bedroom.

8

Get Rid of Him
If You Are Bored to
Death with Him

Mae West once said, "Marriage is a wonderful institution, but who wants to live in an institution?" Unfortunately, a marriage, as well as a relationship, can feel like institutionalized living—an endless run of spiceless days and humdrum nights, until you feel as if you are in a prison without walls. Why do women remain in such situations—for years?

They think it is safe. They'd rather stick to the known, no matter how bad, than venture into the unfamiliar. But is it really safe to do that? Carl Jung says: "We may think there is a sure road. But that would be the road to death. Then nothing happens any longer—at any rate, not the right things. Anyone who takes the sure road is as good as dead."[1]

"Nothing happens any longer—at any rate, not the right things. . . . as good as dead." Indeed, that is the problem. Stay with a man just because it is safe, and nothing will happen—at least not the right things. What *will* happen is you will go on in the same fashion—forever—knowing all the time, deep down in your soul, that you should be somewhere else doing something else.

"Why do you want to leave Joe?" I asked Marilyn, who had been married for thirty years.

Smiling from ear to ear, she said, "I would be free."

"Free?" I asked.

"Yes," she continued. "I wouldn't have to deal with him at all. I wouldn't have to see his face, to talk to him, to have anything to do with him. I would be able to decide what I want to do and when I want to do it. I just can't stand to have him around anymore."

"Well, why don't you leave him?" I asked.

"Safety," she said. "It's safer to stay than to go."

"Why do you stay with Charlie?" I asked Natalie, who had complained that her relationship with her boyfriend of two years was boring but stable.

"It's a sure thing," she said. "At least I know he's there for me. I just don't want to face the singles' world."

And so it goes. But what would happen if a woman took a chance—if she dared to take the path depicted in the Robert Frost poem "The Road Not Taken."

> *Two roads diverged in a wood, and I—*
> *I took the one less traveled by,*
> *And that has made all the difference.* [2]

The women you will meet in this chapter were frightened of change. They were tempted to cling to the known, to stay on the sure road, but instead many of them called forth every ounce of courage within them and took "the road not taken." And for them, that has made "all the difference." Others have chosen the more comfortable road—the path of least resistance, and some of them are wondering what would have happened if they took the road less traveled.

You've Outgrown Him

It's an old story. Two people get together and it works—because at the time, in many ways, they are on the same level: Educationally, philosophically, and financially there is enough agreement to have a pleasant amount of comfort together.

Nothing stays the same. As time goes by, people evolve. Whether they grow more like what they were, and become an exaggeration of their original selves, or whether they expand their thinking and branch out in different directions, they do not remain stagnant. Often, this natural evolution is what causes a previously comfortable relationship to become no longer tenable.

Tara, a nurse's aide, met Cole, a steel worker, when they were both twenty-one. Within a twelve-year marriage they had three children—one after the other. For the first seven years of the marriage, Tara was too busy with the children to think about anything else. But once her oldest child went to school, she decided to return to work and got a job at the local newspaper as a story editor.

> At first Cole was proud of me—his "reporter wife," he called me. But as time went on, and I got promoted to senior editor, my job involved me in more and more travel. He began to resent it openly. "Once in a while, I'd like a hot meal on the table," he would say. In the meantime, whenever we sat down to dinner, the conversation would be, "I dropped a brick on my foot today," or "Damn, it was hot out there," while I would say, "Did you hear that the local government wants to kill that housing project?"
>
> When I spoke, he would yawn and say, "Do you have to take your job home with you? Can't we talk about something else?" In the meantime, he had nothing whatsoever to converse about.
>
> I kept getting raises, until I was making almost double his salary. This seemed to please him quite well—or so I

thought, because he used our credit cards freely, buying anything that struck his fancy—an expensive VCR, stereo equipment, a camera that we didn't need—all sorts of things. When I set up separate savings and checking accounts in my name, just to make sure all the money didn't disappear, he became irate. He said, "Oh, now you're the breadwinner, so I have to ask you for permission?" I didn't do it to insult him; it's just that he was spending money faster than I could make it.

The situation continued to worsen until I found myself avoiding him. The truth is, we had little in common, and I was bored being in his presence; yet I still made efforts to bring him into my world, dragging him to work-related things, such as awards dinners and conventions. He hated them. Each time, at the end of the evening, he would say something like, "I have nothing in common with these people."

Three months ago, I asked him for a divorce. He was shocked, but he had no choice but to accept it. The last I heard, he had already moved in with another woman. Men can't be alone. For all their talk, they are scared to death to make it on their own.

Interestingly, according to some surveys, nearly fifty percent of the people who get divorced do so because they have "fallen out of love"—they have grown in different directions and are bored to death with each other.[3]

Tara is now happily divorced and is going out with a reporter, with whom she laughs a lot and just has a good time. When Tara does make another commitment, she tells me that it will be with someone who, in her own words, fits "the me I am today, and not the me I was twenty years ago."

Are Women More Independent Than Men?

Isn't it amazing that Cole, after being married to Tara for almost twenty years, in a matter of months began to live with another woman? Is it true, as Tara implies, that men are afraid to face life alone?

As a matter of fact, many men do search for a quick replacement once they leave a long-term marriage or live-in relationship, but only if *they* have been dumped. Men who *do the dumping* remain free for a longer period of time.

By way of contrast, women who leave long-term relationships, even those who are dumped, remain single for much longer periods of time than do men. True, we cannot prove that this is not because of the renowned "man shortage," but I dare suggest there's more to it than that. Judging from the many interviews I've had with women, I've discovered that women, once out on their own, even after long-term relationships, begin to treasure and value their freedom and are much more cautious in making another commitment.

In addition to enjoying their freedom, I dare say that some of the women's hesitation to jump into another marriage or live-in situation may be because it doesn't take more than a week or two for a woman to realize that, mysteriously, she is much less fatigued than she was when her man was around. The fact is, it is very unlikely for a woman to find a man who will cook and clean for *her*.

You Were Not in Your Right Mind When You Got Married!

Looking back, many women wonder how they could ever have married the man that they now find themselves having lived with for ten, fifteen, twenty years, or more. They wonder what in the world they were thinking about when they got married. But the truth is, they were thinking the thoughts of a very immature, unevolved, earlier version of themselves. Victoria married Richie, her high school sweetheart of the same age, even though she felt he was too serious and needed to lighten up. But after a few years of marriage, just being around him began to weigh her down. It started to feel as if a heavy stone were resting on top of her all the time.

> If I analyze it, I realize now that I was never really in love with him. I liked him. I was attracted to him, but we never had that "soul" connection. But I stayed with him because, after all, he was a good provider, a good father (I had two children in the ten years of my marriage), and an upstanding citizen.
>
> I felt trapped, and I started eating to vent my frustration. It got to the point where I hated my life. One day, I found myself blurting it all out to my best friend. I heard myself saying, "I'm too young to be this unhappy." She confirmed my thoughts. After a month of agonizing, I told my husband I wanted to leave him. His first reaction was to grimly state, "Where are you going to go with two kids?"
>
> Fortunately, I was young and foolish enough to believe that I could make it on my own, and in spite of a lot of criticism from my family, and anxiety about my future, I did it. On some level, I knew it was a life-or-death issue—the life or death of my personality.
>
> One week after the divorce, I landed a job, got after-school help for the children, and quickly advanced to a managerial position in the garment industry.

But, shortly after that, Victoria made another mistake. She married Stephen, the owner of an elevator company, because he was successful and had a good sense of humor. But as Victoria admits, it was on the rebound, and to prove something to her mother, whom she imagined was sitting in judgment of her failed marriage. Victoria tells us:

The day before my wedding, I got a bad feeling in my gut—I felt like calling off the wedding. All day I grieved—it was as if someone had died. But I brushed it aside and went through with the wedding.

Needless to say, it was a disaster. Before a year was out, I couldn't stand to see him lying around the house in his bathrobe—reading *Playboy* magazine—a fat, aimless blob at the end of the couch. He had no ambition, and we had nothing in common. I determined to extricate myself from the pit I had fallen into.

The second time was easy. I went to a lawyer and took care of business. In the meantime, I continued to advance at my job.

Will I ever get married again? I doubt it. I think that marriage itself kills the reason you got married. I don't think men and women were meant to live together—I think they should visit each other.

Unfortunately, Victoria was not in her right mind either time she got married. The first time, she was too young to know what was right for her. The second, she was bound and determined to right the wrong of her failed first marriage—to find a man who possessed the traits her first husband lacked, specifically, a sense of humor—and to prove to her mother and other members of an invisible audience that she pictured judging her that she was not a loser, a woman without a man.

But in her haste, industrious Victoria forgot to look closely enough at Stephen to become aware of his laziness. Had she done so, she would have realized that they were incompatible.

Is There Any Hope for Marriage?

Is Victoria correct? Should men and women give up on the idea of marriage and just visit each other? Of course not. Marriage can, and often does (thank God), work.

The secret to a successful marriage is to find the right man—the one who is your spiritual match or, to put it another way, your soul mate. Joseph Campbell explains: "If we live a proper life, if our minds are on the right qualities regarding the person of the opposite sex, we will find our proper male or female counterpart. But if we are distracted by certain sensuous interests we'll marry the wrong person. By marrying the right person, we reconstruct the image of the incarnate God, and that's what marriage is."[4]

For a variety of reasons, many of us were not in our right minds—we were not concentrating on the right qualities—when we chose our mates. Instead, we were looking for someone to take care of us—someone with whom to settle down and begin a safe and happy life, without thought of spiritual compatibility. Fortunately for us, and perhaps not so fortunately for our marriages, we grew and evolved. We learned more about ourselves and the world, so that what was comfortable and appropriate then, no longer fits the person we have become.

But what do we do if we have made that mistake—and for some of us, not once, but perhaps twice or more? Do we punish ourselves and add insult to injury by forcing ourselves to stay with that man forever, or do we take courage and leave—even though it costs a great deal of temporary emotional turmoil?

He Needs a Housekeeper and Mother—not a Girlfriend or a Wife

Unbeknown to their brides-to-be, many men plan to marry for the sole purpose of securing a housekeeper, a cook, a secretary, an entertainment director, a baby maker, a "mommy" (for themselves), and more. In such cases, small wonder, once the marriage takes place, there is deep disillusionment on the part of the woman—especially when she finds herself home alone most of the time and bored to death.

Merrie thought that her fairy-tale dream of the perfect marriage had come true when she married the only man she had ever loved—someone she had met in the ninth grade. In spite of her mother's advice to wait until she had experienced other relationships, she married after college graduation, having never dated another man. Merrie says:

> I imagined a storybook life—my exciting, romantic husband, lots of children, the white picket fence, all of it, but I quickly realized that it wasn't going to be that way. Not at all.
>
> Right after the honeymoon, I was awakened to crude reality. The week after we got back, he would leave every night, right after dinner, and go out—either to work out at the gym or to hang out with his friends. Sometimes he would come home as late as two o'clock— even on a weeknight. When I would protest, he would say in an annoyed manner, as if he were talking to a nagging mother, "I went for a drink with the guys. Get off my back."
>
> I was hurt, but I tried to be mellow about it. "I guess he has to have friends," I thought. "Maybe he's just testing me to see if I'll try to force him to give them up." But he continued to go out nearly every night and to act like he was still single. I started to feel more like a mother than a wife. He would throw his clothes all over the bedroom, the bathroom, the living room—everywhere. When I wasn't nagging him, I was picking up after him.
>
> I tried to talk to him about his never being home, his sloppiness, and his attitude that I was his mother or his maid. All he could say was, "What do you think married life is? This is normal. Everyone feels this way!" Then he would take me out to a show to appease me—but the next day, it would start all over again.
>
> The final blow came after I had the baby. He behaved as if it were my baby—and that he was just there to admire it. Finally I told him I wanted a divorce.

Merrie has been divorced for three years now and has gone back to work as a law clerk. She finds single parenting a lot easier than being married because, at least now, as she expresses it, "I have only one child to care for." Rumor has it that Alan has gone back to live with his mother. No surprise there.

Alan married Merrie, not because he was in love with her, but because it was convenient. He found someone to take care of him. I'm sure he even unconsciously enjoyed it when Merrie nagged him about coming home late, spending too much time with the boys, and throwing his clothes around. It made him feel secure—as if he were home again with mommy. Some men never grow up!

The Caretaker Syndrome

Why did Merrie allow herself to be placed in the role of Alan's caretaker—a substitute mother, as it were? Apparently, she had an appropriate role model in her own mother, an example of the many mothers of my own generation (the fifties and early sixties) who felt that it was their obligation to take care of not only the men in the family, but the children as well—and even well after the children had grown up.

Some things change very slowly. Women still place themselves in the position of being solely responsible, not only for seeing to the basic needs of each and every family member, but of in fact holding the family together. "Well, somebody has to do it," you might argue. All well and good. But I would delete the "y" from the word "somebody" and add the letters "ies."

For starters, men need to be taught to take care of their own "little needs," and women need to stop spoiling them. How absurd to hear a man fall to pieces when his wife goes into the hospital, because he doesn't know how to work the washing machine; or to hear him brag to his friends that he's been eating out every night because he does not know how to boil water. And how much more absurd to hear women almost brag to each other about their men when they behave in such a manner, indicating by the tone of their voices how cute it is. There's nothing cute about it. It's downright ridiculous.

But what is behind women's not-so-secret delight that men are rendered virtually helpless the moment they are not there to take care of them? Clearly, it is the need to be needed, and more. All too often, it is the need to have a feeling of importance and purpose. Too many women have placed a man in the center of their lives and made him the sole reason for their existence. Small wonder such a woman will squeal with delight (could it be relief?) when the man expresses inability to function without her. In so doing, he is validating her existence and confirming for her that she has not made a mistake in choosing to build her life around him.

But it is a mistake—every time. A much smarter way to handle a marriage is to think of a husband as a partner and friend who will help you to share life's triumphs as well as life's difficulties, a man who will go shoulder-to-shoulder with you in caring for the family and each other as well.

After all is said and done, when women in general stop offering themselves as caretakers who will save men from having to live in pigsties and who will deliver them from having to eat microwaved TV dinners, men may stop thinking of them as substitute mothers.

It Makes Me Sick to See Him Eat

When a woman is bored to death with a man, when she has passed the point of no return, when in fact she has rejected him as a mate, signs of this rejection appear in the strangest places. Allison, a physical therapist, met Arthur, a podiatrist, in karate class. At first they were just friends, but in time, since all of Allison's friends were already married, she began to think of him as a potential husband. After seven months of going out, he asked her to marry him, and she said yes.

Once we got engaged, however, I started to feel trapped. We would visit those same old friends every Saturday and eat over at one of the couple's houses, and then either rent videos or go to a movie. Other times we would sit around and listen to the men go over old Vietnam stories. I was bored out of my mind. I couldn't help thinking of the Peggy Lee song "Is That All There Is?" . . .

Not long after that, I started to notice little things about him that bothered me—the stupid cap he would wear, his dumb checkered jacket, those old, dirty canvas sneakers from the sixties. (I even bought him a new pair, but he persisted in wearing the old ones, claiming that they had sentimental value.)

Finally, I couldn't stand to see him eat. We were in a restaurant, and suddenly I heard these awful snorting sounds. I looked up and saw that he had his mouth open and was snapping his lips together with each bite. He was devouring his food with such concentration and vigor that you would think he was just released from a prisoner-of-war camp.

I could barely get through the meal, and I made an excuse to leave the table. In the solitude of the ladies' room, I experienced a "moment in time." I looked in the mirror and asked, "Why didn't you notice this before?" I began to panic. I was about to marry a man who repulsed me. Of course, after that, I couldn't stand to kiss him, much less have sex with him.

The wedding was planned. The invitations had been ordered. The hall had been rented. I said to myself, "I can't go through with it." I called off the wedding.

One existentialist philosopher sums it up nicely: "The lack of possibility is like being struck dumb." Once Allison realized that her life would be set in a fixed rhythm, with a man whose boundaries were so completely different than hers and, comparatively speaking, so limited, she was struck dumb at the thought of marrying him. It was after that that her feelings for him began a rapid descent: first the cap, then the jacket, then the sneakers, then the eating, and finally the sex.

Allison was fortunate in that her unconscious took over and caused her to become repulsed by Arthur—otherwise she might have tried to rationalize her misgivings and might have married him anyway.

Different Needs for Stimulation

We have all heard the expression, "One man's meat is another man's poison." Well, so it is when it comes to stimulation. I've invented a saying of my own: "One man's peace is another man's paralysis." When it comes to the need for stimulation and excitement in life, every person has a different comfort zone. Those people who need more stimulation than others experience a feeling of mild depression when things slow down to a calm, steady pace. On the other hand, those people who need less stimulation feel overly stressed when there are too many things going on in their lives. Such people often enjoy the quiet, undisturbed rhythm of a daily routine, which others might call a humdrum existence.

I need a lot of stimulation. If I'm not working on at least three projects, planning an adventurous trip, and at the same time working full time in my major field of interest (such as teaching or lecturing), and if I'm not learning a new sport or hobby, or meeting new people, I actually begin to feel depressed.

Several years ago I was dating a wonderful man who shared with me a similar sense of humor, several sports, a group of mutual friends, and a common interest in dancing and dining out. Yet I often found myself calling him lethargic, and he frequently found himself accusing me of being hyper.

His ideal weekday evening would be his coming home from work, reading the paper, relaxing in front of the television, and then going to bed. My idea of a perfect weekday evening would be coming home from work, going to the gym to work out or going to a judo lesson, and then coming home to play a word game or other board game with him—and then engaging in a stimulating, intellectual conversation.

He was willing to play games and "get deep," but that was only once every two weeks. And he was much too tired to do anything more than relax after a hard day's work. After a while, I felt a bit lonely pursuing my activities—not so much because he wasn't pursuing them with me, but because he wasn't pursuing any activities on his own. In other words, I felt an aloneness because I was made to feel so different in his presence; and he felt an aloneness because he was made to feel so different in mine. Basic compatibility in a crucial area was lacking.

Later, I dated a man with a stimulation-need much closer to my own, and I found that the feeling of aloneness was gone. When we weren't doing things together, we were pursuing our independent sports, activities, and goals, or we were telling each other with great enthusiasm about our latest conquests or defeats. In short, we felt much more at home with each other. Eventually, we went our separate ways, because he had never been married and was interested in beginning a family; and I, at the age of forty-something, was not interested in starting all over again, having already raised my daughter, who was approaching her teen years at the time.

Fortunately, regarding my former relationship, I was able to face a truth about myself and to act upon it—before I made the mistake of marrying a man who was a vision of delight, but who would have bored me to death in less than a year, had we decided to marry.

But not every woman is so lucky. All too often, a woman will allow the passion of the moment to rule the day, and will marry a man even though the two of them have much different comfort zones for levels of stimulation.

There Are No Sparks, But We're So Compatible!

What about when there seems to be a great deal of compatibility, but not much else? Bob and Paula have been going out for over a year now. Bob has just asked Paula to marry him. Paula says:

> There are no sparks flying—in fact, to be honest, there never were. We just liked each other from day one. We met at work, actually in the company cafeteria. We laugh at the same jokes, we like the same movies, we even share the same politics. At first we started going out as friends, then we finally got around to sex. Again, no great sparks there. Pleasant, comfortable, but not really exciting.
>
> I keep saying, "Something is missing." But then I think, "Oh, all that romantic stuff is just in the movies. Maybe it doesn't really exist at all." The fact is, I'm twenty-seven already and all of my friends are married. What am I waiting for? But to tell you the truth, sometimes I worry that I might be making a mistake. Are we really in love? If not, what is love anyway?

Paula's inner voice may be trying to lead her in a different direction—to warn her that she needs more from a relationship than she can have with Bob.

"All that romantic stuff"—the missing sparks really do exist in many love relationships. It's called "romantic love." One of the biggest mistakes many women make is to rationalize it away, claiming that it does not exist, when it may be the very thing they really want and need, often because, like Paula, they are running scared.

Romantic love usually takes place in the beginning of a relationship. It is a feeling of excitement, of intense chemistry with another person, an ability to be completely open with him, and he with you—a feeling that you understand and accept each other in a way that few other people can do, and a sense of love and delight with each other's souls. It is only after a few years of the relationship that the intensity of this feeling normally lessens. This happens naturally, because day-to-day problems and realities force the couple to focus on the very real issues of daily living, and away from the wonders of each other.

But even when romantic love fades over time, it can be rekindled—and couples who have stayed together for many years know this. It's called "working on the relationship," refocusing on each other. However, if the flame was never there in the first place, there is nothing to rekindle.

There is a school of thought among some psychologists which argues that compatibility is enough to sustain a marriage or a long-term relationship, and that romantic love is a wonderful addition but not a necessary component. In a small way, I agree with this line of thinking; but in a much bigger way, I disagree. Let me explain.

A couple can stay together forever, even if they never had the slightest bit of romantic passion between them—if both parties of that couple are satisfied with such a bond. If even one partner, however, feels a need for romantic love, and it is not there, in the long run, in my opinion, the relationship is doomed.

Do You Need the Romantic Fire?

I, for one, could never be happy without the romantic element. If it came down to it, I'd rather be alone with my dreams than with a man who reminded me every day, by his mere presence, that all hope of future romance was cut off. The bottom line is, in deciding whether to bail out of a relationship if you are bored to death, that it is most important to be honest with yourself. Do you need the romantic fire? If you do, and you suppress your needs, you may find yourself walking around in a state of free-floating depression—a sadness that cannot be named.

We often discard romantic love because it can get us in trouble.

If we marry *only* because of it, if we forget to look for common goals and values in addition to romantic love, we are left with nothing once the fire dies down. The point is, to lessen the chances of a relationship dying of sheer boredom, romantic love should be present.

It Doesn't Matter How You Look, He Never Notices the Difference

Berryl has been married to Edgar for seven years. Sick and tired of feeling almost transparent, she says that she could put on the most dazzling outfit, spend five hours in the beauty shop, and make herself up to look like a movie star—or dress in rags, leave her hair in knots, and wear no makeup—and she would get the same reaction from him: "You look fine."

What is the point of fussing with your dress, hair, and makeup for a man such as that? Small wonder Berryl says:

> I find myself envying other women friends of mine who have husbands who are attentive to them, women who are still excited about the prospect of seeing their man at the end of the day. I wonder what it would feel like to get excited about going out with your husband?
>
> Sex? I think he does it just to get release, and I do it just as a favor to him. I'd love to get divorced from him, but I have a little girl. Is it right to divorce a man just because you're bored to death?

Edgar is not the type of man who will give compliments—and some women don't need them. But like many of us, Berryl does. She craves attention and recognition. If she remains with Edgar long enough, she may stop feeling like a woman! The fact is, the two of them were not only never in romantic love; they were basically incompatible from day one. Why did they get married?

As expressed by Berryl, they were "friends," and Berryl didn't know that such a thing as love existed, so she settled for friend-ship. Apparently it is not enough.

But He's a Good Father

Why does Berryl remain with Edgar? Obviously she feels too guilty to leave a man—the father of her child—"just because she's bored to death." Many women feel this way about leaving a man, if, like Edgar, he is basically a good person and especially if he is a good father to their children.

Is it a good idea to stay with a man just because he is a good father to the children, when you feel the way Berryl does about Edgar? Let's look at the pros and cons.

On the one hand, by staying with a man who is a good father, even if he is a boring husband, you will keep the home together and provide the children with a sense of security and continuity. After all, if there are no violent arguments or physical upsets, is it not better that they be spared the psychological anguish of divorce?

On the other hand, children are more perceptive than most of us allow. If a woman stays with a man with whom she is bored to death—and if she feels unfulfilled as a wife, both psychologically and sexually—her frustration and dissatisfaction are bound to come out in many ways, and the children are sure to notice that they have a rather unhappy mother. What kind of a role model will such a woman be providing for her children? Will she not be sending them a message that it is a woman's place to sacrifice her own happiness for that of others? Will she not, in addition, be telling them that, once a marriage, always a marriage—no matter how unfulfilling—and that change is too dangerous to risk?

All things considered, I dare say that staying in a boring, stultifying marriage for the children's sake is a mistake. Children are much more resilient than we imagine, especially if parents are honest with them and share feelings openly and, in addition, show them that they are not the cause of the divorce. (See chapter 9 for more discussion on this subject.)

"I Stay with Him Because I'm Afraid of Getting AIDS"

If you stay in a boring relationship long enough, you will soon be having the safest sex of all—no sex! The fact is, when a relationship is monotonous, the motivation to go to bed with one's partner is usually not there. However, that's when you can get yourself into trouble, and begin doing things you would not ordinarily do. Here's what happened to Autumn after she became engaged to Stan, a good provider who was far from being the man of her dreams:

> I've never been promiscuous, so what I'm about to tell you is completely out of character, but I had sex with two men, behind his back, while we were engaged. The first time it happened was six months ago, when I was a counsellor at a summer camp. I met Phil, another counsellor.
>
> He was exciting and adventurous—and the chemistry was there. One evening, under the stars, we found ourselves in the middle of hot, passionate sex. It was a one-time thing, because it was the last day of camp. I felt so guilty and confused that I refused to see him again.
>
> The next time it happened was with a guy I met in a bar while watching the Super Bowl game. My fiancé was with his cronies, watching the game—no women invited. I went to the local bar—and frankly, now that I think of it, I was hoping to pick up someone and, as luck would have it, I did.
>
> We made eye contact across the bar, and he sent me a drink. Before you know it, we were talking for two hours—then he asked me to dinner. The next thing you know, I was in his apartment, having sex and throwing all caution to the wind in the bargain. It was the best

sex I'd ever had—but after that, I felt confused and guilty again.

What was happening? I'd never been so promiscuous when I was not in a relationship. I could go for months without sex. But now that I was engaged to Stan, I had to go with other men just because Stan was boring. If I did this now, what would I do once we were married? And the best of it all was, my reason for staying with him, to avoid AIDS, was ridiculous. If I stayed with Stan, I'd first *get* AIDS—if I kept up this pace.

Wisely, Autumn broke her engagement to Stan. Sure enough, she settled down into much more conservative sexual behavior and has in fact been seeing someone for three months. Autumn says: "We're only now getting close to having sex, and when we do, we'll use protection, because it will not be a destructive act of self-abandonment."

Why did Autumn suddenly become so sexually indiscriminate when she was engaged to Stan? The fact is, when you're with someone with whom you feel trapped, someone who is stultifying and apparently boring, you feel virtually driven to seek satisfaction elsewhere. By way of contrast, if you were alone and without a relationship, you would feel more content, because there would be no dreadful man to escape from. In short, you would not feel cornered and would have no need to make reckless moves in order to feel free again: You would know that you were free and you would have no problem.

One is reminded of the way a person feels when there is little or no money to be had, and no hope of ever getting a windfall: The person feels compelled to go on buying sprees and spend money on credit. But if this same person were to eventually begin making a substantial amount of money, she might be much more conservative in her spending habits, because now she knows the money is there and can be spent at any time, whereas before, she felt deprived.

The bottom line is, if a woman's main reason for staying with a man is to have a steady sex partner in order to avoid possibly getting AIDS, I suggest that she think again. Such a solution is likely to backfire.

The Balance Scale

Boring relationships are insidious. They can go on forever, because they seem to pose no imminent danger. Yet they take a slow, steady toll on a life. The cumulative effect is ennui, a listlessness that seeps to the core of your being, until you are powerless to act. Before you know it, it's too late. The best years of your life have been spent with the wrong man.

If you have doubts about your relationship, why not try the balance-scale method to help prompt you to action. As below, write the word *Positive* (meaning things you like about him or the relationship) on one side of the page, and *Negative* (meaning things you dislike about him or the relationship) on the other side of the page.

Here's a sample chart drawn up by Tara, the woman you met in the beginning of this chapter. In thinking about Cole, she writes:

Positive	Negative
He's a nice person.	I don't enjoy his company.
We have history together.	He doesn't share my interests.
He doesn't cheat.	We have different values.
He gives me a lot of freedom.	I'm embarrassed to bring him to my peers.
He's a good-looking man.	Sometimes I hate him.
He's father to my children.	He resents my higher income.
	He spends my money too freely.

Don't make a big deal out of it. Just start writing and see where it leads you. There's no need to obligate yourself to be logical. Write down anything that comes to your mind. Tara never expected to write such an extreme statement as, "Sometimes I hate him." When I asked her about it, she said that she was surprised herself and, in fact, at first fought the impulse to write the words on paper; but then, wishing to be true to the nature of the exercise and write exactly what came to mind, she did it. "I learned a lot about myself," she said. "In fact, my feelings about this marriage were a lot more than discomfort. I'm glad I finally faced the facts."

Listen to Yourself

What *did* Tara mean by saying, "Sometimes I hate him"? Did she mean that sometimes she loathed and despised Cole and/or that she wished him harm? Not really. Tara's choice of words showed that she had a lot of unresolved anger. But with whom was she angry? Was it really Cole, who was simply being the man he was when she first met him—or was it with herself, for remaining with a man whom she had clearly outgrown?

After you finish filling out the balance scale, take a good look at each side of the balance. Chances are, your inner voice will have been allowed to speak, and now it may be evident as to how you really feel about your relationship with the man in question.

Your inner voice does not lie. You may rationalize it away, but it will always be there in the background, whispering its truths— remaining faithful to guide you to the path that is best for you. I cannot tell you what your inner voice is saying. Only you can do that. But I can advise you to tune in to it, to let it speak to you, and to follow it. After much wrestling with my conscience, I did it, and for me, it has made "all the difference."

NOTES

1. Carl G. Jung, *Memories, Dreams, Reflections*, ed. Aniela Jaffé (New York: Vintage Books, 1965), p. 297.

2. *Immortal Poems of the English Language*, ed. Oscar Williams (New York: Washington Square Press, Inc., 1952), p. 504.

3. James Patterson and Peter Kim, *The Day America Told the Truth* (Englewood Cliffs, N.J.: Prentice-Hall, 1991), p. 93.

4. Joseph Campbell, with Bill Moyers, *The Power of the Myth*, ed. Betty Sue Flowers (New York: Doubleday, 1988), p. 6.

Reminders

1. If you've outgrown him, don't try to shrink back to his size; admit a sad fact and move on.

2. If you've been playing the role of housekeeper and mommy to a man, small wonder you are bored to death.

3. If things about him begin to repulse you—you're past the point of no return. Travel. And fast.

4. Compatibility is *not* enough. There'd better be some sparks flying too!!

5. If he never notices you, give him notice!

9

Get Rid of Him
If You Are Staying
Only for the Money,
the Security,
or the Children

I'll make this marriage work even if it kills me," say women who are bound and determined to stay married, despite obviously unhealthy situations. Unfortunately, the women are right. The unhealthy marriage—or even relationship, for that matter—may well kill them, if not in body, at least in spirit, if they insist upon hanging in there at all costs.

Why do so many women doggedly stick it out, way beyond the call of duty—clinging to unchanging marriages and relationships that, in their heart of hearts, they would love to escape? In the situation where money, security, children, or a combination of all three are involved, the reason is dread of a possibly more difficult path ahead. The women think: "I'd rather deal with this old familiar devil than face new and possibly worse devils up the road."

Such thinking is normal. It's a part of self-preservation. After all, what woman in her right mind would welcome more trouble than she already has? But there is a fallacy in thinking, "stick to the true and tried, no matter how bad it is." It does not take into account the delicate and sensitive nature of the human spirit, the part of a person which slowly dies if it is forced to endure, on a daily basis, captivity and insult. It is unable to grow and thrive. In short, to remain in a relationship that is detrimental to your basic energy can be similar to allowing yourself to be slowly anesthetized—until your vitality is all but gone. Eventually, you may feel less than alive.

A Living Death

People fall into this trap when it comes to remaining in jobs or even professions that they abhor. Day after day, week after week, month after month, and even year after year, they trudge to work, hating every moment spent on the job, because they are afraid to face the temporary insecurity of change. They remind me of Gregor Samsa, the protagonist in the Franz Kafka novella *The Metamorphosis*, who wakes up one morning and is unable to get out of bed, because, unbeknown to him, overnight, he has turned into a giant insect—a human-sized cockroach.

When the background of the story is explored, it turns out that this man had spent his life at a secure job, but one that he hated—a job that struck at the very core of his human dignity, as he allowed himself on a daily basis to be compromised.[1]

The moral of the story is clear and can be applied to those who remain in marriages or relationships just for the money, the security, the children, or any combination of the three. By choosing safety over self-actualization, by regularly violating the sanctity of their humanity, by continually ignoring the call of the self for escape to freedom, such women eventually begin to feel less than human.

As you read this chapter, I would like you to contemplate the following question: Is it worth the sacrifice of self to remain in a relationship that you have come to dread, just because you are afraid of change?

It's Your Money or Your Life!

Mandy had been married to Noel for twelve years. During that time, she had inherited money and started a lingerie business that became quite successful; and Noel, who had previously been earning a modest wage as an appliance salesman, began working with her. In time, they became extremely successful. But problems soon arose. Mandy says:

> While the business was flourishing, our marriage was going the other way—not because we were too busy for each other, but because he became obsessively interested in pornography, to the point where we couldn't make love without first looking at a film. It didn't stop there. He wanted me to engage in a threesome, and other, what I considered to be, "perverted activities." I got to the point where I felt that when we did make love, it wouldn't have mattered if it were me or anyone else. I was just a body in the bed to fill his strange needs.
>
> I tried to reason with him and agreed to see a counsellor, but he refused and called me a prude, saying that if I were sexier maybe he wouldn't have to resort to outside stimulation. But I knew it was more than that. The man needed help.
>
> Finally, I realized that I must leave him, and I went to a lawyer, whose evaluation of my situation was most depressing. In spite of the fact that I did all the work, and that it was my money which started the now-booming business, I would have to give Noel half of everything if I wanted him out of my life. I couldn't do it. It just wasn't fair.
>
> I hung in there getting more and more depressed each day and even hating to get out of bed in the mornings. I started having panic attacks. My mouth would get dry, the room would start to spin, and I felt as if I were about to fly off the deep end—you know, go berserk in

public. It was horrible. I pictured myself in an insane asylum.

Finally, on the recommendation of a friend, I saw a therapist. After hearing me out for an hour, this woman looked up and spoke the words that will remain riveted in my mind for eternity. "Mandy," she said, *"It's your money or your life."* I stood stock still. It was like a bolt of lightning that went straight to my heart. I don't have a choice. What good is the money if I lose my mind—my life? What will I do with the money then?

That was three years ago. Mandy has been putting a lot of energy into recouping her losses and is now nearly two-thirds of the way to where she was before she had to relinquish half the business to Noel. Instead of feeling depressed about all the hard work she is doing, she looks at it as a challenge and is enjoying her life, as she expresses it, "for the first time in years."

Why did Mandy hesitate so long? Why didn't she simply walk away from Noel, once she realized that she could no longer bear being with him? She didn't think it was fair that she had to give him half the money. But what if she had remained with him? She would probably have continued to have anxiety attacks, messages from her unconscious that something was radically wrong—and, in time, she may have suffered a mental breakdown. Ironically, she would then have lost not only her life, but her money too!

What was it that finally gave Mandy the courage to leave? It was the confirmation by the therapist that her self-knowledge was correct; that she could no longer live with this man and maintain her integrity. Apparently, Mandy knew all along what she "should" do in order to make herself happy and at peace, but she needed the voice of a trusted, respected outside source to confirm that knowledge.

Now You Know How Men Feel

When you come to think of it, perhaps most men who are extremely unhappy in their marriages feel similar to the way Mandy felt about divorce—they want it but are very hesitant to pay the financial price. Yet men very often choose to pay that price because they believe that their happiness is more important than dollars and cents. Perhaps here, we can learn something from the men.

I Don't Want to Be a Bag Lady

Unlike Mandy, Sheila never had any money of her own. She met and married Harry, a very wealthy man, who from day one set her up in a life-style that quickly became more than comfortable—in fact, it became addictive and almost impossible to leave. Sheila says:

> At the time, I didn't want to admit it, even to myself, but I married Harry for his money. How do I know this? If I'm honest, I know that if he—the same cold, domineering, egotistical man—had no money, I never would have dated him, much less married him. Yet I fooled myself into believing that this man was my knight in shining armor, the man of my dreams, someone who would take care of me for the rest of my life.
>
> The first year of our marriage was great—for me it was a storybook world—meeting his high-powered friends, rubbing elbows with "old money," and having him show me off—his young, sexy wife (he is almost twenty years older than me). But in time, I began to feel trapped— stuck in a world with rules and walls—and I wanted to test the boundaries.

When Sheila told Harry that she wanted to go back to her job as an aerobics instructor, he refused to allow it, claiming that it would be too embarrassing for him to have his wife working at such a menial job. In the meantime, they drew further and further apart, and sex became something that Sheila felt she had to do in order to earn her keep. "I resent going to bed with him and he senses it," she says, "but instead of turning him off, it only causes him to insist that I spend hours in bed pleasing him."

One day when she was walking along the beach alone, Sheila began to cry. Tired of the teas, the lunches, and the endless functions, she sat down on the sand and asked herself a hard question: "What do you really want to do? The answer came to me loud and clear," she recalls. "I want to leave Harry. I'd be better off home and poor—or even in New York City with a can of roach-killer spray and a double lock on my door and privacy— than here in a mansion living a life I can't stand with a man I've come to dread."

That night she told Harry she wanted a divorce. He coldly responded that she came into the marriage with nothing and would leave with nothing, and added that he didn't believe she really wanted out, but rather that she was experiencing the "seven-year itch" and would do well with a little vacation.

That was six months ago. Sheila is still married to Harry. She says: "I hate my life, I hate him, I hate his friends. But the thought of being left penniless—I picture myself living as a bag lady in a shelter for the homeless. At least here I have a roof over my head."

Sheila imagines the worst. She envisions herself, not in a modest apartment, which is a much more realistic picture, but in a tenement with a spray can to ward off rats and roaches, or as a bag lady living in a shelter for the homeless. But what are the chances of this really happening? Indeed, they are slim.

Sheila would get a settlement that, even in its most modest form, would allow her to set herself up for a single life—although she would have to sacrifice the life-style she has become accustomed to. In imagining the worst, in telling herself that she will be doomed if she dares to leave Harry, Sheila is falling into the trap of what psychologists call "catastrophizing." While Sheila's fears are understandable and are not completely baseless, there is a convenient, unconscious method to her madness. By catastrophizing, Sheila gives herself an excuse not to take action.

Stop Catastrophizing

Women who are used to the best that money can buy often fall into the catastrophizing trap. The mere thought of not having the luxuries that they have come to take for granted sends them into a panic. Divorce then becomes a fate worse than death—never mind the fact that they feel less than alive in their marriage situation.

If such women were to stop the music and think logically, they would soon realize that, in fact, leaving is not impossible. They would begin to see all kinds of options and would perhaps even become excited by the prospect of setting out on their own.

If you are in a situation where you have to make a decision whether to leave a relationship or a marriage, and your main reason for not leaving is the money—the financial security, pure and simple—use this little checklist in order to give yourself an idea of whether it's worth it.

In the "prize" column, list what you have to gain by remaining in the relationship; and in the "price" column, list what you have to lose by remaining in the relationship. Then weigh one against the other and ask yourself the question: "Is it worth it?" If it is, settle down and enjoy it and stop complaining. If it isn't, take courage and start making some plans.

Here is the list as I imagine Sheila would have filled it out:

STAYING IN IT FOR THE MONEY

THE PRIZE (what you gain)	THE PRICE (what you give up)
Expensive clothing.	Being able to wear the clothing for a man I really love.

Luxurious vacations.	Being able to go away with a man I really love, alone to enjoy tranquility or adventure, or to meet a new man, or with friends for fun and fellowship.
Financial security for the future.	Autonomy. The freedom to decide what I will do with my money, time, and life.

Staying for the Security: I Can't Face Life Alone

Perhaps you have never really been independent. Even if you aren't married, and never have been married, chances are you've always been in a relationship—give or take a month or two, and you remember those miserable months alone as being desolate and empty. You never gave yourself the chance to become strong and self-sufficient, so you are deathly afraid of having no one to lean on.

Sally falls into this category. She went from one relationship to another; while still living at home with her parents, she met and then married her husband. She had never experienced independence of any sort. Now married for eight years, and miserable, Sally says:

> Shane basically ignores me. He's married to his business, and that's fine with him—and it's fine with me too, because I don't love him anymore. In fact, I don't even like him. I wouldn't even choose him as an occasional dinner partner. But leaving him is easier said than done.
>
> I'd love to divorce Shane, but I simply can't face life alone. I have no practice. I don't know how other women do it. I'm scared to death. The mere thought of facing the world alone makes my heart race and my

stomach get a queasy feeling. I make myself sick, because when I look at other women who have done it, I
ask myself, "What's wrong with you?" I must be such a
wimp. Where do these other women get the guts to
leave? I wish I had their secret. If you know it, please
tell it to me now.

The secret is facing natural fears—the fear being alone, of
fending for oneself, and the fear of the unknown—fears that cause
women to choose to stay where they are, no matter how bad it is
(and, as we shall see in the chapter on abuse, even if their very
lives are threatened).

When Feeling Isolation
and Despair

What can Sally, and other women who feel a sense of isolation
and despair at even the very thought of leaving, do? They can talk
to other women who have felt the same way Sally does, and who
made the move.

Sally has given herself a clue to do just this when she says that
she admires other women who have made the move. But she's
saying more than that. In fact, she is saying that she wishes to be
like these women. Psychologists agree that when we admire a trait
in someone else, it is often because we have at least the seeds of
that trait in ourselves, and wish to develop it further. We look at
the admired party as a role model or as a source of strength.
Clearly, then, Sally may not be as far away from freedom as she
imagines.

Group therapy or women's support groups can be very helpful.
By talking to other women, a woman can gain courage for herself.
She can realize that her fears are normal, and that others who felt
the same way took the plunge and lived. A woman may then,
with some fear and trepidation, be willing to take the chance. But

one thing is for sure, if a woman isolates and condemns herself, she only thickens the bars of her jail. She must seek out other people with whom she can share her thoughts. This in itself will begin the process.

One of the best ways to overcome fear is to realize that fears are learned—they are not innate. A newborn baby is not born with the fear of being alone. He or she learns that fear only when the caretaker does not meet a need of that baby (sooner or later, all babies learn to fear being abandoned, left alone to die—they sense this danger, although they cannot yet rationalize it): No matter how conscientious the mother or caretaker is, he or she is not a mind reader and is not omnipresent, and sooner or later that baby will cry and no one will immediately come, and that baby will learn to fear.

Just as the baby learns to fear, so does the child. Mommy is late in picking Jane up, or mommy goes to work and now does not spend as much time with Jane, or a sibling is added to the family and Jane feels neglected. So you see, the fear of being abandoned is learned.

In adult life, the fear of abandonment takes the form of fear of being alone—fear of eternal isolation; and a woman can experience an almost deathlike sensation at even the thought that a man upon whom she has come to depend will leave—forever.

So, too, the fear of the unknown is learned. A two-year-old is not afraid to explore her environment. Sometimes she has pleasant experiences in that exploration. For instance, she will squeal with delight when she manages to put a top on a jar that she has been playing with. But when her explorations lead her to touch a pretty red flame on the hot stove, she screams in terror. She learns that there are also terrors to be faced in the unknown—and that exploration can be dangerous.

The fear thoughts that you learned when you were a baby and a child were perfectly valid for that time of your life, when you were indeed most vulnerable. Now that you are an adult, however, and have much more control over your environment and indeed your life, they are no longer valid, and there's no reason to let them bully you. The fact is, you have a lot more to say about what happens to you now than you did then. When you think about that, isn't it wonderful?

Powerful Self-Talk

What can you do to unlearn your fear, so that you can limit your feeling of isolation and despair, and venture out into the world? You can make a lot of headway by simply talking to yourself. If you are thinking of leaving your man but keep getting fearful thoughts that place you under arrest, here's what you do. Think of leaving. Picture yourself telling your husband or your boyfriend that it's over, and then imagine yourself taking the next step—either asking him to move out or moving out yourself. (If you're not living together, picture yourself no longer spending evenings and weekends together.)

What thought comes to your mind? Catch that thought like a rubber ball. Look at it and say the thought out loud: "I'll be alone every Saturday night, and I'll cry for hours." Now, answer yourself back: "I can be alone for a few Saturdays, if I need the time to get myself together; but if I choose to, I can call a friend and go to a movie, or I can visit a relative, or I can accept a date with someone from the office who might ask me. In any case, even if I am alone, I will not die. I may be sad, I may cry, but, realistically speaking, I will not die."

You might then add: "I may get to catch up on reading some novels and self-help books I've been wanting to read, and I may even rent a video I've been wanting to see. I may even drink some white wine and relax and think about life—and, who knows, I may enjoy being alone."

Your particular fear thoughts and rebuttals will of course be different than the ones above. The examples are only to give you a clue as to the kind of bantering that you can do in your own mind.

Engage in this process for each and every fear thought that springs up in your mind. You'll recognize the thoughts immediately, because they set off an internal alarm. In fact, when you think them, your adrenaline level rises and you may even feel the physical flight-or-fight syndrome. Your heart may start beating fast, your mouth may get dry, and you may even become pale. Every time such a thing happens, instead of cowering in compliant submission, stand right up to that fear by verbalizing it. Say it out loud. Then begin your rebuttal. If you do this every single time a fear thought attacks you, you will soon see that these thoughts are just that—thoughts—and that they have no power to harm you, especially once you prove to yourself by your intelligent self-talk that they are no longer valid and are merely throwbacks to infancy and childhood, when they were valid and appropriate.

The Fear of Rejection

Perhaps the biggest fear of all is not that of being abandoned or of the unknown, but that of rejection. Psychologist Paul Hauk, author of *Overcoming Worry and Fear*, says: "Men and women who can face wild animals, who can do all kinds of dangerous things, simply melt when it comes to going into a roomful of strangers and making small talk. These harmless acts terrify them because they think that being rejected hurts."[2]

But what is so bad about rejection? Would you really die if a man were to say, "thanks, but no thanks"? Of course not. And, in any case, could a stranger really reject you? Absolutely not. What he would really be rejecting is the opportunity to know you. That's all. In refusing to strike up a conversation, he would be saying, "I don't like your facade, and I'm not interested in getting to know you on the inside," or he might be saying, "I am not feeling very sociable tonight," or he might be saying any one of a hundred things. But one thing is for sure: He is not saying, "I reject you as a person." If you thought of what rejection means in this way, you would not be as terrified of the singles scene.

By the way, men have the same fear of rejection as women do—and often they have more, because they are the ones who are obligated to make the first move. The fact is, most men would appreciate a friendly smile and some warm remarks from a woman.

How I Feel About Being Single

I've been single for almost twenty years now. I'm much happier single than I was married. Being single affords me the opportunity for adventure in the area of men. I never know who is coming around the corner!

Sometimes I think it would be wonderful to meet a loving man who shares my values—a soul mate. If I meet him, I will be very tempted to give up my freedom. But then I worry that, even if I marry at the age of ninety, as I'm going down the aisle, I'll be craning my neck to see in the back of the church—looking around to make sure I didn't miss a better deal.

Although I make that last remark with tongue in cheek, I'm quite serious about the value of freedom and the availability of all sorts of interesting men. Once you realize this, and get to know your strengths, you look upon your single life as something to be treasured, not something to be dreaded. You come to the point where you can cope with a man or two passing on you. You even laugh at yourself and say, "Well, I tried. I guess you can't win 'em all." And you pat yourself on the back and go on.

If You Really Want Security . . .

There is no such thing as security in this life. The well-lived life will always be filled with the challenge of change and the dare of chance. In the words of David Schwartz, in his book *The Magic of Self-Direction*: "If you really want security. . . . Go live in some public institution—an insane asylum, a poor house, a jail. There you can be certain of a roof over your head, three meals a day, clothes to wear and cigarette money. You will have absolutely no concerns regarding keeping body and soul together."[3]

Change Can Be a Blessing in Disguise

Rather than a threat, change can be a blessing. It isn't the change itself that has the power to cause trouble in our lives, but how we handle the change. Let me give you an example. At one time, former President Eisenhower was actively pursuing football in his college years, and even had thoughts of becoming a professional player. Then one day he suffered a knee injury that forced him to give up playing football and all contact sports for the rest of his life.[4] Apparently, an unwelcome change turned out to be a blessing in disguise. Had Eisenhower sat around and bemoaned his fate, had he said to himself, "Now that I can't play contact sports, my life is over," he would never have become one of the greatest presidents in United States history.

The fact is, when life throws a dagger at you, you can either catch it by the handle and use it to cut your way through a jungle, or catch it by the blade and cut yourself.

No one is saying that you can't take time to mourn your loss—to gather your forces, to regroup your thoughts. I'm sure President Eisenhower didn't cry tears of joy when he realized that he could no longer play football. The point is, he eventually figured out what he could do with the resources that were still available to him and he moved on with his life. You can do the same.

God Will Punish Me If I Get Divorced

Many people were brought up with various religious prohibitions. Some of these prohibitions are eventually well thought out and become internalized as values that we truly accept as thinking adults, but others are not well thought out and remain external rules of conduct that we feel obligated to obey simply because we were always taught that we must.

Janice is a devout Catholic. She was brought up to believe that once you get married, no matter what happens, you must remain in that marriage: Divorce, under any circumstances, is a mortal sin and is worthy of excommunication from the church. So Janice remained married and miserable for years, until one day she broke away—but not without a lot of soul-searching. Janice says:

> I remember sitting in church as a child and hearing the priest talk about the sacred vow of marriage. I remember how my aunt was excommunicated from the church for getting divorced, and I recall asking my mother why she couldn't go to Sunday mass with us anymore. My mother said that marriage is a holy sacrament, and that divorce is breaking a promise to God—like a slap in his face.
>
> I stayed married to a man who sickened me, for fifteen years—in a marriage that was a mistake from day one. We had nothing in common, except a child that we both adored. How could I commit a double crime against God: break up my marriage and hurt my child?
>
> Well, I did it, and I added a third sin to my repertoire. I committed the big one, the BIG A, with a co-worker. It must have been my unconscious way of getting out of the marriage, because I made no serious attempt to cover my tracks. In fact, it was getting caught that initiated the divorce.
>
> I'm a religious woman, so it really hurt me when I was officially excommunicated from the Catholic Church. I missed God, and church, so I would sneak into churches— any church, just to pray. Each time I did this, I would look up at the ceiling and talk to God. It felt as if I were looking straight to heaven—begging God to hear me.
>
> I gained comfort each time. I felt as if he heard me—he had not abandoned me. I asked him to lead me in the right path and to forgive me if I had done wrong. I felt comforted—not alone. It was as if God were

whispering to me, "Don't worry. I'm not the way people say I am. I don't condemn you. I understand."

Now, three years later, Janice is enjoying a successful career as an exercise therapist in a local hospital. Her son, who is now in college, enjoys a healthy relationship with both his parents. Janice now says of her divorce: "It's the best thing I could have done for all parties concerned; I don't believe God condemns people for getting divorced. Even God couldn't live with some people."

How Dare Anyone Speak for God

It is interesting to note that once Janice stopped listening to what people told her that God was thinking, and she started talking to God herself, she realized that she was not condemned.

I've always wondered how certain members of the clergy could be so audacious as to boldly proclaim the will of God. In fact, I can remember sitting in church as a child of about ten or eleven and thinking, as I watched the preacher deliver his hell-fire-and-brimstone message, "How dare anyone speak for God?" It was at that point that I became suspicious as to whether a lot of the anger was coming from the preacher himself, rather than from God.

People can say all sorts of things about God, but in truth, "It ain't necessarily so." In short, God is bigger than any man's description of him. God, as I understand him, is flexible, and he goes by the individual situation. It is up to each person to make his or her own personal peace with God. (I realize that God has no gender and am using the word "him" as a convention.)

Making the Final Decision

If you are in a situation where you have to make a decision whether or not to leave a relationship or a marriage, and your main reason for not leaving is insecurity or fear of any kind, use the following checklist in order to give yourself an idea of what you have to gain, and what you have to lose, by staying in that relationship.

In the *gain* column, list the benefits of remaining where you are, and in the *lose* column, list the drawbacks of staying put. Then weigh one against the other and ask yourself the question: "Should I take the chance?"

STAYING IN IT FOR THE SECURITY

WHAT YOU GAIN	WHAT YOU LOSE
1. Safety: I don't have to face the world alone.	A feeling of independence and power.
2. Guarantee of not being rejected by men.	The pleasure of meeting new men, and finding out that men have similar or worse fears.
3. Parental approval.	Self-respect.
4. Approval of society (the church, peers, etc.).	Peace of mind and hope for the future.
5. Security: I don't have to deal with change or the unknown.	The possibility of a better life.

Staying in It for the Children

It is not uncommon to hear a woman, or even a man for that matter, proclaim the virtues of staying married for the sake of the children. But very often, if one takes a closer look, the person who makes such statements has more than the children in mind when declaring such virtuous intentions.

Kay has been married to Arnie for twelve years. They have three children—and, as expressed by Kay, "The only reason we are still together is the children." But is that all there is to it? Kay says:

> Before I got married, I was a successful makeup artist— sometimes earning up to a thousand dollars a day. But all of that changed once I started having children. With my first child, sometimes I was able to get away with bringing my nursing infant to the photo shoot—I would keep her in a little cradle nearby. But the clients didn't like it—and since my husband and I agreed that children need a mother at home, I put my career on the shelf.
>
> My husband is an executive in a brokerage house. He's rarely home, and when he is home, all we do is argue about the house not being neat enough, or me wanting to go back to work and hire someone to watch the children. I am tired of being both mother and father to these children.
>
> I don't love him anymore. If the children were grown, I would leave him tomorrow, but children need a father. I don't want my children to come from a broken home. I'm going to try to hang in there until they are grown— another ten years maybe. I have to put my children first. It's only right.

Is Kay really remaining in the marriage only for the good of the children? Let's take a closer look.

When Kay says, "I'm tired of being both mother and father to the children" in one breath, and in the next, she says, "If the children were grown, I'd leave him tomorrow, but children need a father," is she not pointing out the contradiction in her own thinking? The fact is, Arnie is not being much of a father, because he is rarely there anyway.

What may really be stopping Kay is the fear of taking a chance, not the fear that the children will not have a father.

The amazing thing is, if Kay did divorce him, he would probably see the children more. Many fathers come to their senses after a divorce—when they no longer live with their children. They begin to schedule regular, quality time with them. In fact, the children get to know their fathers in a way that they would never have been able to do, had the couple remained married— and at least they will have been freed of having to listen to the continual bickering of their parents and having to live under a roof where tension is always in the air.

It's Not What You Do, But What You Don't Do That You Regret

I have studied the phenomenon of taking chances all my life. What I have learned is, more often, it is not the chances you take that you regret, even if they result in failure, but the chances you don't take! Hugh Downs, the television co-host of "20/20," and former host of the "Today" show, says:

> Making the decision to join "20/20" caused me the most anguish in my career. . . . "20/20" seemed wrecked at that point; its reviews were scathing. If I took the risk, I could imagine how columnists would remind viewers that no one makes a comeback. . . . If I said yes, I knew that I'd have no fallback position. This was it. . . . *but I realized too that I didn't regret anything I'd done as much as what I'd not done* [italics mine].[5]

It is often those who *do* take chances who succeed, and those who don't who fade into anonymity.

I Took a Chance!

I often wonder what would have happened to me if I had not taken the chance and gotten divorced. I remember at the time, it was a heartrending decision. "How could I break up the home when my daughter was only four years old? What would happen to my poor child?" But I was miserable, and in fact, I felt so trapped that I might as well have been in a jail. I can clearly remember coming home from work and wanting to go to sleep—in the middle of the afternoon—just to escape the heaviness of my thoughts. I can recollect sitting on the back stairs of my home and contemplating the sky, and watching the cloud formations, and feeling frozen in time. I can recall, as if it were yesterday, crying out in my thoughts, "Help. Get me out of here. I'm dying."

I realized that the first step in retrieving my life—in finding my path—was to get divorced. I had to forgive myself for making the mistake of marrying the wrong man, and stop punishing myself by dooming myself to a life sentence with that mistake. (See the Preface for more about my history.)

I took the chance. It wasn't easy. When my then four-year-old daughter asked me why we got divorced. I told her the truth—that daddy and I were not happy together, even though we were both good people. We had gotten married before we really knew enough about each other. I then used examples of compatibility—such as someone who likes to laugh all the time, while the other likes to be serious and gets annoyed with too much laughing; or someone who likes to get up late, and gets annoyed when the other is buzzing around early in the morning. I demonstrated this with antics and had her roaring with laughter.

After answering a few questions on who was who (Did I like to laugh and was daddy serious? Did I like to get up late and did daddy get up early? and so on), I added: "Who knows? Maybe it was meant to be that daddy and I married just so that you could be born. Maybe God knew that it would take just that special combination of your father and I to create you." This seemed to satisfy her—in fact, I know it did, because to this day, from time to time, she will bring it up, and always with a smile on her face.

Marthe is now a nineteen-year-old college student. Just the other day she told me that she felt lucky to have me as a mother—that I had been a great role model to her. Not content to leave it at that, and fishing for a compliment, I asked, "What do you mean?" She said, "You provided me with an example of what a woman should be—self-reliant and strong, and not depending upon a man for your existence. Not too many of my friends were that lucky." Needless to say, I was thrilled, and then I thought, "What would have happened if I had stayed with my husband for 'the children'? Would my daughter have been able to say that?"

Marthe also enjoys a wonderful relationship with her father and can often be found talking about his calm, deliberate wisdom. Rather than take sides against one of us or the other, she accepts us as individuals, a fact that I was able to graphically see when, in her freshman year of college, she selected us as the topic for her composition on "comparison and contrast."

We were compared and contrasted in a most delightful manner. I came out as a generous, amusing, friend–vigilant mother, and her father appeared as a calm, spiritual sagelike protector. She then spent a few paragraphs giving examples of my devilish antics, and his serious, almost scholarly approach to life. She ended her composition with: "I imagine that's why they got divorced. They were just two very different people, and I count myself lucky to have them both as parents. When I come to think of it, I share valuable traits from both of them."

Divorce is painful and heartbreaking, and, of course, children are much better off if happily married couples stay together. But when there is a basic unhappiness, staying together can be more harmful to a child than leaving. Children are not easily fooled, and if you are miserable, if you feel trapped and unfulfilled, if you have made a mistake in marrying your husband, and you know it but remain with him, unhappy and unfulfilled, the daily example you give your children is: Once you make a decision, you must stick to it—even if that decision was a drastic mistake.

The Money, the Security, and the Children

Some women give themselves a life sentence to an unhappy relationship because, not only are they unwilling to suffer tempo-rary financial setback and are too insecure to leave, but because they imagine themselves to be eternally responsible for the happi-ness of their children and the man they married. Sylvia is a case in point. Her sexual life with her husband was so bad that she felt driven to have an affair. Eventually she considered divorce, but family concerns surfaced. Sylvia says:

> Since my children were still in school, I figured it would be better to wait until they were eighteen. This way I could also save some money. When my last daughter was eighteen, I told my husband I was leaving. He pointed out that the children needed a home base. "Where will they visit on holidays? Where will they go in the summertime? What would happen to our oldest son, who had graduated from college and was now living with us?" I felt he was right. I was too guilty to leave. I would have to wait until they were out on their own or married.

Easier said than done. Sylvia's husband started to get on her nerves to the point where she dreaded being in his presence. For two years she walked around in a semi-daze, appearing to be almost drugged. Finally, on the verge of a mental breakdown, she sought the help of a therapist, who assisted her in finding the strength to move out—even in the midst of her husband's threats of violence and suicide. Sylvia managed to leave in spite of it all, and now says with delight:

> It's been a month, and I feel as if I've been born again. I rent part of a house in a secluded wooded area. I love waking up in the morning, alone in my own bed. I love not having to watch him put on his pants, snap his belt,

whine for his breakfast. I have joined a yachting course at the local country club, and I'm taking an art course at night.

People have been asking me if I'm in love, or if I've had cosmetic surgery—they don't know why I look so vibrant. Everyone points out the sparkle in my eyes and the glow on my face. I have a message for any woman who is afraid to make the break because of the children. They will be fine without you. You are not doing them a favor by staying. In fact, my son has moved out, has his own apartment, and is planning to marry his girlfriend. My children say they are proud of me for making the move.

Now that I think about it, it wasn't just the children's welfare I was thinking about. I was afraid that I couldn't make it on my own. I let Todd intimidate me also. He knew exactly how to play upon my guilt and fear. The interesting thing is, after the house is sold, I'll have money to buy a condo—and plenty left over. My job is enough to support my modest apartment. What in the world took me so long?

By imposing upon herself the role of martyr or omnipotent caretaker, Sylvia had provided herself with an excuse not to take action. In truth, the real issue was not whether the children needed her to stay married to her husband, but whether Sylvia was willing to brave the world alone. Her husband tried to manipulate her into staying—first by intimidation and then by suicide threats. Once Sylvia got wise to him, and made the move despite his threats, everything fell into place. Isn't it amazing how things work out when you do the right thing for yourself?

You've Got to Give Something Up to Get Something

I've noticed what I can now call a basic truth in life. In order to make a major improvement in life, it is very often necessary to give something up, with no guarantee that you will get anything better in return for your sacrifice. However, time and again, I've seen this principle work: You do get something better in return for the chance you've taken.

This principle has been demonstrated in my own life since my divorce, and in the lives of the hundreds of women I've spoken to. In fact, I have not met one woman who was sorry that she left a relationship in which she was staying only for the money, the security, or the children, but I have met hundreds of women who are glad they did it.

Good News: Women from Every Walk of Life Are Doing It!

Other women have done it—and you can too. Shere Hite points out that, statistically speaking, most of the divorces in our country are initiated by women—and there are an equal number of poor women and rich women who leave. She says: "... most women today are ready to take on extra jobs and face whatever sacrifices are necessary rather than stay in bad relationships."[6]

I'm hoping that this is true. I'm hoping that whether your bad relationship is one with a boyfriend, a live-in partner, or a husband, you will not stay in it just for the money, the security, or the children. As a wise man once said: "If you do what you've always done, you will get what you've always gotten." You can have the best twenty or thirty or more years of your life now, but you've got to take a chance on yourself!

NOTES

1. Franz Kafka, *The Metamorphosis* (New York: Schocken Books, 1968).

2. Paul A. Hauk, *Overcoming Worry and Fear* (Philadelphia: Westminster Press, 1975), p. 11.

3. David J. Schwartz, *The Magic of Self-Direction* (New York: Simon & Schuster, 1965), p. 33.

4. Dwight D. Eisenhower, *At Ease* (New York: Doubleday, 1967), p. 15.

5. Quoted in Walter Anderson, *The Greatest Risk of All* (Boston: Houghton Mifflin, 1988), pp. 89–90.

6. Shere Hite, with Kate Colleran, *Good Guys, Bad Guys* (New York: Caroll & Graf, 1991), p. 158.

Reminders

1. So you're staying in it for the money? Well, think of this. It's your money or your life!

2. Security is a crutch. You must toss away the crutch if you ever want to walk.

3. It's not what you do, but what you don't do that you regret.

4. You've got to give up something to get something.

5. Are you really staying in it for the children—or are you just afraid to take a chance?

10

Get Rid of Him
If He's Chronically
Unemployed

"I'm between jobs right now—I quit because I'm too
talented to waste my time..."
And you end up paying for lunch.
"I got laid off (again)."
And you end up paying his dental bills.
"I'm an entrepreneur, I don't believe in working for some-
one else—I'm in the process of starting my own business."
And you end up buying his clothes.
"I work strictly on commission, and at the moment
things are slow, but I have some big checks coming in."
And you end up paying for the vacation.
"I have writer's block, but my best-selling idea is about
to burst forth."
And you end up paying the rent.

He is always just a little "short," but it's never a permanent
situation. Soon he's going to find a job he really likes, or soon

people who owe him money are going to pay him back, or soon his ship is going to come in—after all, doesn't he play the lottery every day? He only wants you to lay out some money to tide him over.

You love the man. He has a good heart. In fact, if it were not for the money problem, he would be perfect. So many times, you've thought, "This time he's going to get on his feet," but mysteriously, time and again, something always happens to blow the deal—and there he is, back to square one, leaning on you.

What do you do—leave a man in the lurch just because he can't seem to get it together financially? Thinking about the experiences of the women in this chapter may help your decision to become clear. These otherwise intelligent, successful ladies have made what they have now come to realize are stupid mistakes, and they are sharing them with you in the hope that you might not have to go through what they went through.

The Unemployed Creative Artist

He could be an artist, a sculptor, a writer, a musician—one of a hundred creative vocations, a "call" that drives him to believe he must not dirty his hands with plain work. He believes in himself, and he expects you to do the same. But who is paying the bills?

At the age of thirty-nine and—as she was continually reminded by her friends—with her biological clock ticking, Roz was lonely. She had recently broken up with her boyfriend, an older man who was not interested in having children. In a way, Roz was happy to be free, because now, with a little luck, she might just meet a man who could fulfill her greatest dreams: give her a child and take care of her financially. She was as surprised as she was thrilled when she finally met the man who seemed to be her subconscious wish materialized.

She met Gary on line—waiting to get into a concert at Carnegie Hall. When he called to ask her out, she put him off at first. A successful copywriter for an ad agency, making over one hundred and fifty thousand dollars a year, she was concerned about his status as a free-lance writer with no steady income, but Roz finally decided to go out with him.

I don't know how it happened, but we fell head over heels in love. He was the first man who actually loved my body the way it is, cellulite and all. In bed, we couldn't get enough of each other. After three months of mad, passionate romance, he asked me to marry him and I said yes.

What did I know about him? He had an apartment right around the corner from me. It was a typical modest studio—where he did his creative work. He showed me articles and pamphlets he had written, and he told me that he was about to sign a big contract for a book—six figures, he said. I looked at him with dreamy eyes and though, "He's a creative genius." I pictured us married, with a hideaway in the country—him writing the Great American Novel and me looking out into the lake, my adorable children by my side, and thinking, "How lucky I am."

But getting back down to earth, now that I think of it, I should have seen signs before the wedding. Why didn't I question it when I had to lay out the entire sum for our reception because his money was "all tied up"? Why did I believe without a shadow of a doubt that he would pay me back later?

As it turned out, not only did he not pay me back the money for the reception, but once we were married, he borrowed money—a little bit at a time, and, in addition, I paid all the bills. What was the problem? He said he had writer's block, the excitement of the marriage and all.

I found myself picking on him all the time—and we began to argue a lot. What used to be great sex turned into resentful sex because, in the end, I saw him as a leech. I would nag him about getting a real job, and he would say he didn't want to prostitute his talent—like I did. (I wrote copy for various companies. He thought that was selling out.)

After five months of his excuses, Roz consulted a lawyer and had the marriage annulled. Gary has moved back into his old apartment, and Roz is alone and happy to be so. She says: "It was an expensive but valuable lesson. I'm out ten thousand dollars, but it was well worth the price of getting rid of him. Just think of what it would have cost me if I didn't swallow my pride and have the marriage annulled (it was hell admitting this to my friends because they had all warned me)."

When Neediness Determines Your Choices

What was going through Roz's intelligent, logical mind when she decided to marry this man—a man she knew only five months, and who demonstrated well before the wedding that he was not only not planning to share responsibility when it came to finances, but that he would be leaning heavily on her for support? What was she thinking about when she ignored her own previous standard for a potential husband—a standard which insisted that any man she marry be well-established financially?

It was her neediness. Sometimes it is virtually impossible to avoid being swept away by a romance that would not otherwise have happened had one not been so "thirsty" at the time. Like someone on a desert island whose tongue is slaked and swollen from dehydration, Roz did not stop to negotiate the details of the quality of her water when she suddenly came upon an oasis. She drank her fill. It was only *after* her thirst was quenched that she was able to discover whether the water contained impurities which could cause serious problems.

When Roz met Gary, she was starving for love and affection,

and sexual and physical acceptance. Tired of apologizing for her cellulite, Roz's delight when her body was perfect in Gary's eyes was perfectly understandable. No man had ever made her feel this way. In addition, he was young and virile and seemed to be a perfect candidate for father of her children.

How could she listen to her well-meaning friends when they so rudely interrupted her fantasy with something so cruel as the facts? Any information that contradicted what she was feeling was automatically deleted. Roz was unable to even hear them. She was too busy concentrating on how Gary made her feel to stop and see what he really was. Her unconscious reasoning was: "How could this man be bad, when he makes me feel so good?" So she would automatically X out any information which would contradict that feeling. Logic and analytical thinking go flying out the window when driving needs are being met.

What finally brought Roz's feet back to the ground? Once she was forced to see that she would be supporting this man, her sense of equity was offended and she began to resent him. Her actions from that point are admirable. Instead of trying to fool herself into believing that things would change, she cut her losses and moved on.

If you have found yourself in a situation with a man where you were being used, rather than condemn yourself, realize that it was a natural thing for you to do at the time and try to understand yourself. Ask yourself what you were trying to accomplish when you made that choice, and why it seemed right at that moment. If you do this, you will quickly realize that all you were doing was trying to take care of yourself—attempting to fill a need, and in that sense, it was really a survival instinct. You will be able to gain insight into yourself, and, rather than waste energy condemning yourself, you can go on in life, a wiser woman; and the next time you find yourself about to melt and throw all caution to the wind, you will at least keep one foot on the ground.

The Entrepreneur

Some men simply can't work for someone else. They must strike out on their own—be their own boss. While this is all well and good, what happens when Mr. Capitalist is continually borrowing money to pay for dinner? Would it not be better for him to, at least temporarily, join the labor force? Nicole had this experience with Erwin, manager of a retail clothing store, who quit his job so he could "think," as he put it. After all, how could he be creative if his mind was always bogged down with the day's nonsense from a robotic, menial job?

After the first few dates, Erwin began asking Nicole to pay for dinner—promising to pay her back triple once he got his own business started. "At first I didn't mind, but then I began to resent it," Nicole recalls. "The next thing you know, he wanted me to lend him the three thousand dollars I had saved, to help buy the stock for a clothing store he was planning to open."

Nicole lent him the money and lost every penny of it. But when that business failed, he quickly asked for another loan, and then another. Nicole asked her father to finance him this time, but, as she later rejoices, he refused. Nicole explains:

> In the meantime, he was always broke, and I ended up paying for everything, "just until I get on my feet," he would say. He kept a record of everything I spent on us, saying that he would pay it all back once things got rolling.
>
> After two and a half years of this, I could no longer ignore the facts. I kept thinking, "Help. I'm sinking. Get me out of here before it's too late." But I felt powerless. I was attached to him. We had spent every night together for the past few years, either at his place or mine. Also, I was confused. At times I thought I was being too hard on him—too impatient.
>
> Finally, I realized that I could never change him. I had to face it. I had spent three years of my life with

someone who I had come to despise. He was unrealistic, unfocused, and immoral in the bargain. (I had watched him con and lie to people, and listened to his rationalizations long enough to know this.)

Nicole got rid of Erwin indirectly. Her sister had mentioned that there was a job opening in a designer dress shop near her house. Nicole applied and got the job—even though it was far from where Nicole lived. Travel soon became a chore, so Nicole's sister asked her if she would like to move in with her. Nicole accepted, and soon Erwin began to complain about the inconvenience. Nicole began meeting and dating men whom she met on her new job. Then one day, Nicole got into an argument with Erwin, and rather than try to smooth things over, the way she usually did, she "let it explode into a breakup," as Nicole expresses it. Nicole explains:

> Once it was done, I fought every impulse to go back with him. I kept reminding myself of the life I would have to lead with him. Always waiting for that never-arriving ship to come in.
> A few years later, I met a wonderful man—a lawyer. We have been married for two years and I'm about to have our first child. We are so happy together it's hard to imagine how I could have ever even thought of marrying someone else. I often wonder what would have happened if I stayed with Erwin—even for another year!

Sometimes you must let something go in order to find something new. If Nicole had clung to Erwin, if she had not been willing to take steps in moving out of the relationship, chances are she would still be shelling out money and subsidizing his dreams, rather than enjoying a life with someone with whom she apparently has much in common.

When the Student Is Ready, the Teacher Arrives—But Perhaps He Was Always There, and You Just Didn't See Him

Nicole's escape began as a wish—almost a silent prayer: "Help. Get me out of here. I'm sinking." Such thoughts perhaps triggered the unconscious process of moving away from Erwin.

It appears to me that when you are seeking to move toward the light, when you are straining toward the right path for your life, the universe itself will rise up to help you—but you must be alert to take advantage of these opportunities.

Let me explain. Is it really the universe that suddenly helps one in such a situation, or is it the individual who is now willing to take advantage of opportunities in the universe which were always there, but previously ignored? It is quite possible that most of us, like Nicole, take advantage of opportunities in the universe, indeed see opportunities in the universe, only when we are ready to see them.

Nicole took advantage of the opportunity to put physical distance between herself and Erwin by taking a job far away from him. She took advantage of the second opportunity to get away from him by moving in with her sister. She then cooperated with the universe by being willing to go out with other men. All of this made the fourth and most difficult step possible—the final breakup, when she took advantage of the argument in order to end things. Then all of her previous experience, coupled with the knowledge of how difficult it was to get away from him in the first place, enabled her to put into practice the fifth and repetitive step—the continual refusal to fall back into the trap of dating him again, no matter how much she missed him.

By first willing herself free, and then, step by step, taking advantage of opportunities to be free, Nicole was able to extricate herself from the kind of relationship from which many women never escape.

What to Do When You Are Tempted to Crawl Back

Nicole was able to resist going back to her negative relationship by, in her own words, "fighting every impulse to go back with Erwin, and remembering the life I would have with him." Apparently, for Nicole, this memory was enough to prevent her, in a moment of weakness, from crawling back.

But what if a mere memory alone is not enough? What if you find yourself missing him—to the point of almost physical pain? When you feel this way, what are you really doing? You are remembering the good things about the relationship, the things that comforted you, the things you enjoyed—the excitement you experienced—to the exclusion of the bad memories, which are equally valid.

Let's face it, if the relationship was so great, why did it end in the first place? (Notice I said "end," because even if, in your case, he left you, there were evidently problems that you probably didn't need, and you are most likely very lucky to have had him do the work. Now you owe it to yourself to stay rid of him!)

In order to balance the scale and see the relationship in proper perspective, it is only fair that you take a hard look at the darker side as well as the lighter side. You've been basking in the sentimentality and the nostalgia of the wonderful aspects of the relationship, as it were—teasing yourself, saying, "See? Now you won't have that wonderful feeling anymore. Now you won't have that fun anymore. Now you won't feel loved anymore."

Think of the things that you hated about the relationship. Remember every time you felt anger and rage toward him. Recall every time you were disappointed with him and felt that he let you down. Reminisce about the many nights you cried yourself to sleep, or the days you went to work depressed, thinking that he would never change and that you were doomed to life with a loser.

Here is a simple checklist that may help you to put things in perspective, and to stay happily put in your place the next time you are tempted to crawl back. Write down everything you loved about the relationship in the left column, and everything you hated about the relationship in the right column. Then take a hard look at the results. I've used what I imagine Nicole would have written down, had she decided to commit her mental checklist to paper.

RELATIONSHIP CHECKLIST: WHAT I LOVED, WHAT I HATED

LOVED	HATED
1. His good looks.	He was always broke and continually borrowed money from me.
2. His charm.	He was dishonest: He lied to people—and to himself.
3. Sleeping with him every night.	He was unrealistic about business situations—a hopeless dreamer whom I would end up supporting.
4. A guaranteed date every Saturday, and for holidays and family events.	His continual excuses and false promises.
5. Someone to talk to when I was lonely.	The disappointment and anger I constantly felt.

Now think hard. If you take him back, you will be taking the bad with the good. Is it worth it?

One final thought. If you do go back, realize that you may well end up terminating the relationship again, for the same reasons you ended it this time; and then you will have to go through the trauma of leaving him all over again. Is it worth it? Is that what you really want to do with your emotional time and energy for the rest of your life? Why put yourself through the leaving process again and again and again? Why not let this one painful time be it?

Healing with Time

I want to offer a word of comfort to women who may presently feel that the pain of the missed relationship—bad things about it notwithstanding—is just too much to bear. What I am about to say may seem to be somewhat of a cliché, and for that reason you may be tempted to ignore it. But clichés were coined for a reason: They were developed because they represent generally agreed upon observations about life.

"Time is a great healer." It really is. But how much time must go by before you start feeling better? There is a simple formula for healing in relationships, as I see it. The first week is the most difficult. If you can get through that week without going back, you are halfway there. Then, every day, you feel a little better.

The second part of the formula is quite fascinating: the part that deals with how long it will take before you are completely over your relationship—a time when you will feel absolutely nothing when you think of that man. It seems to me that it takes exactly as long as the relationship itself lasted before you are completely free of any feelings for that man. Let me explain.

If you were in love with a man for three months, and then break up with him, it will take you three months before you can say, "What was I so upset about?" If you were going out with a man for two years and then break up, it will take two years before you feel absolutely nothing when you think of him. If you were married to a man for five years, it will take five years before you feel no pain when you remember him.

Of course, this is not a formula cast in stone. It's a simple observation on my part that has held true for me, and for many of the women I've interviewed.

Now don't throw this book across the room. I'm not saying that if you were with a man for fifteen years, you are doomed to pine away for him for the next fifteen years. Of course not. You will be able to go on with your life within a matter of months—and in a year or two, you may even be in love with another man. What I am saying is, the sore spot may not be completely calloused over until the same amount of time you spent in the relationship has gone by.

Let me add one more thing. Of course, everyone is different. You may be able to get over your lost loves in half that time! I hope you do. If you've had some experience in this area, I'm very interested in hearing from you. Please write to me and tell me if my formula has proven true in your situation—or if it has not. I'd love to know.

The Prima Donna

Some men are chronically unemployed because they are "too good" to work at just any job. They must have *the* job, the employment that is worthy of their talent. In the meantime, someone has to pay the bills. Blanche had this experience with Lance, who answered her ad in the personals. He sounded like her dream come true in his letter, but he hadn't sent a photograph, so you can imagine her delight when she discovered that he was absolutely dashing.

The first two times they went out, Lance took Blanche to the best restaurants, telling her that he was in his family's silkscreen business. But after that, he seemed to continually prefer dining at home—particularly at Blanche's house, where she would not only cook but supply the food as well, and he would show up in rather threadbare clothing. Blanche explains:

> It turned out that the suit he wore on our first few dates was borrowed from his brother. He was always broke. Finally he admitted that his family business had failed and that he was looking for a job.
>
> Over the next three months he turned down at least six jobs. It was never *the right one*. This annoyed me. How dare he be so fussy. If you have no job, for God's sake, take anything. Respect yourself. You have to pay

your rent, don't you? Not Lance. He simply moved back
in with his parents while he refused to "settle."

In spite of all this, Lance asked Blanche to marry him and, in
spite of it all, Blanche accepted, but under the condition that he
get a job within the next month. They agreed to get married in a
year—as long as Lance was true to his word. But as time passed,
Lance continued to turn down job offers, declaring that he was a
special person, and that the openings were all beneath his dignity.
In the meantime, he would gleefully say, "Thank God. Only in
America—my unemployment checks can keep me alive forever."
Blanche was furious. She recalls:

> I realized that this wasn't going to work out. I had left a
> lot of my property at his house (actually, his parents'
> house), my computer, my fax machine, and so forth, so I
> asked for them back and then told him it was over. He
> begged me to give him another chance, but I refused. I
> knew I had to cut it off now or I would end up sup-
> porting him for the rest of my life.

Lance is now married to a nurse who works nights—a woman
who is paying the bills just until Lance "finds the right job."
A man like Lance, I suspect, will always be waiting for the right
job, tailor-made, to magically come along. It seems highly unlikely that he would even dream of starting at the bottom and
working his way up to some position that he could eventually
create for himself.

Ain't Nothing Going on
But the Rent

In my opinion, unemployed men cannot afford to be prima
donnas. I'm sure Blanche would have had more respect for Lance

if he had worked as a security guard, taken a job as a supermarket clerk, or even mopped floors—any honest employment. Let's face it, ladies, someone has got to pay the rent. As a matter of fact, if I were Blanche, I would have gotten a copy of the song whose words go: "You've got to have a J-O-B if you want to be with me, ain't nothing going on but the rent," and sung it to him on a regular basis, until he got the message—and if he didn't, I would have traveled!

By way of review, here are the excuses of the four unemployed men discussed in this chapter. If you have heard any interesting excuses, please add them to the list.

FAVORITE EXCUSES OF UNEMPLOYED MEN

1. "I'm about make a big business deal..."
2. "My money is all tied up but..."
3. "I'm planning to open a business. I need time to think..."
4. "The only jobs I'm offered are for idiots... I'll wait until the right job comes along."
5.
6.
7.
8.
9.
10.

He Works for a Commission

Other men *do* work—but not really. They seem to be stirring up quite a cloud of dust with their goings and comings, but when the dust settles, very little net income has resulted from their efforts.

When Adrianne first met Charlie, she was quite impressed with his independence and guts. He worked as a real-estate agent, strictly on commission, and was doing rather well. She admired a man who could depend solely upon his talent to make a living. But once they got married, Adrianne began to see the darker side of the situation. She says:

> When we got married, I knew he worked on commission and that there would be ups and downs in his paycheck. Since I'm a teacher, my pay is steady—so we figured we could manage when times were bad.
>
> But I never knew how bad things would get—and how comfortable he would be about us living on my salary. In the past year he made about one-fifth of what I make, and it didn't bother him a bit. All he could say was, "Thank God *we* have your job." Hmmph! "*We* have your job." I resent that. I feel as if he let me down. When I married him, I was under the impression that he would soon be earning enough so that I could get pregnant, quit my job, and devote myself to full-time motherhood. And here he is being so thrilled that he doesn't have to worry about his money, because "we always have mine."
>
> I never told him how I felt. Don't ask me why, but I just thought he would rise to the occasion and drive himself to earn a living. But he just sits by and blames the economy, never thinking to do something else.
>
> I don't know what to do. We're still married, but I'm always picking on him—and he's always lashing out at me. My mother says, if I realize that marrying him was a mistake, I should face it now and get a divorce—before I waste my life with a man I'll have to support.

Putting Your Cards on the Table Early in the Game

Admittedly, Adrianne made a mistake by not leveling with Charlie about how she felt about his earnings or about her own ideals concerning full-time motherhood before they got married. It is most important that a couple clearly understand what is the agreement or contract between them before they make such a serious commitment as marriage. (Interestingly, some couples are now setting down such details in their prenuptial agreements; something that is, I feel, a poor substitute for an open, honest conversation between two people, where trust can be established.)

Having failed to have such a conversation before marriage, they could have had it later. Instead of quietly seething and building up a mountain of resentment against Charlie, Adrianne could have put her cards on the table. She could say something like: "It does not comfort me to hear you say, 'Thank God, we always have your salary.' In fact, I resent being the one to shoulder most of the financial burden when there is nothing stopping you from looking for a full-time job. I feel disappointed in you, because I was hoping to become pregnant and to stay home with the child. I was expecting you to be willing to support us." It would also be a good idea for Adrianne to point out that the two of them should have had this conversation before marriage, and that she is not placing all the blame on Charlie.

In any case, if Adrianne doesn't speak up soon, it may soon be too late. She may build up such a resentment for Charlie that when she does speak, it will be to tell him that she has rejected him as a man, and that she wants a divorce.

The bottom line is, men are not mind readers. If you feel a certain way about finances, then say so. Don't expect your man to somehow magically know your expectations.

I made this mistake with my former husband. I secretly resented the fact that he was earning half of what I was earning, and that he seemed quite content with the situation. Yet, rather than confront him with my feelings, I buried them and seethed until I had built up such an anger toward him that I could not speak a civil word to the man. Finally, one day I lashed out at him, accusing him of being insensitive and uncaring. The poor devil did not know what hit him and could not figure out from which left field my tirade was coming. When I finally expressed exactly what was bothering me, dutifully he got a second job to supplement his income, but then *he* became angry.

Needless to say, things went from bad to worse, and we eventually got divorced.

The Man Who Is Always Being "Let Go"

Some guys get all the breaks, while others seem to get a bad deal no matter what they do. But is it really just bad luck? Burt, a lovable guy who was a zoo keeper when Shannon met him six years ago, thought so. As it turned out, Shannon, a botanist, would be spending six years examining Burt's excuses. He would get fired or laid off every few weeks and would blame everyone but himself for his bad luck. People were against him, plain and simple. No one wanted to give him a break. The boss favored other people, and on and on and on. But in the meantime, he came to work late, was absent a lot, forgot to do things he was supposed to do, cut out early, took long lunches, and started arguments with his co-workers. Then, when he was the first one to get laid off, he cried, "Not fair." When I asked Shannon why she didn't dump him long ago, she replied with sadness:

> He's the only man who could make me laugh—the only guy I could really talk to—who listened and understood. And I'm the only woman who has ever understood him. I wanted to marry him. In fact, we were unofficially engaged. But my brother kept telling me, "Get rid of him, Shannon. It's not going to get better."
>
> Two months ago, after he was fired again, I tried to help him to see the part he played in it. He began defending himself and saying that nobody understood him. Sick to my stomach of his endless excuses, I told him I didn't want to see him anymore.

Shannon realized that she was dealing with a full-grown man who was operating with the mind of a boy—an immature child who believed that the world was truly against him. Knowing full well that he would want to lean on her as a mother and a caretaker, wisely, she ended the relationship. She says:

> I'm enjoying the singles scene more than I expected to. Men are so cute. They really work at getting women to like them. I never realized how many men there are out there trying to meet women. In fact, there are as many "desperate men" as there are women, but the next time I get involved with a man, I'm going to make sure that he's a responsible guy who is well-established.

It isn't easy to give someone up—even if they are not employed—especially if they have other virtues and are meeting some of your compelling needs. Shannon needed a friend and a companion, but, what is more, she needed to be needed. In a sense, she enjoyed playing the role of mother. But another side of Shannon knew that playing mother was not enough to satisfy her needs as a woman. She wanted a responsible man who was willing take charge of his own life. She realized that there was little chance of Burt ever doing this and, as painful as it was, wisely, she let him go.

Listen, Listen, Listen

If you are in a relationship with a man who is not right for you, chances are friends and family have tried to warn you, and chances are you've resented their interference. If this is true, instead of waving them away, why not stop at least to consider their words. There is no harm in listening to what they have to say. Listening is not doing. No one will force you to take action. But if there is a message in those words, at least you are giving yourself a chance to get it.

And to those of you who are reading this book for someone

else—a friend or a relative who needs to get rid of a man—I encourage you to not stop talking. You'd be surprised. Your words just might be registering, and at the right moment, as for Shannon, they may just serve their purpose.

Disabled or Dishonest?

What does disability have to do with unemployment? After all, a man who is collecting disability checks is earning an income, is he not? Yes. But what happens when you know that the man in your life has faked his disability and is collecting money just so that he can loaf around all day while you go to work? That's what happened to Miranda, who after six years of marriage to Verne, an electrician, found out that he was, in her view, not only lazy but dishonest.

As it turns out, after being involved in a minor accident at work, Verne decided to "milk it," as he delightedly expressed it to his wife, and claim permanent disability. Now, this thirty-eight-year-old man spends his days playing basketball in the local school yard, surfing on sunny days, going to the movies, and, in general, just hanging around. Miranda bemoans her fate:

> All of this, while I drag myself to work every day. I'm a waitress and I have to put up with a lot of abuse from customers, all day long. When I get home from work, it irks me to see him sitting there in front of the TV, chomping on a hero sandwich, while I take off my shoes and rub my feet.
>
> I confronted him time and again, and I even admitted to him that I cannot respect a man who does not work for a living, much less is cheating his company on a daily basis. Every time I say this, he gets angry and says, "The company owes me. I worked and slaved for them at a near-minimum wage all those years. Anyway, everybody does it. I would have been a fool not to."

I'm still married to him, but I have no respect for him. I don't know what to do.

A Conflict of Values May Be Irreconcilable

The real issue with Miranda and Verne is a conflict in values. After six years of marriage, Miranda has been forced to see another side of Verne, a side which points up that the two of them have very different standards of right and wrong. Miranda's dislike for deception and dishonesty, coupled with her belief in the work ethic, has rendered it all but impossible for her to remain married to Verne.

Perhaps you've met a man like Verne—someone who has taken advantage of an opportunity to be paid without working. Perhaps he has sued someone wrongly just to collect the money so that he would no longer have to work and is someone who is also content to lie about and just relax—with no apparent purpose in life. Something within you may have recoiled. Perhaps you said to yourself, "I don't respect you," and perhaps you have moved on quickly.

But what would you do if your man showed none of those traits when you first married him, but began to demonstrate them after a few years of marriage? Would you stay with him in spite of your growing misgivings, or would you find it necessary to leave?

I, for one, could never stay with such a man. My basic set of values, the work ethic that I was taught to believe in and follow, an ethic that I later absorbed and put into practice in my own life, would cause me to see that I had made a dismal mistake in marrying this man. If I were Miranda, I would tell Verne exactly how I felt, and unless it turned out that Verne was really just going through a midlife crisis, and had temporarily taken leave of his senses and his values as well, I would give him the bum's rush.

It must be stated, however, that if a woman is doing her

homework, she can often detect such attitudes before a marriage takes place.

Early Retirement

Early retirement can be a blessing—or it can be a curse. Lila, a travel agent, had been going out with Tony, a police lieutenant, for a year, when to her amazement he announced that he was retiring. Lila says:

> At first I thought he was kidding. How could a man in his late forties retire? He said he was burned out on police work and needed a change. Naturally, I assumed this meant that he would get another job—maybe open his own business or something. But I was wrong. His only intention was to live the life of Riley—to sit around, play sports, and just relax.
>
> When I protested, he told me not to worry. He said, "Think of how lucky you are. I can cook you dinner every night, and after we're married, if we have a baby, I can watch it while you go to work. We won't have to hire a sitter."
>
> These words did not make me happy. In fact, they made me sick. In my mind, a self-respecting man would never be content to sit home on his butt while his wife went out and worked.
>
> He was good to his word. Once he retired, he spent most of his time watching games on TV or playing golf with his friends.
>
> I lost respect for him. I know what you're thinking. Why couldn't he stay home and cook and clean and mind the children while I went to work? But I wasn't brought up that way. To me, a man should be a man.
>
> I've heard a lot about women's lib and role switching, but it's just not for me. I called off the engagement,

thankful for the fact that all of this happened *before* and not *after* we got married.

Lila is smart to be honest with herself. She is not impressed with the fact that Tony is willing to cook and take care of a child. She realizes that she needs to see the man in her life working. Role switching is uncomfortable for her. The fact is, even in this day and age, many women do not appreciate leaving the house at the crack of dawn while their husband is snug in bed sleeping, even if they know that he will soon be up cooking and cleaning, and I am one of them.

If I were Lila, I would insist that Tony either go into some other business or get another job. If he refused, I would tell him that we have very different ideas of roles for men and women, and that these differences in thinking are irreconcilable.

Just Who Should Carry the Log?

When it comes to the issue of "carrying the log," the most important thing for you to do is to be honest with yourself. Would you respect a man who would not or could not at least carry his weight when it comes to finances? Would you be willing to earn most or more than half of the income? In short, what is your standard of equity when it comes to financial matters?

There are some women who can cope with working to either completely or partially support a man, particularly if that man is contributing other things to the relationship, such as taking care of the home and the children. In such role-switching situations, where both a woman and a man are content with this arrangement, all well and good.

However, if I meet a man who prefers to remain at home and cook and clean while I go out to work, I will run as quickly as possible in the opposite direction. It's not for me—and I must add, from my interviews and general observation, even today, such couples are in the extreme minority.

In closing, I would like to add that, for me, a relationship with a man who is not a financially successful achiever is out of the question. As the saying goes, "Water seeks its own level," and since I have reached a certain level of success in life, and have developed in myself character traits and values that I think are worthwhile, I look for similar qualities in a man whom I could eventually come to love enough to marry.

Reminders

1. The creative artist, the entrepreneur, the perpetual student— God bless them all, with a real job. Otherwise get rid of them.

2. Disability, early retirement, or Prima Donna: If you have completely different values when it comes to work and earning money, get rid of him.

3. Put your cards on the table early in the game. How do you really feel about supporting a man?

4. If you've entertained some leeches of your own, rather than blame yourself, realize that it's easy to do foolish things out of momentary neediness. Forgive yourself, then pick the leech off your back, throw him out, and learn from your mistake.

5. The next time you meet an unemployed man, no matter how gorgeous or charming he is, remember to sing him this song: "You've got to have a J-O-B if you want to be with me, ain't nothing goin on but the rent."

11

Get Rid of Him
If He's Married to
Someone Else

Everything about him is perfect, except for one thing—he's married. When you're not thinking about this little fly in the ointment, you are as happy as can be. But you are forced to come down to cold reality when, time and again, you realize that you must share your man with another woman—someone who in fact has first choice when it comes to his time.

A part of you would like nothing better than to get rid of him, but another part of you would like to leave things the way they are—because the very thought of living without him sends you into a panic. How did you get yourself into this situation in the first place? Certainly, you didn't plan it that way—or did you?

Some women get caught up in a fling with a married man—something they expect to be a meaningless affair that will not last, but it does—and before they know it, they are in love. Resentful of the fact that they have to give him up, the one man who in every way (except for the marriage) is perfect, they continue the relationship, until they are so deeply entrenched that it is nearly impossible to leave.

Other women fall into cheating situations with married men completely innocently. The man, in the beginning, lies to them and is quite good at it. By the time these women discover the subterfuge, it's too late! They are hooked.

Other women go out with a married man because they believe that the man is unhappily married, that they are the only one who really "understands" him. The only reason he's staying with his wife, they believe, is for the children. Once they grow up, "we will be together for life," they tell themselves. The only problem is, it rarely happens.

Still other women repeatedly get involved with married men. "What can you do?" they say. "The good ones are all taken." But is there an unconscious method to their madness? Could it be that, deep down inside, they are in conflict as to whether they want to make a commitment? Perhaps a married man suits their purpose to a *T*.

Whether going out with a married man is a one-time experience or a pattern for you, as you read this chapter and discover what happened to other women, I hope that you will be inspired to take action.

It Was Just a Foolish Fling

Darcy, an architect, would see Ryan, a construction worker, on the train every day. They would smile at each other and leave it at that. This went on for a year, with Darcy often thinking, "I wonder if he's shy. Maybe I should make the first move." Finally, one day the train was delayed, and Darcy found herself standing next to him. They got into a conversation, and Ryan told her that he was unhappily married and had always been attracted to her. He asked her out to dinner. Darcy explains:

I don't usually go out with married men, but I was lonely and bored with my life, so I accepted. On our first date, there was so much electricity between us that I don't even remember the dinner conversation. We ended up in my apartment, kissing passionately.

We said good night—without making another date. But the next day, when we met on the train, he agreed to come over to my house that evening. It was the beginning of a five-month relationship that could have destroyed me.

At first it was very exciting. Our attraction was mainly sexual, with very little soul connection. But after a while, as we shared our hopes and dreams and began to bare our hearts to each other, we fell in love. My life began to revolve around the stolen moments I had with him. Finally, the very thought of him sleeping with his wife drove me mad. I began hating her—and feeling guilty for it at the same time. After all, how would I feel if I were married and some woman was going out with my husband?

I started nagging him to spend more time with me and asked him to get a divorce. In the meantime, my work was suffering—I was no longer creative, and I neglected a few projects and ended up losing them. People started to notice. One friend said, "The sparkle is gone from your eyes. What's wrong?" I was sick of leading a double life.

One evening after their date ended in a crying bout regarding her having to play "second fiddle," Darcy dropped Ryan off in the usual spot, a few blocks from his house, and they kissed good night. The next day, a Saturday, Ryan was supposed to spend the afternoon at Darcy's house watching old movies, but, instead, Darcy got a phone call from him. "It's over. My wife saw me getting out of your car," he said. Darcy was furious.

I jumped in my car and drove to his house in a wild rage, planning to go straight upstairs and confront him in the presence of his wife. Did he think he could dismiss me just like that, as if I meant nothing to him—after all the love and emotion I had invested in him?

But just as I arrived at his door, before his wife could see me, he was coming down the stairs. He signaled me to turn around. Then he asked me to follow him in my car. I did. We finally parked, and he got into my car. Tears were streaming down his cheeks. It was raining outside, and ironically there was a Willie Nelson song playing on the radio, "Blue Eyes Cryin' in the Rain." I looked at his blue eyes and thought, "I am doomed." This big, beautiful, muscular man was crying over me— and his wife. He confessed to loving both of us, and said he didn't want to get a divorce and that he had chosen his wife over me.

I wanted to be angry, but something in his voice made me understand. I could tell he loved me, but he was torn. On the one hand, I wanted to curse him out and blame him for everything—to have a tantrum, to threaten to expose him, to slap his face. But I knew I was wrong. Perhaps this was inevitable. I should have seen it coming.

After kissing him good-bye. Darcy went home to, as she expresses it, "lick her wounds." Although it was in the middle of the afternoon, she sat in a hot bath for an hour, crying and thinking, and working it out. The pain was so great that she could actually feel her heart ache—physically. She wondered if anyone really did die of a broken heart. Then, slowly, Darcy's spirit began to heal. She says:

I put my energy into my business, and soon I was working on new projects. In a month, the pain was bearable. In two, it was much better. In three, I was almost happy. In four, I was nearly myself. In some ways I even felt better—freer than ever in my life. It was as if a heavy burden were lifted off my chest.

Then he called and said he couldn't live without me.

He wanted me to be his woman on the side. He even suggested that we have a baby together. I was disgusted. How pitiful. He had not moved an inch. Here I was, getting on with my life—I'd moved way past him—and he was still thinking I would sacrifice my life for him. I had gotten used to living my life in the clear light of day. There was no way I would go back to the shadows again. I turned him down.

It's Like Having Your Feet Tied and Trying to Walk

Five years later, Ryan still calls Darcy, begging her to at least see him one more time. After asking about his family, she politely turns him down. "I would never put myself through that again," she exclaims. "The guilt, the misery, it's just not worth it."

As Darcy finally realized, leading a double life is a drain on creative energy. Involvement in a relationship that requires continual cover-up is the same as having your feet tied and being asked to run. You can't do it. Guilt can have a paralyzing effect.

In fact, studies show that people with a guilty conscience often step on their own feet when it comes to success in life. When opportunities for success come along, they unconsciously blow the deal, because deep in their hearts, they believe that they don't deserve to succeed. In fact, such people regularly put obstacles in their own way, in an unconscious effort to punish themselves for a wrong they believe they have committed.[1]

The fact is, everything we do that we believe is wrong is recorded in our unconscious mind as clearly as if a score were being kept. It is just as if an indictment were written against us. Each indictment serves to weigh us down, until it becomes more and more difficult to succeed.

On the up side, however, every time we take action that coincides with our value system, it is as if a mark were recorded in our favor, in the "positive" column. Our self-esteem and our belief in ourselves increase, and we welcome opportunities for advancement.[2] Notice that once Darcy got out of her relationship with Ryan, she began to take on new projects.

Quite a psychological system going on! It's almost as if God were too busy to keep a record of everyone's deeds, good and bad, so he provided us with an automatic unconscious bookkeeping system. We punish and reward ourselves, like it or not, in accordance with whether or not we live up to our own values.

Sisterhood: If We Refused to Do It, with Whom Would the Men Cheat?

It is interesting to note that Darcy did feel some compunction about going out with someone else's husband. In fact, she felt guilty, and I think many women who go out with other men's husbands do too—as, in my opinion, well they should. After all, as Darcy so simply expresses it, "How would I feel if I were married, and some woman was going out with my husband?"

We women have for too long allowed ourselves to be typecast into the role of catty competitors with each other, when, in fact, most of us feel a sense of sisterhood, a kindred spirit among us. If we would allow ourselves to fully experience the true empathy that we feel for each other, if we would, instead of suppressing our natural compassion for one another, let it rule our behavior, I doubt very much that we would conduct an affair with another woman's husband—no matter how dashing, debonair, or charming he might be.

After all is said and done, perhaps the words of the Bible are best to guide our behavior when it comes to going out with another woman's husband: "Do unto others as you would have others do unto you." In other words, if you wish that, when your husband would try to date another woman, that woman would set him straight by saying, "How dare you betray your wife in this fashion?" and turn him down cold, and if you wish that every single woman whom your husband approached would do the same, then do that yourself when another woman's husband approaches you.

By the Time I Found Out He Was Married, It Was Too Late

When Amy met Lee, they hit it off so well that, in a week's time, they were seeing each other almost every night, weekends included— and in a matter of months, they were sleeping together at least twice a week—either at Lee's apartment in the city or at Amy's home in the suburbs. You can imagine, then, Amy's dismay when after six months of going out, Lee confessed that he was married and had a wife and five happy children living in a nearby town. Amy says:

> He told me he didn't love his wife and that it was merely a marriage of convenience, but that he could never get divorced because of strict Chinese family tradition. He begged me to stay in his life forever—as his "real wife," as he put it. He promised to take care of my every need.
>
> It made me sick that he had lied to me, so I broke it off. But that night I cried myself to sleep, thinking, "It's just not fair. Why should I have to suffer this way?" In the middle of my crying jag, at 2:00 A.M., he called and said, "I love you. That's why I lied to you. I knew you would drop me if I told you the truth. Don't throw this away. This is meant to be. Neither of us will ever be happy without the other."
>
> I agreed to go back with him. That was seven years ago. Now he's paying all my bills. We still see each other at least three times a week, and sometimes we even

travel together. I often resent not being able to live a normal life—but I can't let him go.

In spite of her continual pleas that Lee get divorced, he refuses to do so on the grounds that it is Chinese custom to remain married, no matter what, and that it would be a disgrace to his family name if he broke that custom. He also tells her that it is understood in Chinese tradition that wealthy men have concubines—and, in fact, they are a status symbol.

I know that Lee claims to be old-fashioned, but I'm wondering just how far back his fashion goes. Could it be that he's living in the Middle Ages? I know of no such tradition among the Chinese—at least not in recent history. In any case, what made Amy decide to continue her relationship with Lee? What went through her mind that night when she had resolved to end it and then changed her mind?

Wake Up to the World: Life Is Not Fair, Never Was, Never Will Be

While it is true that Amy had no way of knowing in the beginning that Lee was married (he did have his own apartment in the city) and it is true that by the time she found out, six months later, she was already emotionally involved with Lee, why didn't she end it then? She said to herself, "Why should I have to suffer this way? It's just not fair."

Isn't that an interesting concept: "It's not fair that I suffer this way"? And who says it isn't fair? Where is it written that, in life, people should only suffer in certain ways and on certain occasions? (The unspoken assumption here is: only when they "deserve" it.)

Let us all wake up to the world. The fact is, life rarely, if ever, is fair in that way. In fact, much of the experience of life is learning some hard lessons after having to experience emotional pain—

and, it is hoped, growing from those lessons because, in spite of the pain, we find the inner strength to make the right choice.

And what is the right choice? It is that choice which will enable us to look in the mirror and say, "I respect myself." It is that choice which will, in the long run, provide us with peace of mind and self-value. But what is more, it is that choice which usually, in the end, is best not only for our psychological well-being, but for our physical and material well-being as well. Let me explain.

Feeling cheated, as Amy feels, takes a physical toll. The stress of living with anger can in fact cause the start of many diseases—cancer, heart trouble, and so on. In addition, who is to say that if Amy had let Lee go that night, six and a half years ago, she would not have met a wonderful man whom she could have all to herself? What's more, speaking of the material aspect of it, who is to say that the man may not have been even better off than Lee financially and that she would never have had to deal with money pressure again?

But what about now? After seven years, is it too late for Amy to leave? Of course not. In fact, contrary to popular belief, sometimes it is easier, not more difficult, to leave a dead-end relationship after many years than it is in the beginning, because after the lapse of so much time, you know for a fact that nothing will change, and you can look at your life and decide whether you want to spend the rest of it doing exactly what you are doing.

Financial and Emotional Dependence

In closing this discussion, I cannot help but comment on one of the biggest pitfalls into which so many women fall—that of financial and emotional dependence. We'll discuss financial dependence first.

Once Amy allowed Lee to begin paying her bills, she became,

in a sense, his property—never mind what he was or was not thinking, but in her own mind. If a man is paying your bills, you owe him something, do you not? In addition, you will have to think that much more carefully before leaving him, because questions such as, "Can I make it on my own?" come into play, and "Is it worth the financial struggle I will have to endure?" will plague your mind.

What am I saying—that no woman should let a man pay her bills? Of course not. As a matter of fact, I wish I could find someone to pay mine. But the fact is, if I do find such a man, I'll never be foolish enough to cease and desist from either earning my own money or at least having the power to begin earning my own money. I'll go a step further. As a matter of fact, if the man I am committed to gets out of hand, I want to be able to say, "Get out of my house before I call the police"; and if he doesn't go, I want to be sure that when the police do come, it is *my name*, and not his, that is on the deed!

In summary, if a man is paying all the bills, unless you have a real understanding with a man that you are contributing equally—even though your contribution may not be financial—and unless you trust that man implicitly, I say, have your own source of income. And in the case of Lee, and any "cheating" man for that matter, how can you trust him implicitly? It can't be done.

What about the emotional element? Amy had allowed herself to become psychologically dependent upon Lee. She convinced herself she was so much in love with him that she could not function without him. She was wrong. As we all know, we can and do learn to live very well without men who, at one time, we thought we would be willing to die for. In fact, if you come to think about it, I'll bet you can think of someone with whom you were once madly in love, and who now does not even have the power to make your heart increase its beat by one stroke.

For more advice on dealing with emotional pain, see the section, "When tempted to crawl back," on page 202, and read chapter fifteen.

He's Unhappy at Home—He Said He Would Get Divorced!

Perhaps the most common trap for women, when it comes to falling in love with a married man, is that of the "poor misunderstood husband"—the man who no longer loves his wife but who is staying with her just until the children grow up. Such a man is in love with you—not his wife. You are the only one who really understands him.

But there is something *you may not understand*. This man may have an agenda quite different than the one on the surface; and, in the end, you may find yourself quite disappointed—and indeed, out in the cold.

Here's what happened to Jessica, who waited in vain for Grant to marry her after his children had grown up. She met him after a vacation in Barbados. At the supermarket, their cars were parked side by side, a matched pair—the same make and the same year—only hers was white and his was black. "This must be a sign," he said, and invited her to dinner. She was still high from the vacation so, impulsively, she accepted.

At dinner, he told her that he was unhappily married and that his wife didn't understand him. He said he was staying married just until the children grew up, and that *he and his wife had an unspoken understanding* that they would both go out with other people. All this, he said, was agreed upon just so the money which would otherwise be wasted on a divorce and two separate living quarters could be squirreled away for the children's education.

When he dropped all of this on Jessica, her heart sank to her feet. She thought of ending it right there—but then she rationalized, "It doesn't matter. I'm not in the market for a husband right now anyway." In spite of it all, the two eventually become lovers, friends, and even business advisers to each other. They were inseparable.

That was ten years ago, when his children were nine and ten, and he promised to get divorced as soon as they were in college. Indeed, he kept his promise, at least half of it. Jessica reports:

He got divorced all right, but as soon as he did, he dumped me. I'm so furious with him that I'm thinking of dropping a dime on him. I may just call his wife to tell her about the whole thing. She should know what a worm he is. All those years he cheated us both—he deceived his wife and he led me on. I wasted my life fantasizing about our future together, and what does he do once he finally gets divorced? He says he doesn't want another commitment yet, and that I'm starting to remind him of his wife—putting pressure on him. I'm so furious I can't even think straight. But I guess you could say I'm lucky in a way. If we did get married, he would be cheating on me!

Why Affairs Rarely Lead to Marriage

Jessica let ten years of her precious life slip away while going out with a man who said that he was staying married just for the children. Most men who make such claims usually do one of two things: They either find other excuses not to get divorced once the children are grown, or they do get divorced, but when they do, they drop the affair person and remain single forever or eventually marry someone else.

Grant fell into the second category. Having gotten divorced, the last thing he wanted to do was to replace his wife. "Why exchange one bondage for another?" he must have thought. But there's more to it than that. Very few affairs survive the change in the relationship that inevitably takes place after a divorce. With the need for clandestine meetings and stolen moments of love in out-of-the-way motels gone, the relationship must be conducted in a more practical fashion. Missing the excitement, many couples split apart.

There is yet another element involved. Once an affair is over, a man who has been cheating on his wife for years often does not want to marry the woman who has been party to this deception. He would rather find someone who will allow him to forget the shadowy past. He wants to begin the future with a new person and a clean slate. All too often, like Jessica, the affair person is left out in the cold—and furious.

But My Wife and I Have an Understanding!

Don't you just love it when a man asks you out, tells you he's married, and then, as Grant told Jessica, adds, "Oh, it's all right. My wife and I have an understanding." My answer to such men is always the same: "Oh, really. How wonderful. Then when I call you at home, she won't mind taking messages for me—in case I want to change our meeting place."

Needless to say, I have never gotten the okay to do such a thing. But what I have gotten are a host of reasons why I must, under no conditions, call the home. Seemingly legitimate excuses are given, such as "sensitivity" (we don't want to throw it up in each other's faces) "the children," and so on. But no matter what, I am never, under any circumstances, given permission to live the affair in the clear light of day, and, mysteriously, in spite of this "understanding," the man is never willing to frequent restaurants where anyone who may know his wife would be.

It never fails. No matter how many questions I ask, I am never allowed to find out for sure whether this man indeed has an open marriage; and for this reason, I never go out with such a man. As discussed on pages 222–223, how could I do that to another woman?

Why Are All the Men I Fall in Love with Married?

Abigail, a gemologist, was in love again, and she knew she was in trouble. "Why is it that every time I meet the perfect man, he's married?" she thought. "Could it be true that all the good men are taken?" When Abigail first spotted Timothy, a salesman, at a jewelry convention, he was in the process of giving a speech, and she liked him right away—the in-command way he spoke, the sparkle in his eyes, his enthusiasm, and his boyish charm. She left the convention hall fantasizing about him, and then forgot about it.

But later that night, she met him at the coffee shop and struck up a conversation that lasted until dawn. "When I finally got to my room," Abigail recalls, "I went to sleep in a reverie—and knowing full well that he was married and that I was in trouble—again."

After a year of going out, Abigail and Timothy had a big blowup over his not being able to take her out on her birthday, and they broke up. Abigail concludes: "I just can't win, can I?"

Abigail can win—if she faces the fact that her continually getting involved with married men may not be just a coincidence. The fact is, if a woman has a pattern of involvement with unavailable men, there may be something else going on—an unconscious plan that needs exploration.

Mental health professionals agree that some women who repeatedly become embroiled in liaisons with unavailable men are in conflict with conscious and unconscious desires. Consciously, such women want to have a man all to themselves, but on an unconscious level, due to fears stemming from early childhood, they are compelled to run the other way. The solution: to choose "safe" men who are perfect potential mates, except for one thing—they are already married.

Time and again, such women are frustrated when things don't work out. They decry fate, they proclaim that all of the good ones are taken, but on a deeper level, a very real need is being met—the need to remain unattached.

What makes these women so afraid to make a permanent commitment? Their reasons are as diverse as the personalities involved. Perhaps one woman saw her father abandon her mother when she was a child, and she fears the same thing will happen to her. Another woman may fear being stuck with one man, because her mother felt trapped with her father. Another woman may have had to compete with her mother for her father's attention, and now she may need to continually relive this childhood experience in order to feel excitement with men. The possibilities are endless. The most important thing to remember is, if you are repeatedly involved with married men, it's a good idea to probe into your own motives and find out what they are. It's a good bet that such a pattern is not merely a coincidence.[3]

Looking for Love in All the Wrong Places

There is nothing whatsoever wrong with looking for love. The trouble comes when we look for it in the wrong place. Women who go out with married men in an effort to fulfill a love need remind me of the character in a book of Sufi wisdom. The main character, Nasrudin, meets a man who is in the street and on all fours—apparently in desperate search of something. Unable to contain his curiosity, Nasrudin stops and initiates a conversation:

"What are you looking for?" asks Nasrudin.
"My keys," the stranger replies.
"Where exactly did you drop them?" asks Nasrudin.
"In my house," the stranger replies.
"Then why are you looking for them out in the street?" Nasrudin asks.
"Because there is more light out here," the stranger replies.[4]

A woman who is searching for love and who becomes involved with a married man is, in my opinion, just as foolish as the stranger in the Sufi tale who is looking for his keys in the street—even though he knows he dropped them in the house—simply because there is more light out there.

When a woman thinks it will be easier to find love in one place than in another, she may look there, even though, in her heart of hearts, she knows that she will never find it in that place. Where will she find it? Getting back to the Sufi tale, she will find it where she lost it, "in her own house," or in herself. You see, if she would take the time to love and value herself, she would no longer be willing to settle for the crumbs that fall from a man's table. She would believe that she deserves the full pie, and she would get it.

When Therapy Is Needed

If you are continually getting involved with married men and are unable to find out what your own motives are, it may be difficult or even impossible for you to break the pattern. And, after all, why should you be expected to trek along thorny emotional paths alone? It is difficult and often scary, but it doesn't have to be that way, with the help of a mental health professional.

Years ago, people were afraid to go to therapy. They imagined that only sick or seriously disturbed people would do such a thing. But times have changed and, these days, most people realize that going to a therapist has no more of a stigma than going to a foot doctor if you experience discomfort in walking, to an eye doctor if you can't see, or to a cardiologist if you have chest pains. They realize that it is as smart to take care of mental pain as it is to take care of physical pain—even smarter, because it is the mind, after all, and not the foot, the eye, or even the heart, which rules and directs the life.

It's Usually a Losing Game

In summary, in my opinion, aside from the ethical issues involved (after all, I realize that you may not share my moral convictions, and why should you?), to go out with a married man is to put yourself at a great disadvantage. There are several reasons for my saying this.

Even if the man eventually divorces his wife and marries you (which is unusual), what you often have is a heritage of guilt and anger. There are usually shadows of his and your guilt—often coupled with the anger of the people who have gotten hurt as a result of your joining together (his ex-wife, his children, his family). That bad energy will be in the background of your relationship forever.

I'm not saying that it is impossible to overcome the obstacles, or that no couple can survive a marriage that has resulted from an adulterous situation—I'm just saying it's very, very difficult, and it would be better to avoid it.

NOTES

1. Franz G. Alexander and Hugo Staub, *The Criminal, the Judge and the Public* (Glencoe, Ill.: Falcon Wing Press, 1956), pp. 40 and 139.

2. Joyce L. Vedral, *I Dare You* (New York: Holt, 1983), p. 38. Abraham Maslow discusses this subject at length in his book *Toward a Psychology of Being* (New York: Van Nostrand, 1968); specifically, on p. 5.

3. Yahuda Nir and Bonnie Maslin, *Loving Men for All the Right Reasons* (New York: Dell, 1982), pp. 13–17. For those who wish to attempt self-analysis, this book provides helpful ways to determine patterns of self-destructive behavior in women who continually date married men, behavior that is caused by a conflict of wish versus need. The authors suggest ways to correct such patterns.

4. Idries Shah, *The Pleasantries of the Incredible Mulla Nasrudin* (New York: Dutton, 1971), p. 93.

Reminders

1. A fling with a married man may snap back in your face—like a boomerang.

2. If all women refused to go out with married men, with whom would these married men cheat? Let's stick together, ladies. If he's married, throw him out the door before he comes in.

3. Promises, promises. Even if he does divorce his wife, more than likely, *you* will *not* be the one he marries.

4. If he says he has an understanding with his wife, ask for her phone number!

5. If you've been "burned" by a married man, get out of the fire—and just for the hey of it, why not drop a dime on him on your way out?

12

Get Rid of Him If He Abuses You— Physically, Verbally, or Emotionally

There are a variety of ways in which a man can abuse or mistreat a woman. The most obvious and apparently most dangerous is physical abuse because, in such cases, one's immediate life is threatened. However, the other types of mistreatment, verbal and psychological, can be just as damaging over time. As a matter of fact, the three usually go hand in hand. In this chapter, you will read about women who have experienced all three—in various combinations and to different degrees—and perhaps you will learn from their mistakes and be inspired by their courage.

Why do women remain in abusive relationships with husbands and even boyfriends when, on a daily basis, they must suffer continual assault—physically, verbally, and emotionally? And what kind of a man would engage in such behavior?

The Abusive Man

Men who hit women to "keep them in line" do so because they suffer from very low self-esteem. By placing someone weaker than they are in fear of them, they temporarily gain a feeling of power—a sense of respect—a fleeting respite from the haunting thought: "You are weak and worthless." The act of hitting a woman gives such a man instant recognition. For a moment, the world revolves around him, as his victim gives him her full attention—as she begs for mercy, as she cowers in the corner, waiting for the beating to end. While she is begging, he is onstage—finally, he is king.

But for how long? It's only a matter of hours before he feels twice as lowly—now that guilt is added to his woes. "You are the scum of the earth," the voice says. "You are a worthless worm," it repeats; and in a desperate effort to quiet the voice, he goes out to buy atonement gifts for his victim. When his victim accepts the gifts, the burden of guilt is lifted.

But just as his power was short-lived when he was doing the beating, so is his feeling of expiation. In a matter of days or even hours, when something else comes up in his life to remind him that he is weak and powerless, when anything happens to him that can be construed as disrespect, whether it be from his wife or girlfriend, or from some outside source totally unconnected to her, he beats her again—and the cycle begins anew.

Men who beat women hate themselves and would probably love to beat or even kill *themselves*. But self-preservation and a combination of other psychological factors prevent them from taking this course of action, so they divert their anger and find an easy mark, a scapegoat. That scapegoat is always someone relatively defenseless—and more often than not, it is the woman in their lives.

One wonders if sometimes the abuser's actions are not a misguided attempt to be heard—a way of begging "help me," a cry to touch and be touched—but what a way to communicate!

The Nonabusive Man

In contrast, a man of high self-esteem has no need to bully anyone. He respects himself and is not on a mission to gain appreciation. He can cope with differing opinions and, in fact, respects other people's right to disagree with him.

He can afford to be giving and loving, because he is not afraid that in so doing he will appear weak or be taken advantage of. He can do all this with ease, because his energy is not continually being diverted in an effort to protect his ego against imaginary assaults.

In fact, I believe there is a direct correlation between a man's ability to treat women with dignity, respect, and kindness and his self-esteem. The more secure a man is, the more he values himself, the greater will be his capacity to love and respect women (and people in general, for that matter).

In short, it is a man of high self-esteem, a man who believes that at his very core he is good, and not rotten, who is a nonabusive man. Such a man is not afraid of loving. Such a man is not afraid of women.

The Abused Woman

When it comes to abuse in male-female relationships, it takes two to tango. A woman who remains in an abusive relationship with a man also suffers from low self-esteem. Deep down inside, for a variety of reasons, she believes that she is not worthy of better treatment, and that in fact she is lucky to have anyone at all.

If such a woman has never been independent, never paid her own bills or run her own life, she could be terrified of leaving. She may fear that if she strikes out on her own, she will be worse off than she is now. In fact, she may experience the thought of leaving as worse than the physical pain she has to endure in the beatings; and she may experience the thought of leaving as the sensation of death itself. If she is an independent, career-driven woman, she may be fearful of the uncertainty of leaving a "secure" situation.

On another level, perhaps she feels that she is somehow to blame for her husband's or boyfriend's behavior. "I must be doing something to provoke this," she says. "What's wrong with me? Why can't I figure out what it is I'm doing—and stop it?" Because she feels as if she is to blame for the abuse, the abused women often takes great pains to hide her situation from others. "I must not let anyone find out how despicable I am," she says. "The least I can do is keep this private."

What in the world would make a woman think this way? Up until very recently, society itself was in full cooperation with such views. The victim herself was blamed for somehow provoking the abuse. Clichés such as the "nagging wife," the "demanding shrew," or the "unfaithful seductress" have been thrown around rather freely. In fact, it was not unusual to find police officers arriving at the scene of an abuse case accepting these excuses from a man who had just violated "his woman." Perhaps the officers would secretly or even openly understand why a man would "be provoked" to hit a woman. Remarkably, an unspoken code of ethics was in operation—a cooperation of certain males—a silent understanding that, every once in a while, a woman needs a reminder, just to "keep her in line." An amazing conclusion, since many of the women who allow themselves to be abused are not aggressive, pushy women but, rather, reticent, fearful enablers. Such women would never dream of fighting back with any significant force and in fact are willing accomplices in their own victimization.

Birds of a Feather

It appears to me, and psychologists confirm this, that, not so accidentally, people of high self-esteem usually find each other and eventually get involved in relationships or marriage—and people of low self-esteem often do the same. In fact, the phenomenon also seems to hold true for people of middle self-esteem. In other words, when it comes to self-esteem, apparently birds of a feather flock together.

There is good news in this finding, is there not? If a woman has low self-esteem, she can raise it, and she will then be more likely to shun a future relationship with an abusive man.

But what if she has low self-esteem and is *already* involved with an abusive man? Is it a catch-22 situation, a puzzle with no solution? Of course not.

For such a woman, one way to instantly raise self-esteem is to, by a courageous act of will, walk out of an abusive relationship. Some of the women in this chapter were able to do just that—and everything went uphill for them after that. Others were not so lucky; but they too may have their day of awakening. Where there is life, there is hope.

Physical Abuse

Approximately one out of every ten American women is beaten by the man in her life.[1] Katherine is one. She never dreamed that she would one day fit the description of a "battered woman." A well-known fashion model with a beauty so striking that people would stop and stare at her in the street, she married her male counterpart—a stunning actor who told her that he worshipped the ground she walked on.

Katherine says:

> I met Etienne on a movie set. He's a Frenchman and was in town to film a section of his latest film. I was in the movie for a cameo appearance. He approached me and told me that he had always been in love with me—from my photographs in French magazines. He told

me that I was the woman of his dreams—that he had my pictures plastered all over the walls of his home back in France. I was flattered, because this man could get any woman he wanted by just snapping his fingers.

On their first date, the pair spent the whole night talking—until the wee hours of the morning. Katherine was surprised to see how much she had in common with Etienne, and how much he understood her after only one day. It was something that seemed destined.

Their budding relationship continued that way for the entire week. When Etienne wasn't shooting, they were in each other's arms. By the end of the week, they knew they would be together forever. "Neither one of us had a commitment to anyone else at the time, so even though we only knew each other for seven days, we got engaged," Katherine says. A month later, Katherine found out she was pregnant, and a wedding date was set. Katherine recalls:

> It all happened so fast that no one had time to think. Even my mother saved her warnings. What could she say? I was pregnant, and I was marrying an up-and-coming actor. Maybe it wasn't so bad after all.
>
> We looked like the perfect couple—physically beautiful, completely in love. Everywhere we went, people blessed us. Except for an occasional scary temper outburst, Etienne was the perfect mate. I had no other clue as to what would happen in the future.

It wasn't until the baby was born that Etienne showed his true colors. His entire personality did an about-face. He became volatile and nasty and began putting Katherine down, calling her "dumpy" and other names. When the baby would cry, Katherine would want to pick her up, but he would scream: "Your whole life revolves around that f——ing baby. Why don't you let her cry for a while? She won't die." "This really hurt me," Katherine says. "I couldn't understand why he didn't feel the same way I did about the baby. After all, it wasn't my baby, it was our baby."

It got to the point where Katherine was under constant pressure
when Etienne was around. She felt as if she had to be careful not
to pay the baby too much attention in his presence. She told her
mother about it and was told it was normal, it would pass. "Some
men are like little boys," her mother said. "They feel jealous when
their wives pay more attention to the baby than to them. But
don't worry. He'll get over it."

But he didn't. It got worse, and finally, one day, when Katherine
didn't have her husband's breakfast ready on time, and was
sleeping, he exploded. Katherine explains:

> He pulled me out of bed and called me a lazy pig. When
> I raised my head to defend myself from his grabbing me,
> he slapped me so hard my head twisted around, and
> later, I had a strained neck. I just stood there looking at
> him—in shock and horror. I ran into the bathroom and
> locked it, and cried and waited until he left.
>
> I made up my mind to pretend it never happened.
> After all, it never happened before, why should it
> happen again? But it did. Again and again and again. If
> the house was a mess, if the baby was crying, if dinner
> wasn't ready, if I asked too many questions about why he
> was late, I got a slap in the face. It got to the point
> where I was constantly plotting to make sure everything
> was just right so that I wouldn't get hit.
>
> I know why he loses his temper so much. He has a lot
> of pressure with the acting and all. And he doesn't mean
> to hurt me. He just forgets himself and takes it out on
> me. Every time he hits me he's sorry, and he brings me
> flowers and gifts and he looks so pitiful and cute. He says
> he loves me more than life itself and promises never to
> do it again. My heart softens to him. I love him, he's the
> father of my child, he's a good provider. We lack for no
> material thing.
>
> But to tell you the truth, right after a beating, I do
> think of leaving, but then I chicken out. I realize that I
> could be worse off alone. Go? What would I do? I'm too
> old to model—and my looks are gone. How would I hide

these black-and-blue marks? I'm hoping that he'll mellow out as he gets a little older.

When a Man Is Competing with a Baby Because *He* Is a Baby

It is not unusual for a man with previously hidden emotional problems to demonstrate them once a child is born into the family. To an emotionally insecure man, a newborn baby is not just seen as a competitor for his wife's attention, that baby *is* a competitor.

How so? Such a man is so emotionally unevolved that he is a baby himself, and feels compelled to compete with a baby just the way a two-year-old would compete when a new baby enters the family system and upsets the balance of attention-giving. Etienne is as angry as any two-year-old would be, and would like to take a whack at the baby, the intruder, when "mommy" isn't looking.

But since, physically, Etienne is not a baby but in fact a full-grown man, he realizes that he cannot take out his anger on a helpless infant, and he transfers his anger to his wife. Although a woman, and not as strong as a man in most cases, at least she is full grown and not completely defenseless. In addition, he feels justified in doing this because, as he sees it, she is the cause of the trouble. How dare she upset the blissful balance and bring this intruder into the home? In sync with his two-year-old thinking, Etienne forgets that he had any part to play in the creation of the baby.

The Seduction by the Repentant Abuser

Why doesn't Katherine leave him? Time and again, she succumbs to his gift-giving and charm—a weapon commonly used by men who batter women. It is a manipulative technique that can keep a woman trapped for years.[2] Each time a gift is given, or charm is used, some time is literally bought. But why does it work time and again? Are women really that easily fooled?

By the deadly combination of manipulation, a woman's insecurity, and wishful thinking, women in such circumstances are made prisoners of relationships that can eventually destroy them. Afraid to face the world alone, and often with children in the bargain, such women, like Katherine, are afraid that they will have no means of employment and that their children will starve to death if they leave the man.

Things *Will* Change: They Will Get Worse!

Wishful thinking such as that engaged in by Katherine—that the man will mellow out as he ages and gradually abandon his abusive techniques—is just that: wishful thinking, with no basis in fact whatsoever. In fact, it is well-established among mental health professionals that, unless they seek professional help, abusive men become more, not less, abusive with time. And even with professional help, once a pattern of abuse has been set in a given relationship, it will probably continue. The best chance such a man would have, even with professional help, would be to begin a new relationship with someone with whom no abusive pattern has been established.[3]

Tina Turner Did It

What are the chances of Katherine ever leaving Etienne? Surprisingly, they are not as slim as you might imagine. Katherine may come to a breaking point, where she's no longer able to put up with Etienne's ill treatment. Other women have left abusive men, even after twenty years of mistreatment. Tina Turner is a case in point.

For twenty years, the now-independent Tina was a member of the famous duo "Ike and Tina Turner," during which time she endured continual beatings, womanizing, and verbal abuse at the hand of Ike. This well-kept secret was broken when Tina escaped from Ike, and broke the duo and the silence at the same time. But why did it take her twenty years to do it?

It was low self-esteem. Tina felt unwanted from the day she was born. She says: "The fact is, I had no love from my mother or father from the beginning, from birth."[4]

With little or no love as a child, Tina's self-image was damaged to the point that she was willing to accept mistreatment from Ike as par for the course. She was happy enough to receive what scraps of love she could get when Ike was in a good mood and treating her well. But what was it that changed? Why did Tina suddenly get the strength to leave Ike?

Apparently, one day, she finally acknowledged something very important about herself—her inner strength. She says: "I realized that I take his best lick. . . ."[5]

In that revelation was Tina's escape. "If after all his beatings, I am still alive and my spirit is not crushed," she must have thought, "I am stronger than I realized. I can find the strength to walk out on him." And she did. The rest is history.

Had she remained with Ike, where would Tina Turner be today? Surely, she would not be the popular recording star as we now know her. If lucky, she would still be alive, but probably a distant memory of an old rock-and-roll couple from the seventies.

The Price Some Women Pay

Some women have to pay even a greater price than did Tina
Turner. They have to leave their country. Margaret, who lived in
Scotland and was married at seventeen, had to get on a plane with
her three young children and a few dollars in her pocket in order
to be free of her abusive husband. She says:

> Joseph had beaten me for years. At first I hid my bruises
> from my family, but finally it became impossible. When
> my father realized that my husband was beating me, he
> consoled me by saying: "Men get that way sometimes,
> especially when they're drinking. Just learn to stay out of
> his way when he comes home drunk."
>
> I tried that, but it never worked. If I left the house
> with the kids, he would be waiting for me when I
> returned, and he'd be twice as drunk. If I hid from him,
> he would find me and curse me out for not having his
> dinner on the table, and throw things at me until he
> would wreck the house—again.
>
> I tried to get help from neighbors and friends, even
> the local clergy, but there wasn't much they could do.
> They advised me that my husband was a good provider
> (he worked in a steel mill and brought home a paycheck
> every week) and told me that I should count my blessings.

One morning, after a particularly vicious beating, Margaret
found herself staring at her reflection in the mirror—looking into
her own eyes. She saw deep pain and, under it, warmth and love.
She also saw a twenty-nine-year-old woman who looked forty. "I
don't deserve this life," she said to herself, and she made up her
mind to leave.

When Joseph was at work, Margaret took the children to the
airport, bound for the United States, with just a small suitcase
containing the bare necessities and the clothing on their backs.
The children were three, seven, and ten.

Five years later, Margaret works as district manager for a large hotel chain. She is married to a golf pro. She says: "He treats me like the Queen of England. I could not imagine being happier than I am now. But I shudder to think of what would have happened if I did not take that step and leave my country, my family, my friends, everything."

What can be said about Margaret, except that perhaps not so miraculously (she may have simply come to that point), she found the courage to run for her life, and the lives of her children.

Time and again, I have noticed this pattern. It is often when a woman comes to that point, where she's had about all she's willing to take, that she ventures out and risks whatever she must—even though there is no guarantee that things will be better—because in her mind, nothing can be worse than the way things are. And time and again, I've noticed that once such a point is reached and the chance is taken, an old door is closed and a new door is opened.

Verbal Abuse

Verbal abuse, although not an immediate threat to life and limb, can be a long-term threat to one's mental and physical health. It can place a woman in such a state of turmoil and raise her tension level to a point where she can attract a variety of life-threatening diseases, and perhaps suffer a mental breakdown.

Myrna has been married to Dean, who has a history of verbally abusing his wife without the slightest provocation, for twenty-six years. "Let me give you an example," Myrna explains:

> I might as well start with last night. We were coming home from a visit to friends. I had been driving for an hour when my car overheated. I decided to try to keep going until we got to an exit. Immediately, he started yelling at the top of his lungs: "You idiot. Now you're

gonna wreck the motor. What a dingbat you are. If they put you in a fish tank, you wouldn't be able to swim out."

I turned to him and said, "What do you suggest I do?" He said, "That's right. Ask me. We all know that you don't have a brain of your own." So I pulled the car over to the shoulder of the road and turned off the ignition and started to cry. Then he said, "That's right. Just sit there and cry. That will solve everything." He shoved me over and tried to start the car. When it wouldn't start, he looked at me with hatred and said, "Now you've really done it, you idiot. Now we'll be stuck here forever."

Used to his attacks, his eighteen-year-old daughter sat by in practiced silence. Myrna recalls with pain:

For example, the other day when he came home, he wanted to make a call, but when he picked up the phone, our daughter was talking on the upstairs extension. "Get the hell off the phone," he yelled. "You're always talking to those damned air-brained friends of yours." Then he clicked it down and, one second later, picked it up again. She was saying good-bye to her friend, but that wasn't good enough for him. "Get off that phone before I come up there and rip it out of the wall. I pay the bills around here, and I have the right to use the phone when I want to." She hung up on her friend mid-sentence, and he made his call.

Later, Myrna very calmly asked what was the emergency. As it turned out, he had to call the architect (they were in the process of having their house remodeled). When Myrna asked why it couldn't wait, all he could say was, "When I want to make a call, I want to make a call. I don't want to sit around and wait for the phone in my own home."

Myrna is now in the process of divorcing Dean, but why did she stay with him this long? "Well, he has a lot of good qualities," she says. "For one thing, he's generous—never complains about the way I spend his money, and he also gives me lots of freedom. I come and go as I please." You're better off alone!

But as I see it, as the biblical proverb states: "It is better to live in the corner of a housetop [an attic] than to share a mansion with a contentious [crabby] man."[6] The additions are mine (I've combined two biblical translations), and I have taken the liberty of changing the word "woman" to "man." I'm sure God would agree that the proverb applies to the male as well as the female gender.

What good is it to be living in the lap of luxury, but without a moment's peace? Would it not be better to have a modest apartment and tranquility than the best that money can buy and constant turmoil?

Most women agree that it would. In fact, I have never yet met a woman who has regretted leaving an abusive man, even if it did mean quite a plunge financially. Once the deed was done, each and every woman expressed joy and delight with her newfound autonomy and would never give it up again—not for any price.

Emotional Abuse Resulting from Drugs and/or Alcohol

The emotional abuse that I will discuss here is connected with substance abuse. (Other types of emotional abuse have been covered in chapters two, four, five, six, and eleven.)

Emotional abuse comes in various forms—but whether overt or subtle, the end result is mental torment. If a woman is married to, living with, or even going out with a man who keeps her psychologically on the edge all the time, and the reason for her being kept on that edge is her mate's misuse of controlled substances, she may decide that the relationship just isn't worth the price.

Dee and Darryl, who had been in love as far back as the sixth grade, continued their romance until they married in their late teens. Shortly before their wedding, they had tried cocaine and liked it, but because they only "snorted" on the weekends, they were not worried about getting hooked.

But shortly after marriage, Darryl began getting more and more involved with the drug, while Dee began to taper off. Finally, Darryl was spending half his paycheck on cocaine, and hanging out with his drug compatriots into the wee hours of the morning. In the bargain, Dee found out that she was pregnant. Thinking that, certainly, this good news would straighten Darryl out, she tells us:

> I couldn't wait for him to get home from work so that I could tell him about the baby. I was so excited that I cooked a special dinner and set the table with candles and all. But when I broke the news, all he could do was look at me with a cold stare and say, "That's *your* problem."
>
> The next day he apologized and promised to quit coke and start saving money, but two days later, he was stoned out of his mind again. I can't remember how many fights we had over his spending all of our money on drugs, or how many times I fooled myself into believing that this time, when he promised to stop, he meant it. I only know that one day, I found myself packing my bags and leaving.

Dee moved in with her mother, but Darryl did not give up. "He called incessantly, promising to change his ways, 'for the baby'." Dee says: "I was very tempted to believe him again, but then I realized that if anything, I owed it to the baby to be strong, and not take him back."

I dare say that it was the "baby"—the insecure, seemingly helpless part of Dee—that might have felt it needed to keep Darryl in her life, and not the baby growing inside of her. In fact, when Dee realized this, she was strong enough to refuse to take him back—and was able to see through Darryl's appeal to her on the grounds that the baby needs him.

Some women are fortunate and can make hard decisions such as Dee's quickly. Others take longer and pay a higher price.

Abigail married Joel right after they both graduated from college, and they got off to a wonderful start—professionally and financially. Abigail landed a job in an art gallery as director of display, and Joel became an accountant for one of the biggest firms in town.

His career was on the rise until he turned to alcohol to help him cope with chronic back pain. Abigail explains:

> At first he drank in moderation—a drink or two after dinner. Then it increased to a couple at lunch, and, finally, he would down a few in the morning—"to ease the pain," he said. We began to argue about his drinking problem. I loved him so much that I couldn't let this happen to him. I brought him to my family doctor, who recommended the best surgeon in the country. We flew out there, but the answer was the same. There was nothing physically wrong with him.

After five troubled years, Abigail couldn't stand it any more. She told Joel that she could no longer live with an alcoholic, and threatened to leave if he didn't go to AA. Although he yessed Abigail to death, Joel did nothing about it. Finally the drinking problem got so bad that, at times, neighbors would have to bring him home because he would be found wandering on their lawns and in their backyards. "I felt terrible because it was like abandoning a sinking ship. But I had no choice—it was either jump ship or go down with it," Abigail says. "I've been out on my own for two years now, and finally I can think straight. It was foolish of me to believe I could heal him with my love. All the love in the world can't cure a person unless he cooperates."

The fact is, it was not Abigail's job to save Joel—even though she did marry him "for better or for worse." It was her loving duty to encourage him—even lead him to seek help—but it was not her responsibility, nor was it in her power, to reform him. The old saying, "You can lead a horse to the water but you can't make him drink," applies here.

Your Relationship Is a Failure—Not You!

If you have been involved in an abusive relationship, and up until now you've felt like a failure, think again. Your entire worth as a person is not based upon your track record in that relationship.

You can do something to help make yourself feel like a success, however; and that is, walk out if you're still in an abusive relationship. It's never too late. No matter how many years you have wasted, there is still time to enjoy a productive, fruitful life.

The good news is, once you've been through an abusive relationship and have gotten out by your own free will, and received some counselling, chances are you'll never get into another one again. [7]

Help in Getting Out

There are some lovely words in this chapter—wonderful words of advice. But it is easier to read a book and say, "amen to that," than it is to put those words into action. You may need assistance in getting out.

Call telephone information for the local female-abuse hot line, and call the line and tell them your situation. Another possibility is the "mental health center" listings found in the yellow pages of your telephone directory. They will give you the number of centers for spouse abuse. Many of these services are free.

In a less desperate situation, you might try your local chapter of the National Organization for Women, or your local college or community college and ask to speak with a counsellor regarding female abuse.

Another idea is to speak to your minister, rabbi, or religious leader—or a supportive family member or friend. Then talk to a lawyer who has been recommended by someone you trust. In any case, your first step in getting out will be to tell someone else your problem. You may have to test the waters on a few people.

If your first confidant does not offer help, does not understand, don't stop there. People are human, and there is no guarantee that they will be able to give you the best advice, so if you don't get the help you need from one source, keep going until you get a hold of the rope that you can use to climb out.

How Do Women Ever Get Out?

What do all the women who did leave have in common? They got to a point, and then they took a chance. They were willing to shoot now and ask questions later, in a manner of speaking. They ran for their proverbial lives, and let the devil take the hindermost. And, in fact, the devil took their husbands, not them.

Each of these women had a moment-in-time experience, the proverbial straw that broke the camel's back, and it caused them to say enough, and, against all odds, they were able to escape. For this reason, I don't write anybody off. I never say, "never." I never say, "That's a hopeless case."

NOTES

1. This information can be found in the following books: Lenore E. Walker, *The Battered Women* (New York: Harper & Row, 1979), p. xv; Susan Forward and Craig Buck, *Obsessive Love* (New York: Bantam, 1991), p. 170. It is interesting to note that abuse experts consider a woman to be battered if she is beaten by the same man more than once.

2. Walker, *The Battered Woman*, p. 29.

3. Ibid., p. 26.

4. Tina Turner, with Kurt Loder, *I Tina* (New York: Morrow, 1986), p. 16.

5. Ibid., p. 163.

6. Proverbs 21:9.

7. Walker, *The Battered Woman*, p. 28. Dr. Walker offers encouraging words to women in abusive relationships and points out that many women *have* learned from experience.

Reminders

1. If a man values himself, he will value you. Abusive men suffer from very low self-esteem. They need lots of help from a professional—not from you. Get out while you're still alive.

2. Most abusers are very sorry after the fact—until it happens again. They will apologize until Kingdom Come, and repeat the offense for the same length of time.

3. When an abuser promises that things will change, he is right. They *will* change—for the worse.

4. Verbal and emotional abuse can be just as, if not more, devastating than physical abuse.

5. Remember, it's the relationship that is a failure, not you.

13

Oh, What a Catch!

We've already discussed men who have been given a fair chance, but who have been weighed in the balances and found wanting—men who should be dumped! But what about other men who come along—those who seem to be a great catch, and indeed believe that they are God's gift to women, but who are in reality the bane of all women? In the following paragraphs, we'll talk about men who are potential nemeses and, like fish who are clearly pests, should be thrown back into the sea as soon as they are identified.

After that, we'll talk about what is a catch—and how to find out what are and are not important qualities to look for in a future relationship.

The Blowfish

The blowfish is a diminutive creature. In fact, he's so small, most experienced fishermen throw him back into the water as soon as they see him on the line—knowing full well that such a fish could never make a meal.

If you've caught a blowfish, you might have been fooled into thinking he's bigger than he is, because when this fellow feels threatened, he puffs himself up to more than twice his size. The blowfish man is an insecure person who believes that he must aggrandize himself in order to be accepted.

Perhaps someday you will meet a blowfish. Here are his identification marks:

1. He wears his possessions (everything is imported or of designer origin) as badges of honor, from his one-of-a-kind watch to his suit, which cost well into the four-figure range.
2. He takes you to only "top ten" restaurants, where he is always recognized as a man about town by not a few "important people." He is apparently more interested in you as a showpiece than as a person.
3. He keeps the conversation light and superficial. Should you try to discuss philosophy, feelings, his background, or anything of substance, he becomes annoyed and changes the subject.

Who knows? Under all that puffery could lie a lovely person. But he cannot chance your probing, for fear that you will discover what he believes to be the truth about himself—that he is a worthless loser. Perhaps he behaves this way because he was regularly and cruelly criticized as a child, and he has learned that it is not okay to be himself.

If you meet this fellow, save yourself the time and throw him back. You will spend a lifetime trying to get to his substance, and even then, you may never succeed.

The Dogfish

This long, slender, spiny creature is a member of the shark family—as dangerous as he is inedible. He'll leave you with serious wounds if you're not on the lookout. But how will you know it if you've reeled in a dogfish?

1. He is divorced—with a wounded ego and a lot to prove. He spends an inordinate amount of time with his children, trying to make himself believe that nothing has changed and that he is still a full-time father. He has conveniently located his "bachelor pad" a few blocks from his former home.
2. He's a handsome fellow whose belief that he is a good catch is sustained by the "desperate women" he brags about—women who try to pick him up in restaurants, at work, and even in supermarket lines.
3. He quickly makes his relationship one-on-one, insisting upon cooking for you and encouraging your cooking for him. Before you know it, you're dreaming of marriage, but the moment he smells such sentiments, he is gone without apology or worry. He's sure that, should he ever want a commitment, there are thousands of women who would snap him up in a minute.

The dogfish is a dog indeed. He has no guilt about your pain. He believes in his heart that you were a fool if you read too much into the relationship, although he has given you every reason to believe that there could be a future with him. It was his enjoyment of the feeling of commitment without the actual tie that fooled you. You didn't realize that the woman in a dogfish's life is only a comfortable stand-in, while he works out his psychological problems concerning his divorce and his children.

The Jellyfish

The jellyfish, a gentle work of art with fragile, umbrellalike beauty, floats freely about and can be scooped up by hand. But watch out. You would be better off looking but not touching, because those who handle the jellyfish come away with a nasty rash—and more.

Perhaps you have met a jellyfish. You didn't know it at the time. See if any of these characteristics ring a bell:

1. He has not lived in one place for very long; nor has he kept one job for any length of time. Like the "rambling man" of the country-and-western song, he thinks of himself as footloose and fancy free.
2. Although you have known him only a few days, he tells you that he has fallen in love with you—and means it. You are flattered and, unwisely, you brush aside the little voice that whispers, "Too much too soon. Something is rotten in Denmark."
3. Because he's gallant, optimistic, sensitive, and intuitive, your defenses are down; so when he asks you to lend him money to start a business, to have his baby, or to do some other "wild thing," you agree. But shortly after, if the going gets rough for any reason, this man who has promised you the world has run away and left you holding the bag, the baby, or the bill!

Jellyfish men may have been treated without discipline as children. Instead of appropriate criticism at the right time, their parents probably admired them for their adorable antics, no matter how destructive. Now that the jellyfish man's out on his own, rather than face his responsibilities or the consequences of his actions, he floats away to more pleasant waters.

The jellyfish. As gentle, well-meaning, and sensitive as he seems, he will leave you with more than you bargained for.

The Scorpion Fish

This colorful sea creature looks more like a large precious stone than a fish. He's so fascinating to look at that a fisherwoman may be lured into mounting him as a treasure to be saved. But this fellow has venomous spines that will sting and even poison. Have you ever met a scorpion fish?

1. He is gorgeous beyond description—in face and physique. You cannot believe your good fortune when this breathtaking man of movie-star quality takes an interest in you. But he suffers from a deep-rooted inferiority complex and needs to be worshipped and admired, so he is often seen in the company of women he believes to be less good-looking than he is in face or figure—women who revere him.
2. During the course of the first or second date, he cannot help but talk of former lovers—"conquests." He uses a practiced come-hither look to seduce you into his bedroom. If you refuse to have sex with him on the first or second date, he has a tantrum; and if that doesn't work, he drops you.
3. If you fall for his charm and begin a sexual relationship, he will use you until he has gained the ego satisfaction he so desperately needs to temporarily fill a vacuum in the center of his being—where self-esteem is lacking. He can infect a woman with bitterness and suspicion toward men because he loves her and leaves her.

Perhaps the scorpion fish was such a good-looking child that everyone, including his parents, forgot to emphasize his positive inner qualities. This fellow grew up believing that his only value was external. He has little awareness of the importance of integrity, loyalty, and human kindness. He thinks of himself and others as objects.

The scorpion fish. All that glitters is not gold. (In all fairness to the many loving, well-balanced good-looking men in the world, I must add that, of course, not every man with stunning looks should be viewed as a scorpion fish.)

The Crab

This ten-footed crustacean moves along the ocean floor sideways, with quick bursts of speed—yet a clever fisherwoman can whisk him into her net. But rather than having a delightful meal (crab meat, after all, is a delicacy), a woman may be in for an unpleasant surprise when she discovers to her chagrin that, rather than her dining on this shifty creature, he will dine on her. His chief characteristics?

1. You are attracted by his power, his money, and his success, not his looks, and imagine yourself living in the fashion of those seen on "Lifestyles of the Rich and Famous."
2. For all his money, you notice that he is tight with anything that could cost him a cent. For example, he turns down the heat to near freezing, shuts lights every time he leaves a room, and in a restaurant diligently goes over the check for the fifth time, hoping to catch an error that may save him a few cents. He is a hoarder and a collector. He saves stamps, coins, cars, and more.
3. He rarely if ever buys you a gift, although you buy him plenty; and you discover that all of his ex's ended up investing what money they had in his business.

I went out with a crab once, and I remember clearly the day I told him it was over. As he was getting ready to leave, I asked him to wait a minute. I ran into my den, where I kept an old flyswatter. I then began flailing it about wildly, batting away at imaginary insects. "What the hell are you doing?" he asked. "When you open your wallet, the moths fly out," I replied, and continued to dance around, flailing the swatter above his head and in front of his face—at this point laughing hysterically at my own joke. Needless to say, the man left my house shaking his head and wondering whether he should call the mental ward.

What motivates the crab? Why is he so frugal—so watchful over every penny—although he has more money than he could ever spend in a lifetime? Chances are, it was his upbringing—which has now become a part of his personality. He may have been rebuked as a child for not turning off the lights when he left a room, or not looking for the best deal when buying his school supplies. He may also have endured continual warnings from his parents, such as "waste not want not," and may have been given the clear message that material wealth is the only guarantee of survival.

This man has spent his life piling up wealth and then hoarding it. It is highly unlikely that he will ever change his ways, because he believes, "If I let down my guard and start spending, I'll soon be on skid row."

The crab. When you first meet him, you think, "Oh, what a catch," and dream of the lovely meal that awaits you. But you will quickly find out that you were indeed dreaming, and that not only will you never get *his* money, but if you marry him, he may take whatever money you have and add it to his ever-growing coffers.

The Chameleon

This water creature is not of the fish family, but rather of the lizard family. Nevertheless, even though most women aren't fishing for him, many have found one in their net.

This slow-moving creature changes position so subtly that one never realizes exactly when the movement took place. One minute he's here, and the next he's there—although you never see him stir. Not only does he move subtly, but he also changes colors at will, depending upon his environment.

How can you tell if you've met a chameleon?

1. You wonder if you imagined certain conversations. Ground you covered thoroughly must be trod and retrod. Nothing is ever settled.
2. One day he tells you he loves you and wants to marry you; the next day he's elusive and shies away from even the thought of a

commitment. Then, two weeks later, he's talking marriage again. First he's going to start up a business, and the next week he thinks it's a ridiculous idea, and later he changes his mind again, and so it goes.

3. He makes promises he intends to keep, but, later, he feels no obligation to follow through because he has moved on in his own mind. He expects others to automatically understand this, so if you dare to question his actions, he becomes angry and defensive.

What is the chameleon's problem? He's flighty and indecisive, afraid to take risks. The moment he decides to take some specific action, especially action that requires a major commitment, he gets nervous and backs away. He seems at times manipulative, but the truth is, he does not plan to tease others with his on-again off-again behavior. He has little confidence or trust in his own intelligence. Deep down inside, the chameleon thinks very poorly of himself.

Perhaps he behaves this way because of his position in his family when he was a child. He may have been the least intelligent son in a highly intelligent family, where his opinions and ideas were not valued. Clearly, in some way, he was regularly disrespected as a child and now lacks the confidence to make a decision and stick to it.

The chameleon. You could spend a lifetime trying to nail him down—but to no avail. He changes his mind as often as he changes his moods.[1]

What Is a Catch?

What is a catch—and how will you know him if you meet him? Simply put, a catch is a man who shares your basic values, a man who can love and is open to being loved in return. But, more than that, a catch is a man who can live up to at least your minimum standard of what a man should be. But how do you find out what your standard is?

There are really some very simple guidelines. Look for a man who possesses at least the main positive traits possessed by your father or male role model(s). Let me explain.

It is a well-established psychological truth that we begin to decide what is desirable and good in a man from the moment we see our first man (usually our father). If that man remains in our lives as we grow up, we continue to decide what we like and do not like in a man, based upon traits that he possesses which we perceive to be positive.

If our genetic father, for whatever reason, should not be there, we will use a substitute male role model, or models, as our guideline, and will in fact make up a composite list if necessary. These substitutes may be composed of uncles, male cousins, male companions, or even our mother; or they may reflect characters from television, books, magazines, and comic strips. In short, as we grow up, no matter what our particular environment, we all develop an ideal image of a future mate.

If you look back at your love life, it should be no surprise that most, if not all, of the men you have loved—or with whom you've had intimate bonding-type relationships—possessed at least some of the positive traits possessed by your father or male role model(s).

I'll use myself as an example. My father was generous, highly intelligent, and witty, but above all he was extremely loyal and dependable. He was generous and kind and tough at the same time. He was sensitive to others, and romantic. He treated my mother with great respect. In fact, he adored her. So, quite naturally, when I look for a man, I am going to hope to find at least some of these traits possessed by my father.

For example, I may meet a man who is brilliant, but will leave me in the lurch when trouble comes; and he may be dour, with no sense of humor, but wealthy, and he may pursue me until I finally decide, "Oh, what the hey," and I marry him. But I may later reject him because he does not possess basic traits that I have come to think of as bare necessities in order to build trust and confidence in a man—and in order to open myself to an intimate soul connection with him. All the brilliance and wealth in the world, for me, may not be able to make up for loyalty, generosity, kindness, and a sense of humor.

Let's experiment. Make a list of the positive traits that your father or male role model possessed:

1.
2.
3.
4.
5.
6.
7.

You may include physical traits as well, but we are looking here mainly for personality and value traits.

Your next step is to take a run-through of your history and think of all the men you dated for any length of time—men with whom you felt an affinity, or men with whom you fell in love. Think of each and every man and list the positive traits of each of them. I'll use myself as an example:

1. *Steve*   Loyal and dependable, muscular, sense of humor, generous, intelligent.
2. *Rick*   Easygoing, loyal and dependable, sense of humor, generous, strong, sensitive to others.
3. *Joe*   Intelligent, loyal and dependable, sense of humor, sensitive to others, romantic, muscular.
4. *Paul*   Loyal and dependable, spiritual, masculine, generous, high integrity, intelligent.
5. *John*   Sensitive to others, loyal and dependable, muscular, sense of humor, generous.
6. *Ryan*   Sensitive to others, generous, sense of humor, muscular, loyal and dependable, sensitive, romantic.

Now make your own list:

NAME   POSITIVE TRAITS
1.
2.
3.
4.
5.
6.

Now look at the list and find the traits that the men have in common. You will probably see that these are also traits possessed by your father or the male role model in your life as a child.

Again, I'll use myself as an example. I notice that each and every man I've loved was "loyal and dependable," and "muscular," or at least "masculine," and all but one possessed a sense of humor.

Your basic requirements in a man, then, are the traits that all or nearly all of your former loves possessed—traits that your father also possessed.

Analyze your own list. What traits do each or most of the men possess that your father also possessed? These are your basic requisites in a man.

BASIC REQUISITES
1.
2.
3.
4.
5.

Again looking at my list, I notice that most of the men were intelligent and sensitive to others, as was my father. These are priorities in a man. I may or may not be able to live without these traits in a man. Look at your own list. If two-thirds of the men have a particular trait, list it under "Priorities."

PRIORITIES
1.
2.
3.

Again, looking at my list, I can see that half the men were generous, as was my father. Look at your own list and find the traits possessed by approximately half the men. These traits will fall into the list, "Important." Look at the men in your accounting and make your list here:

IMPORTANT

1.
2.
3.

Again, looking at my list, I notice that only two of the men were romantic, as was my father. This trait will fall into the category of "It Would Be Nice." Look at your list. If you find a trait repeated only once or twice, list it under "It Would Be Nice."

IT WOULD BE NICE

1.
2.
3.

If you want to have a lasting, intimate relationship, look for a man who has at least the bare minimum—the basic requisites—positive traits possessed by your father or male role model and also possessed by every or nearly every man you've ever loved. This man should also possess some of the priority traits and even some of the important traits. If he also has the it-would-be-nice traits, then lucky you.

Quite naturally, this is not a magical formula. There are many additional components that come into play. But it is an interesting basic guideline, and, more often than not, it holds true.

Let's Not Be Too Picky

A word of caution is in order here. Many women (myself included) get carried away with our list of requisites, and not only do we demand that the man of our dreams possess *all* the positive traits of our father or male role model, but *all* the positive traits of every man we have ever dated, plus a whole list of other traits that we have seen in men on television or read about in books.

If you insist that a man possess every single positive trait imaginable, you will of course remain safely alone. (Perhaps that is the unconscious method to your madness—you really don't want to share your life with anyone, so you deliberately make the requirements so high that no one man could possibly live up to them.)

It is important to consider another aspect of the *qualities* we are asking the man of our dreams to possess—and that is *quantity*. Rather than expect a man to have, for example, one hundred percent of a given trait, why not allow him to have a certain amount of that trait, and read it off to human error if he dares to fall short in that category once in a while. For example, if your list includes the trait "sensitive to others," and the man of your dreams is from time to time insensitive but in general is sensitive, learn to be realistic and to forgive him an occasional lapse. The same holds true for any trait. We are all human, so let us not expect the man of our dreams to be perfect. It just can't be.

What am I saying? If you mean business, and if you would really like to meet a man with whom you could enjoy life, you will have to give up at least some of your ideal traits, and you will have to be flexible when those ideal traits which *are* present are not apparent at times. As long as the basics are there, your relationship will have a healthy chance of working. In other words, don't be so picky as to make it impossible for yourself to ever find a man with whom you can share your life.

Other Kinds of Catches

You don't necessarily have to have a long-term relationship with a man for him to be a catch. A catch can be any man who is a pleasure to be with—for whatever time you choose to be with him. He can be fling who is fun for a while. In such a case, of course, the man does not have to possess the same amount of positive traits discussed above.

Some women are happy at the moment (and some forever) without a deep, committed relationship with a man. They prefer to remain single and free, and to enjoy the adventure of an occasional fling. What is wrong with that? Nothing. As long as the relationship brings more pleasure than pain, as long as it adds rather than detracts from a woman's life, such a relationship is a catch, and should be treasured.

And by the Way... You Don't Need to "Catch" Anything— You Are the Catch

Alexandra Penney interviewed hundreds of women and asked them what is most important in life. She discovered that "... a majority of women would agree, probably not publicly though, that a man is first on the list."[2]

How sad that even in the nineties, a man is still often the most important thing to a woman. Is a woman the most important thing to a man? Of course not. His career, his accomplishments, his long-term goals—these are his priorities. A woman fits into the picture only as she suits his life-style.

As long as women think in terms of *getting* a catch, and not *being* one, they will be doing an awful lot of fishing and an awful lot of untangling of the lines. Instead of worrying about catching a man, instead of making it your main goal in life to find a man, I would suggest that you concentrate your energies on developing your own potential to the fullest. Then, when you do meet an interesting man, your question will not be, "Do I measure up?" but instead, "What do I think of him?" Your immediate concern will be to use your judgment, based upon what you see and hear, as to just what kind of a man this is—and whether you wish to have further dealings with him.

And may I add that it is an exercise in foolishness to waste your energy thinking about the statistical shortage of men to women. If you go about the business of being and celebrating yourself, you will in fact meet so many men that you will wonder if the statisticians have somehow made a mistake and reversed the numbers. You will have more men courting you than you know what to do with. Your problem will be knowing which ones are worthy of your precious time.

NOTES

1. Herbert T. Boschung, Jr., et al., *The Audubon Society Field Guide to North American Fishes, Whales & Dolphins* (New York: Knopf, 1983). The information about the fish discussed in this chapter has come from this wonderful and informative book.

2. Alexandra Penney, *Why Men Stray, Why Men Stay* (New York: Bantam, 1989), p. 11.

Reminders

1. All that glitters is not gold. Some men who seem to be catches are really dogfish in disguise—and worse. Better throw them back before you get bitten.

2. To find out if a man is a catch, see if he possesses the basic requisites of what you value in a man. If he doesn't, don't waste your time.

3. The question is not, "do I measure up to him," but, "does he measure up to my standard?" Remember: *you* are the catch.

14

Who Is Over the Hill?

This chapter is not just for "older women," but for younger women as well. It's very important that younger women learn early in life that the clock is *not* ticking away, and that they will not be over the hill once they reach forty. As a matter of fact, the good news is, the opposite is true.

Women over forty are often more beautiful and charming than they were in their twenties, and in better shape. They are more relaxed, more self-assured, and, indeed, because everything is no longer a life-and-death issue, they are more fun. Women over forty can afford to live and let live because they have been around for a while, and they understand a few things. In fact, if you haven't approached forty yet, you have a lot to look forward to.

Physically, women over forty can be in better shape than they were when they were half their age. I've seen hundreds of examples of this—and I'm one myself. You too can be an example—if you're not one already—and you can do it in a matter of months; but more about that later.

Sexually, women become more desirable as they age, because they come into their sexual peak in their thirties, and remain there for years, while men peak sexually in their teens, and go downhill from there.

As far as men are concerned, women over forty can pick and choose among younger, older, or same-aged men. We stand in the middle—so we can go in any direction.

The truth of the matter is, women over forty are not over the hill—not psychologically, not physically, and certainly not sexually. These days, women can remain in full throttle well into their sixties—and beyond. The decision is theirs to make.

In the following paragraphs, we will take a look at the advantages that women over forty have in three areas: the physical, the sexual, and the psychological. We'll discuss the myth that has been perpetuated about women—that they become less desirable to the opposite sex as they age—and we'll talk about why some women over forty enjoy going out with men twenty years their junior, while others choose men in their own age category.

Physically

If a woman follows a reasonable and intelligent workout program (see the Annotated Bibliography, page 310, for information about my fitness books: *Bottoms Up*, *The Fat-Burning Workout*, *The Twelve-Minute Total-Body Workout*, and *Now or Never*), she can look better than she did in her twenties. She can perfect the shape of her body beyond what it was at its most perfect natural form. How so?

Genetics go just so far. Even if a twenty-year-old woman is as thin as a reed, chances are she doesn't have the perfect figure. Her hips may be too big, her waistline may be too thick, her thighs may be rather shapeless, her buttocks may be too flat, her shoulders may be curved downward too much, her arms may be weak, or she may have other imperfections. But she is happy, because she is young and she is thin. Often, the most she will do in the way of fitness will be to diet and do a little aerobic exercise, which will help to keep her thin but will do nothing to change her shape.

The fact is, her shape could be improved—if she worked out with weights as described in my exercise books. But why should she? It is not an emergency situation. She doesn't yet know what it is to feel the downward pull of gravity. She's doing just fine the way she is, and she knows it.

When a woman begins to age, things change dramatically—muscle and bone atrophy a little, every year after thirty, and posture and shape take a downward slump. Unless you do something to reverse the process, even if you are as thin as a rail, you begin to take on an older, more matronly look. It is only by working out with weights the right way that you can not only get back what you lost but, in fact, this time, put it in all the right places and shape it just right. In essence, instead of aging, you with be "youthing," and then some![1]

An older woman, in a matter of months, perhaps for the first time in her life, can have high, round, tight buttocks, attractive hips, shapely, sexy thighs, perfectly formed calves, sensuous upper-back muscles, a narrow-looking waist, and a flat, well-defined stomach. She can have shapely shoulders and pretty biceps and triceps. Not only will her arm (elbow to armpit) not jiggle when she raises it, it will be ultrafirm.

I am most fortunate because I discovered the secrets of champion body builders in my mid-thirties. I took their techniques and modified them and used them on myself so that I transformed my own body. I then helped thousands of other women to do the same (a large majority of them are well over forty—yes, even sixty and older). These women now have better bodies than they did when they were in their prime. The physical and mental stimulation of the workout also adds energy and optimism to a woman's life—so she really feels and thinks younger.

A muscular body is a shapely, sexy body—because muscles are curves. True, overbuilt muscles make for bulky, masculine curves, but in order to get those muscles you have to work with very heavy weights for hours each day. In order to get the feminine muscularity

I am talking about, you only have to invest twenty to forty minutes, four to six days a week.[2]

But why are we talking only of women's bodies? Men's bodies go over the hill too. In fact, I dated a man fifteen years younger than I, ten years ago, when I was thirty-eight and he was twenty-three. Now he is thirty-three and I'm forty-eight. Today he sports a beer belly and walks with a shuffle. In fact, he's no longer the "young stud" he thinks he is. Yet, will society say that a thirty-eight-year-old man is going over the hill—no matter what he looks like? Of course not. But more of that later.

Sexually

Women have been led to believe that they are sexually less desirable as they approach forty and older—while men are supposedly more desirable. Nothing could be further from the truth.

The fact is, women don't begin to peak sexually until their mid-thirties, while men pass their sexual peak in their teens and begin a steady downhill slide from that point on. If we look at the figures logically, sexually speaking, the ideal match for a woman of forty-five would be a man fifteen to twenty years her junior. (Some of you ladies know what I'm talking about.)

But there's more to it than just sex, and that's why you don't see every older woman sporting a younger man on her arm. We'll talk about the pros and cons of older women and younger men later in this chapter.

Getting back to sex, let's be more specific. If a forty-five-year-old woman goes to bed with a twenty-five-year-old man as opposed to a forty-five-year-old man (all other things being equal), the younger man will get hard immediately, stay that way indefinitely, and, once he experiences orgasm, he will often be ready to go again within the hour. Not necessarily so with a man her own age or older.

In fact, when it comes to aging and sex, nature has played a rather cruel trick on older men. For all of their good intentions, they simply cannot perform the way they did in their younger days; whereas women can perform better and better as they get older and older, not just because they peak sexually at a much later age, but because of obvious reasons such as not having to get or stay hard in order to experience orgasm or to satisfy a partner.

So, once and for all, let it be known: Sexually speaking, it is the men, and not the women over forty, who are going over the hill. Let the men over forty stop deluding themselves into believing that, sexually, they are prized possessions. (It never ceases to amaze me when an older man invites me to bed, obviously out of pure lust for my body. What makes him dream for a moment that, if I were in it for the sex alone, I would pick a man his age? Why would I not choose one of the many charming, adorable young men who regularly throw themselves at my feet in the hope that they might get lucky?)

But what about technique? How many times have I heard an older man say to me, "But younger men don't know what they're doing"? Either that is a nice defense, or such men are projecting their own former behavior onto the young men of today. I don't know how young men behaved thirty years ago. Perhaps then most of them did do the "Slam, Bam, Thank you, Ma'am" tango. But today, things are different. Most men over twenty-one have learned a thing or two about sex, and as any women who has had experience can tell you, most of them can in fact teach older men a thing or two about making love.

Psychologically

The forties and beyond are indeed the best years of a woman's life. By this time, she has gained confidence and wisdom. She can cope with disappointment and loss, and she realizes that she can survive. She can maintain a sense of humor in the face of difficulties, as she calmly tells herself from experience, "this too shall pass." She can afford to lose, because she's lost before and lived through it, so she is no longer desperate. In fact, she faces life with a devil-may-care attitude—an attitude that is intoxicating to others, especially to adventurous men.

Many older women have just begun careers, and for the first time in their lives are getting a whiff of the sweet smell of success. They feel all of the energy and enthusiasm of one who is beginning an exciting enterprise. They believe that the world is their oyster—just waiting to be devoured.

In contrast, too often, single men who are well into their forties, or who are fifty or older, are rather pessimistic in their view of the world. Many of them have plodded the career trail for too many years to be buoyant, or have struggled up the ladder of success only to slip down too many times to be optimistic. Often, these men are counting the days until they can retire from their jobs. They have a "down" energy level, while their female counterparts can have an "up" energy level.

In addition, some of these men are divorced and have been shelling out alimony and child-support payments for years. They are angry with women and are on guard against them—believing that women are parasites, out to get what they can. Men who sport such mentalities are no treat to be around. Small wonder that older women often seek out younger men, who naturally have a more sanguine outlook on life.

A younger man, who has no such antagonistic ideas, can have a soothing effect on an older woman—a woman who would never have thought of going out with a man younger than herself when she was in her twenties or thirties. Forty-something-year-old Dixie Carter sums it up nicely: "Now listen to me—before you find your true love, don't rule out men in their twenties. They'll help you heal up your heart. When you're in your thirties, you're too old for them. But when you hit forty-something—ta da! Interesting men just fall from the trees!"[3]

Society Says: Older Men–Younger Women, Okay; Older Women– Younger Men, Not Okay. Why?

If an older man has a younger girlfriend, that's just fine. But if an older woman has a younger boyfriend, the first thing you hear is, "Who is she kidding—what is she trying to prove?" It doesn't matter that the woman and man look great together, that they are psychologically, sexually, and physically a match, or that they enjoy each other's company. It just isn't accepted—at least not by society in general. Why?

The myth that women are over the hill after forty (not so long ago, the imagined age was thirty) is very ingrained in our culture: Even if people clearly see that a woman is not over the hill (she is obviously in great shape, full of energy, and is sexy), and that the younger man on her arm seems to be madly in love with her, they don't want to believe it. Instead, they assume: "She must be paying his way," or they insist: "It will never work out—one day he'll look up and see how old she is, and leave her for a younger woman." In other words, they refuse to believe their own eyes because everything they have heard tells them that it can't be true.

But why don't we hear these same arguments when we see an older man with a younger woman? The answer is simple: money. Up until now, men have ruled the purse, and they have ruled the world. It has always been acceptable for a man to, in a sense, buy a woman; so why make comments such as, "He must be paying her way"? Of course he is. And no need to worry that she will leave him for a younger man. As long as he is paying the bills, she is his.

Older men can "buy" younger women, without shame or apology— but older women cannot do the same. In fact, they don't have to, because younger men, even those who make half the money of an older woman, are often happy to pay for dinner and then some. Why? Younger men enjoy the company of older women. They can relax in the presence of an older woman because she is compassionate and understanding, and not critical or demanding. What? Are you thinking "Mother substitute"? Not quite. Let us just say, an older woman can provide the best qualities of an ideal mother with the best qualities of an ideal woman or lover. Who could resist such a combination?

Younger Men Versus Older Men— the Pros and the Cons

If younger men and older women are such a great match, why doesn't every older woman simply get herself a younger man and live happily ever after? The truth is, for all the good things about it, such a pairing may not be a match made in heaven.

For one thing, younger men are not usually financially secure yet, so an older woman may find herself at least partially supporting him as he advances in his career. While in and of itself, there is nothing wrong with this, most older women have more traditional values when it comes to who pays the bills, and they usually do not like to be placed in this position.

In addition, younger men are often not established in a career yet, and may even stop working to return to school, in order to qualify for a different profession. This can be quite unsettling to a woman who has children of her own in college. The last thing in the world she may want to do is to be married to a student.

Then there is the very real problem of children. Most older women have already had children, who are now grown and who are adults themselves. To start a family again (even if it is physically possible) is not something they would relish.

Then there is the mentality of the younger person, which cannot be escaped. Older people have come to grips with the philosophical issues that plague all thinking people as they come into maturity. While there are many exceptions to the rule, and, in fact, some younger men are more mature and indeed in many ways "older and wiser" than older men, most younger men are still grappling with these matters and may want to engage in lengthy and tedious discourse. Topics of the sixties, dressed in different colors in the nineties, are now grist for the mill of endless discussion. Most often, an older woman will wisely steer her young lover away from such debates, but because she cannot always be on guard, once in a while she will find herself in the thick of it, and while he's saying, "I disagree," a mile a minute, she will be saying, at least in her own mind, "Let's just be happy," or "I wish he would shut up."

Then there is sex. For all the positive points mentioned above, there is a drawback to being married to a younger man. While sex with a younger man can be a refreshing change in the beginning, and making love three times a day, every day, a treat—after a while, one can become tired and wish to be left alone. But an eager young lover does not feel that way. Either because he wants to prove that he is the great Don Juan of the century, or because his sex drive is out of control, he won't give a woman a moment's rest. So as she lies in bed with her young and eager beau, she says to herself, "Lord, will that boy ever go to sleep?" and she wonders if she would have been better off with old Milt.

And then there is history that you lived through—events that he knows about only from reading books. You find yourself asking him things like, "How did you feel about the war in Vietnam?" or "What was your position on the Watergate scandal?" But you check yourself mid-sentence, because it suddenly dawns on you that he was only five years old at the time or not even born yet.

Music can be a problem too. You may be able to tolerate hard rock or even disco, but after a while, it gets on your nerves. He may mildly enjoy music of the fifties, jazz, and Frank Sinatra—but after a while it gets on his nerves. You find yourself having to put up with his music; again, you wistfully think of old Milt, who went with the flow.

And then there is the dancing. Your young man may have no idea what it means to dance with a partner—except of course to do the hustle, if he was old enough to learn that dance. You want to do the lindy, the fox-trot, the merengué, or even—yes—the old "Lindy-hop" but he has no idea what you're talking about. He thinks it's something from the big-band era, and he sometimes wonders just *how* old you are!

And then there is the physical fact of aging. You look great for your age—you are in better shape than women ten years your junior, but some things just can't be changed. Those spots he thinks are freckles are really liver spots, a sure sign that the clock is ticking away, and you wonder when he will notice the vulturelike skin in multiple folds hanging from your elbow, a condition that cannot be remedied, either by exercise or cosmetic surgery.

You are tired of wearing makeup to bed, or rushing to get up before him to put it on first thing in the morning. You'd love to go au naturel, but you don't want him to see how old you look in the morning light—and again you wistfully think of old Milt, who was in the same boat as you, and who has worries of his own about aging.

Because of all of the above, many women in their forties and older choose to pass on a younger man. They know that older men who are on their level, physically, psychologically, and sexually, are few and far between, but they continue to search, because if they find one, they will have found a great treasure—a man who has all the qualities to make for a compatible and wonderful life together.

NOTES

1. "20/20," 10 May 1991 (New York: Journal Graphics, Show no. 1919), pp. 7–8. John Stossel of ABC News interviewed Dr. Sydney Bonner, Director of Osteoporosis Services of the Cooper Institute, and Dr. William Evans, USDA Human Nutrition Research Center. These doctors offered studies which gave proof that working with weights (techniques such as those described in the workout books listed in footnote 2) could enable one to double muscle strength in eight weeks and increase bone density by two and a half percent in ten months.

2. If you want to get in shape in record time, get a copy of my book *The Fat-Burning Workout*. You can do it at home with a minimum of equipment in as little time as four twenty-minute sessions per week. If

you want to start out more slowly—to get accustomed to body-shaping movements—begin with *The Twelve-Minute Total-Body Workout*, and in three months advance to *The Fat-Burning Workout*. *Now or Never* requires an hour, four days a week. You can do it in a gym or at home, and you will get bigger muscles than with the above two books. When my latest book, *Bottoms Up!*, is available, get a copy for a special emphasis on hips, stomach, and buttocks. See the "Annotated Bibliography of Joyce Vedral Books," page 310, for further information.

3. Celeste Fremon, "Interview with Dixie Carter," *Moxie*, February 1990, p. 51.

Reminders

1. Physically, men's bodies age just as quickly as do women's, only some men remain quite appealing to the opposite sex, and this appeal is directly related to the size of their bank account.

2. When you see a younger woman with an older man, you can rest assured, she's not going out with him for the sex.

3. Sexually, it is the men who go "over the hill" as they approach forty and fifty, while women are in fact in their sexual prime. This may be one of the reasons women sometimes choose men ten or more years their junior.

4. Psychologically, men often go over the hill much sooner than women—because of job burnout, and/or bitterness for having had to pay child support or alimony, while many women are optimistic because they are just beginning a career.

5. So who is over the hill?

15

Fifteen Ways to Leave Your Lover

Okay. You've made up your mind. You've decided that you really want to get rid of him. But it's easier said than done. Just when you begin to end it, all sorts of worries arise in your mind, and you think, "I just can't do it." The following suggestions may help you to set the wheels in motion.

1. Challenge Your "Can'ts" with "Why Nots?"

We don't realize how we can place ourselves under arrest with our own words. Every time we say "I can't," whether we say it aloud or only in our mind, we "hear" ourselves, and our unconscious mind interprets it as fact. In essence, when we say "I can't," again and again, we are giving ourselves the wrong instructions. But we can reverse the instructions.

Every time the words, "I can't leave him," come to your mind or your lips, immediately challenge those words with the question: "Why not?" Make a list of all the reasons you allegedly can't leave him. Then challenge every one of those reasons with "Why not?" Then, after each reason, write the words, "It's all up to me. Of course I can."

In addition, challenge the answers to your "Why not?" list. For example, if you've been married for fifteen years, and your "Why not?" list includes: "I'm too afraid to be alone," challenge that answer with, "What will happen to me if I am alone that I am afraid of?" Suppose the answer is, "I'll be sad, even depressed." Then say, "What will happen to me if that comes about?" Once you see your answers, you will realize that even though you may have some discomfort for a while, you will be able to cope and eventually to thrive.

You can also help yourself by remembering past fears and how you took action anyway, and lived. For example, you may remember that you were afraid to apply for that job, because you dreaded being turned down. Suppose you did get turned down. What happened? Did you die? Of course not. You were disappointed, but you continued to persevere until eventually you landed a job. Think of other times when your fears proved to be greater than their power to harm you. Perhaps you were afraid to move from a former home into a new neighborhood, and it worked out just fine; or you were afraid to learn to use a computer, and now you are a whiz; and so on. Think of anything that you did, big or small, that you once thought you could not do. Then write, "Of course I can leave him."

As you continue to challenge every "can't" with a "Why not?" you will quickly realize that indeed you can get rid of him, and the decision is in your hands, not in the hands of some mysterious force out there.

2. Remember Your Possibilities

Some women are so used to being dependent upon a husband or a boyfriend that they honestly believe that if the man in their lives were gone, they would not be able to survive. I challenge you to remember your possibilities. For one thing, you do live in America. Let me explain.

I have a habit of writing in the margins of books as I read them. In a sense, this writing activity allows me to answer back, as I read what the author has to say. I was recently reading a book written by Dr. Susan Forward, *Men Who Hate Women and the Women Who Love Them*, when I came across a passage quoting a woman who was telling Dr. Forward about her mistreatment by her husband. She says:

> Jeff kept me penniless, but he'd spend anything on himself—a boat, new skis, new cars, the best tennis rackets, the best running shoes, custom-made suits and shirts. Meantime, I drove an old wreck of a car. If I needed new shoes, he'd blow his stack and say I was sucking him dry. I kept thinking he should have been ashamed to have anyone see me in that car, but he just blamed me and said it was my fault for not keeping it up properly.[1]

My note in the margin reads: "Why don't you leave him? This is America! There are endless possibilities here."

What did I mean? In short, she was not stranded in the Brazilian rain forest; nor was she abandoned in the Saharan desert with only Jeff to depend on. She could pick herself up and walk out—and start her own life. As unsettling as such a move might be, would it not be better than for her to endure daily anger and humiliation, as she continues to live in the dependent, regressive, and, indeed, self-imposed state of childhood? And what could be more uncomfortable than this?

How ridiculous to sit there and feel sorry for herself because she must drive "an old wreck of a car," when her husband buys the best "tennis rackets, running shoes, and custom-made shirts." Are husbands now our parents? Is there no recourse but to sit by and whine, or to passively tolerate the treatment? Of course not. The fact is, we do live in America (if you are a European reader, your country is equally civilized, so the same applies to you). There are opportunities for women. It's a matter of taking some initiative—if you want to—if you choose to be the master of your own destiny.

3. Realize That Solitude and Freedom Are Priceless Gifts, Not Punishments—and Then Do It

Many women are afraid to leave a man because they dread the thought of being alone. But most often, the very thing they fear may be exactly what they need the most—precious, solitary time to think, to feel, and to just be.

If the thought of sleeping alone, of waking up alone, of living alone, fills you with apprehension, take courage. Once you try it, you'll find it can be the best gift you could give yourself.

When you sleep alone and free yourself of the negative energy of your previous bedfellow, you will find yourself waking up in the morning with a new feeling of refreshment. Why? When you sleep with a negative person, his hostile spirit and your reaction to it can drain your energy—all night long. You wake up feeling enervated instead of revitalized. You don't believe me? Wait until you see how much more energy you will have in the morning once you stop sleeping with that negative man.

There are more bonuses to waking up alone. How delightful it is to make that first cup of brewed coffee—to smell it from the shower and to know that you can linger over the morning paper until *you* decide to get a move on—because there will be no intruding voice to disturb your choices of tranquility, your peaceful routine.

How invigorating to be able to decide, on a whim, at six o'clock on a spring morning, as you wake up to the sound of chirping birds, to go for a walk or a run and greet the rising sun as you inhale the intoxicating aroma of the mimosa trees. "How lucky I am to be alive," you think. "How happy I am to be what I want in myself," you rejoice. And you are higher than you have ever been in your life.

And the rest of the day, and evening too, are yours to enjoy. With no one there to distract you—no one to turn on the television when you don't want it on, no one to demand that you make him dinner, do this chore, answer this question—finally, you can be your own woman. If you please, you can just sit and watch the rain from the window, as it pounds against the pavement and brushes the trees, and you can let your mind drift wherever it may go.

On the weekends, if it pleases you, you are no longer obligated to share your precious free time. You can go places alone—to think. How priceless is the opportunity to walk along the shoreline of a nearly deserted beach and look out at the endless ocean. Just watching the billowing waves that seem to go on to infinity can give you a new outlook on life—it can put you in touch with eternity. You can walk away understanding, at least partially, what it means to surrender to the will of the universe.

Oh, the beauty of solitude. No matter where you live—whether it be in a modest apartment that you can keep as neat or as messy as you please, or a large country home that you can fill with items you've collected from your travels, whether it be a small icebox that you keep empty all the time, or a large refrigerator stacked with your favorite goodies, it is home-sweet-home, your home, and no one can take it away from you or tell you what to do in it.

Oh, the precious value of silence. What a gift it can be to not have to hear anyone's voice—or listen to anyone's problems, if you don't want to. And how wonderful it is to know that, at any point in time, you can choose to break your solitude and go out and socialize with people—but the choice is yours, and yours alone.

You will think not once, not twice, but a hundred times before you give up your solitude and freedom. In fact, some man is going to have to make you an offer you can't refuse before you even consider trading your independence for a life with him. It's going to have to be really worth your while.

4. Practice Visualization, and Then Do It

It has been demonstrated time and again that mental picturing, or visualization, works. Athletes are able to improve their performance skills by as much as fifty percent, without ever picking up a ball or a racquet, or moving a muscle. Just by repeatedly running through the movements ahead of time in their minds, they are able to make a major difference in their performance.

If you have been thinking about leaving the man in your life, but are afraid that when the time comes you will retreat in fear, you can help yourself with mental picturing. Play a movie of the scene ahead of time. Include all the details—where you will be standing, what you will be wearing, the expression on his face, and so forth.

Decide exactly what you will say, and what his possible reaction will be. Then see yourself answering his reaction with firmness and resolve. Imagine yourself thinking of backing down—of being tempted to weaken—and then picture yourself suddenly becoming angry that you were about to retreat, and imagine yourself becoming even stronger and following through. See yourself being happy once he is gone, and imagine yourself catching every temptation to weaken, just the way you would catch a rubber ball. Picture yourself looking at that temptation and identifying it, and throwing it back—saying, "No. I'm not going to fall into that trap again."

Play this movie over and over again in your mind. Then, when you feel you've had enough practice, lower the boom on him. This time it will work. You'll see.

5. Use Psychological Judo, and Then Do It

Many women want to leave a man, but they just can't seem to find the right time to do it. One way to do it is to let him do it. In judo terms, use his own force against him, or let him "throw himself." Let me explain.

As a former judo player (brown belt in Kodokan judo—a sport I took up immediately after my divorce as a positive outlet for my energy), I learned how to throw the biggest, the strongest, the most powerful men—not by using my own force, but by using their force against them. In fact, my favorite throw, "tomoe-nage," is a classic example of this method.

You and your opponent have a grip on each other's *gis* (thick fighting uniforms) and are walking around in semicircles, waiting for a chance to throw each other. You push your opponent hard, and without thinking he pushes back—it is a natural reaction. The moment he does that, in a flash, you place your foot on his stomach and fall on your back, while you lift his body in cooperation with its already-forward force—helping him to fly through the air, over your head.

Time and again, I've succeeded with this throw—catapulting men up to a hundred pounds heavier than myself through the air. You can do this with a man you want to get rid of by simply waiting for the next time he starts an argument with you; and then, instead of defending yourself or resolving the fight, go with the force. Agree with him—about how bad you are, or how bad the relationship is, and end it. He'll never know what hit him, and before you know it, you're free and clear. Then when he tries to get back with you, stand your ground. You'll be out of a bad situation and he will have done the work for you!

6. Two-Step (Not Twelve-Step) Your Way Out

While it's always nice to get support, and to provide ourselves with a buffer before we make a radical change in our lives, sometimes it's better to just take the old-fashioned way and go cold turkey. Instead of going to a support group or to therapy, or instead of analyzing the thing to death, bite the bullet and cut it cold. In other words, do the two-step instead of the twelve-step. Step one: get tough. Step two: get out!

People do all sorts of seemingly impossible things without the help of others, when they are determined to do so. In fact—all the special stop-smoking programs notwithstanding—ninety-five percent of the smokers who actually quit do so on their own, without any outside source of help whatsoever.[2] Are you surprised? I'm not. I *never* underestimate the power of the human will. You'd be amazed by what you can do once you *decide* to do it.

And what stops you from amputating the relationship from your life the way you would amputate a gangrenous arm or leg? Fear of psychological pain. But will emotional pain really kill you? Of course not.

The fact is, when it comes to psychological growth, more often than not the adage "no pain, no gain" applies. You must endure some growing pains if you want things to change. But are they really pains? Are they not in essence just a new form of concentrated energy—a temporary loss of the security of our daily, but perhaps stultifying, routine?

Most often, you have to give something up in order to get something. For a time, you may feel empty and uncertain as to your direction, but it is a necessary time. As you go through the period of deprivation, as you realize that once the man left, you did not die—in fact you survived and even thrived—your inner strength will increase and you will realize that you can do other difficult things too. You will find yourself being more willing to take other chances that require temporary discomfort.

Before you know it, you'll see a change in your pattern of thinking. Instead of choosing the easier path, the path of least resistance, more and more often you'll choose more promising roads—ones that will lead you to greater success in every area of your life. Soon, as a matter of course, when confronted with apparent obstacles in life, instead of crumbling you will rise to the occasion and overcome.

All well and good. But how do you handle the actual pain? How do you cope with the very real emotions that will assail you, once he is gone? The answer is cooperation.

Don't try to escape, avoid, or deny the pain. Instead, flow with it—join it. Lie on the couch and let yourself feel it. Say out loud, "Yes, this really hurts." Tune into its heartbeat. Dance to its music rather than outside of it. Go with the rhythm of its tide rather than against it.

You'll feel like the cowboys in the country-and-western songs who lament over lost loves. It hurts, or it is just an intense feeling that seems like pain—but there's a high with it, a feeling that you've gone to the depths and have survived—and have freed yourself from anger and fear. Soon you will begin to feel stronger, more independent, like a champion.

7. Make Up a Balance Sheet, and Then Do It

Maybe you're not really sure you want to leave him. Thoughts keep popping into your head, such as, "He's not bad all the time—he does have some good qualities." Well, it's time to know, to find out how you really feel; and then, if it's a bluff, call it.

Make up a balance sheet of the good and the bad—the pleasure and the pain. Be openly honest. Then see which side outweighs the other. If you see that the pain is much more than the pleasure, the answer is clear. It's time to get out! (See p. 203 for an example of this balance sheet.)

8. Pursue a Goal, and Then Do It

One of the most common reasons a woman finds it difficult to leave a man is that she has made the mistake of building her life around him. She has no real goal in life except to keep her relationship intact. Small wonder she finds herself in fear and trembling at the mere thought of confronting him. No wonder she is so angry at the thought of having to live life without him. Who wouldn't be upset if her very life were about to walk out the door?

You may not have completely built your life around a man, but, even so, he may have come to dominate a lot of your time, so much so that you have neglected your personal wants or goals. One of the best ways to give yourself the strength you need to walk away from that man is to rediscover what you really want to do with your life, and then start to do it—if necessary, in small steps.

Ask yourself to think wildly: "What is it that I've always wished I could do?" If nothing comes to you, put it this way: "Is there anything I really would have liked to have accomplished or become, but didn't?" An answer will come to you. "I always wanted to become proficient in jazz dancing," or "I always dreamed of playing the piano," or "I wished I could have become a lawyer, but I was afraid it was too much work."

More than one idea will probably pop up. Choose one for the moment—the idea that is most exciting to you, and also the goal that you feel you can begin to pursue immediately.

For example, you may want to become a lawyer, but at the moment you have three young children and very little money. You would have to take out a tremendous bank loan to go back to school—and baby-sitting would be very difficult. So you put that goal aside temporarily, and pursue a lesser goal—jazz dancing. It's much easier to get a sitter once a week than to work around the obstacles mentioned above.

One step at a time has been the secret of many self-help organizations, among them AA. It is a formula that seems to work very well. Take the first step by making some phone calls. If it's jazz dancing, call some local dance studios and find out the schedule and the prices. Arrange for a sitter. Set up your first dance session. Whatever the goal, taking the first step will greatly empower you.

If you've chosen a goal that is dear to your heart, you'll be amazed to see how motivated you will be in pursuing it—even in the face of obstacles. Once you accomplish one goal, you will be energized to pursue the next, and the next. You will tackle bigger and bigger goals and will gain more and more strength.

Before you know it, that unnecessary man will drop from you like a scab from an old wound; and if he doesn't drop off of his own will, you'll "pick him off." He will simply have lost his function as a substitute for your finding your own self.

9. Make a List of Your Assets, and Then Do It

Leaving that man may be more terrifying than it has to be—because you're not taking into account what you have going for you. Take the time to think about abilities you have that can eventually earn you money—and, indeed, a better relationship someday. Ask yourself, "What is it that I am talented in and enjoy doing?" Your next question will be, "How can I turn this ability into something that people need?" This magical combination—your talent and consumer demand—will become profitable, if you put the combination out into the marketplace.

When you come to think of it, anyone who makes money does that. Writers have talent to write, and they write books that people want and/or need to read. They enjoy their work because they are using their talent to help people, and, at the same time, they make money because they are meeting a need.

Merchants do the same. A businessman may open up a boat shop because he loves being in a nautical atmosphere and has a flair for boats. He also wants to make money. People come to his shop to buy boats because they want to enjoy their vacations on the water. He loves his work so much that he gives them special service—and he beats his competitors, some of whom have gone into the business, not because they love it, but just because they want to make money.

You see the formula: Do what you love to do and are talented in doing—and give people what they want and/or need.

People in your life are assets too. Think of everyone you know who is even remotely in your corner. List all the relatives, friends, and acquaintances who could possibly be counted on to offer you moral or other support—no matter how little. Added up, it will come to a lot.

First, list the people who you could call, those who would take five minutes to talk to you if you were feeling lonely or depressed. Now list the people who you believe would be willing to spend some time with you—perhaps three hours to go to a movie, or to come over and help you to accomplish a chore. Then think of one person you know who would come through for you in a pinch—someone you could count on. Chances are you'll be surprised to find that you are not really alone.

Your skills and strengths and the people in your corner added together are invaluable assets. Don't undermine them. They are the solid rock of the foundation that makes you a self-sufficient person. Once you realize that you have assets of your own, you will be less terrified of leaving that man.

10. Improve Your Self-Image: Get in Shape, and Then Do It

We are all very critical of our own physical appearance, and sometimes this self-criticism prevents us from leaving a man. We tell ourselves, "I'm too fat. Nobody else would go for me," or "I'm too old—my time is passed," or "I've never been sexy—and I really look dumpy now. Forget it."

But you don't have to feel that way. You can turn it around. There are things that will bring about an immediate change in your appearance and your thinking, and things that will take a little longer. Let's start with the immediate, because you'll need them to energize you for the things that will take a little longer.

If you're badly out of shape, you are probably so depressed that you don't really believe there's any hope of getting a beautiful body again. In order to lift your spirits, before even starting on the workout and diet plan, I want you to do a few things that will net instant results and will remind you that you've still "got it."

First, go for a makeover. Call the nearest major department store and ask for the cosmetics department. Find out if they give makeovers. Often, they do, and they are free. You are not obligated to buy the makeup that they use in the makeover unless you are pleased with the results.

Another idea is to call a photographer and ask him to put you in touch with his makeup artist. Then call the makeup artist and ask for a consultation. Look at her portfolio. Then ask what changes she would suggest as to your hair and makeup. If you get a good feeling about her, go for it. It's daring but exciting, and it just may change your entire image of yourself.

Most women can benefit greatly from professional help in the area of bringing out the best in their physical beauty. In fact, the movie and television stars that you see got a lot of help. Most of them looked a lot different when they first started acting.

Your next step will be to consult a fashion coordinator. Again, a large department store should do the trick—one that has a healthy interest in fashion. Bloomingdale's, Lord and Taylor, Bergdorf Goodman, or Saks Fifth Avenue are examples. Such stores have a special service where you can consult with a fashion coordinator who will help you to select clothing suited to your physique, your personality, and your budget. You can achieve a whole new look in a matter of hours.

I go to the Fifth Avenue Club in Saks Fifth Avenue, where I sit and sip Perrier, while the coordinator runs around and collects clothing and accessories that she believes will look great on me. There is no charge for the service, and there is no obligation to buy anything.

After you've gotten these lifts, you will be ready to tackle your body. It doesn't matter whether you're fifteen, fifty, or a hundred pounds overweight. You can transform your body in less than a year. In fact, you can look better than you've ever looked in your life!

By using the body-shaping techniques outlined in my fitness plan, you can reshape your body and perfect it beyond its natural form. Let me tell you what I did for myself, for my sister, and for thousands of other women.

Even at my thinnest, I never had the ideal shape. My hips were too big, my waist was too thick, my legs were rather shapeless, and my arms were too thin. But I thought I looked great, because I did get a reaction from men when I would strut on the beach in my 1960s bikini. In fact, I would never have embarked upon a fitness program had I not started to turn into a mound of cellulite after I got married. At the same time, my sister had evolved into a fatter version of myself. I decided to do something about it—for both of us.

In three to six months' time, if you follow the routine in my best-selling book, *The Fat-Burning Workout*, you too can have a brand-new body. The best part is, you don't have to devote every waking moment to exercise. All it takes are four or five twenty-to-thirty-minute sessions weekly. I guarantee the results, but you must follow the routine exactly.

If you're only ten pounds overweight, you'll reach your goal much sooner. If you're a hundred pounds overweight, it will take a little longer—perhaps a year. But no matter. With time and effort, you'll get there just the same. And you won't just lose weight. You'll reshape your body and replace fat with feminine muscularity.

Take a hard look at yourself and set a target date for getting in shape. Once you set a date, make up your mind to leave your man on that date. You will have the confidence to do it, because getting in shape helps to change your self-image. Finally, you'll have the courage to give him his walking papers.

11. Cross Water or Go to a Luxury Health Spa to Clear Your Mind—Then Come Back and Get Rid of Him!

You may want to leave your boyfriend or husband, but you may still be a little confused as to how and when to do it. For some reason, I have always found that crossing water clears the mind.

If you can afford it, get on a plane and go anywhere that crosses water—preferably to an island, where you can then be surrounded by water. This act, in and of itself, can be a symbolic or psychological distancing—a stepping away from the problem.

While you're on the plane, rather than getting into a conversation with your seatmate, try letting your mind run free. Relax. As the plane soars through the air, as it crosses water, you will find yourself thinking new, freer thoughts. You'll begin to see your life in a different perspective. As you arrive at your destination, completely relax. Take in the new environment. With the pressure off, things will soon become clear.

By the time you arrive home, to your amazement, you'll have a much clearer idea of what you want to do and how to do it. I have no way of proving that this works. I only know it does—not just for me, but for many people I've interviewed.

If you can't or won't cross water, going to a luxury health spa can be just as effective when it comes to clearing the mind. A week or even a long weekend of pampering can work wonders to help you remember who you are and what you want out of life.

For ultimate pampering, choose a spa that specializes in massages of all sorts (total-body, cranial, foot, hand, and so on). Be sure that they offer a combination of herbal wraps, facials, scalp treatment, aromatherapy (treatment with oils), hydrotherapy (underwater massage), and thalassotherapy (treatment with seawater and seaweed). You don't have to get every treatment, but you want to be able to pick and choose among a variety.

If you want to work out at the same time, you will want to choose one that offers a balance of fitness activities and pampering treatments. I recommend that you skim through Pam Sarnoff's *The Ultimate Spa Book* (New York: Warner, 1989) and select a spa that is conveniently located and that is within your price range. Then call the spa and ask for brochures to be sent to you. I've been to La Costa, Cal-A-Vie, and Canyon Ranch (Arizona branch) and loved all three.

When you go to the spa, let your mind run free. As you're being pampered and preened, suddenly it will come to you: "I deserve to be nurtured and loved." You will find that, as you return home, a new resolve has been born.

12. Get a Taste of the Single Life—and Then Get Rid of Him!

Whether you are married or just going out with someone, you can get a taste of the single life without actually cheating (committing adultery).

Go out with your girlfriends and flirt a little. Let yourself see that there are plenty of men out there who would be more than willing to pay proper attention to you.

Don't stop there. Flirt at work. Go to lunch with a male colleague. Get the feeling of what it will be like to be treated with respect and special attention. You'll like it.

Arrange a "singles" vacation, either alone or with a girlfriend. I like Club Med. (Avoid the clubs that have family plans. Your goal is to meet single people so you can get a taste of the fun and excitement you've been missing.) Club Med is nearly a guaranteed place to have a good laugh and meet available men at the same time—and it isn't all that expensive, as far as vacations go. The best part is, everything is included in the price—food, air fare, the works.

What? You're getting depressed just thinking of it? You're saying, "What's the use? There's nothing out there. I'll never meet anyone like Joe again." Well, I'm glad to say you're right. Of course you won't meet anyone like him. You'll meet someone better. Let me explain.

You see, up until now, you tasted vanilla ice cream and you loved it. You said, "Wow. I love vanilla. I would never want to live without vanilla ice cream." But that was because you didn't know any better. That was before you tasted strawberry, chocolate, butter pecan, and pistachio.

The fact is, you have no idea how wonderful you will feel about that unknown man who is coming around the corner. After all, you didn't know how you would feel about the last man you fell in love with (the man you are with now) until you met him, did you? Your real life will begin the day you get rid of him.

13. Practice Cognitive Self-Therapy, and Then Do It

Chances are you really want to leave that man, but every time you think of leaving, you are assaulted by fear thoughts that prevent you from taking action. Cognitive self-therapy will enable you to catch these thoughts before they depress you into believing that you are powerless. Here's how it works. You teach yourself to engage in rational thinking.

You have just begun to pick up the phone to call your boyfriend of six months to inform him that you no longer want to see him, but before you can dial the number you experience an awful feeling.

a) Ask yourself, "What am I feeling?" (Identify the emotion.) You decide it's fear.

b) Ask yourself what thought triggered the fear. You decide that you had thought, "If I make this call, this will be the end. I will be completely alone."

c) Next, ask yourself what will happen if you are alone. You think:

I will be sad.
I will cry.
I will be depressed.
I'll never meet another man.
I'll shrivel up and die.

d) Now challenge each statement on your list (c, above) with rational thinking. Ask yourself, "Do I really believe that? How likely is it that it will happen?" On a scale of one to ten, rate how much you believe that each will happen. Then place the number next to each thought—indicating the probability of such a thought: 0 = no probability; 10 = one hundred percent probability. For example:

I will be sad.	9
I will cry.	9
I will be depressed.	8
I'll never meet another man.	2
I'll shrivel up and die.	0

e) Now cancel out the things on your list that you've decided have a zero possibility. Out goes "shrivel up and die"!

f) Now look at each item on your list and say to yourself, "What will happen if that happens to me?" Then answer the question. Do this for each item listed, even if the chance of it happening is remote.

I will be sad.	So I'll feel the angst and cry in my beer. I may call some friends.
I will cry.	When I've cried myself out, I'll blow my nose and get busy with my life.
I'll be depressed.	I'll call my mother. I'll speak to a therapist. I'll go to a fun movie and forget my woes for a while.
I'll never meet another man.	So I'll enjoy my single life. I'll develop my talents and have adventures—and will anticipate the mystery of the future. But at least I'll have my self-respect.

g) Finally, ask yourself: "Are the things that I ultimately fear capable of destroying me?" You will quickly realize that they are really dreadful imaginings created by the fear itself.

What is the point of cognitive self-therapy? You can understand, redirect, and reshape your thinking, rather than let your fearful mind-set control you. You can get a grip on yourself so that you can take action which will improve your life.

Once you discover that the way you view the world is created by your thoughts, you will begin to realize how much power you have to actually change the way you feel. In essence, you will find that you can "unparalyze" yourself when you want to take action, by challenging your unreasonable, automatic thoughts rather than simply letting them take you over.

The end result of such practiced control is release from the debilitating bondage of fear, and the freedom to decide what you want to do with your life.[3]

14. Go for a One-Session Therapy Boost, and Then Do It

Many therapists agree that a single session may be all that is required to solidify a person's resolve to leave a destructive relationship.[4] In fact, contrary to former popular belief, when a person is facing a difficult crisis, the urgency of the situation is often motivation enough to help that person change very quickly.

Of course a single session would not work to cure more deeply rooted problems, such as personality disorders or neuroses of any kind. In addition, it will of course not be enough to master self-understanding skills. (You can increase self-understanding in one visit but not master the skills of self-understanding.) However, it may well be enough to give you the impetus to make the move. Whether to seek further therapy can be a completely different decision, once the leaving is accomplished.

15. Go to Regular Therapy, and Then Do It

I never cease to be amazed at how many people shy away from therapy when they could gain so much by going: peace of mind, increased self-esteem, greater joy in living, improved life-style, and an increase in both personal and professional gratification.

Many people resist going to therapy because they believe taking such action would prove, once and for all, that something is wrong with them. However, the opposite is true.

Statistics show that there is no evidence that people who are in therapy are any less balanced than those who are not. In fact, mental health professionals agree that those who go to therapy are generally mentally healthier than those who do not go, because people who go are striving for even greater mental health.

Who should go to see a therapist? Not just those who obviously need it—the severely depressed, the suicidal, the violent, and the out-of-control—but those who feel stuck, who seem to repeat a pattern of self-defeating behavior.

Your therapist will provide a "hospital for your mind," a place where your psychological needs can be met and where you can slowly begin to heal—a place where you can take yourself apart, see what you are made of, and then slowly and lovingly put yourself back together again.[5] In therapy, you can finally let your hair down. You can express any emotion or desire without fear of being judged or condemned.

In the end, when you confront the problems of life, you will be able to say, "What do *I* think of this," instead of being compelled to ask, "What would *my mother* say?" or "What would *my father* think of this?" In short, effective therapy will help you to finally be yourself.

Let's not undermine the fact that going to therapy takes courage. It is scary. You will be treading on unknown territory— ground that you cannot see, but that you walk on twenty-four hours a day—the ground of your mind. But to avoid therapy out of fear is as foolish as it is to avoid a medical doctor out of fear—both can cost you extended and unnecessary pain.

For example, if a man cannot remove a splinter from his toe and he notices that it is becoming infected, he can choose to either go to the doctor immediately, or wait in the hope that it will go away. If he goes before it becomes serious, he can save himself the fever and the time off from work that will accompany a serious infection.

The analogy can be used when it comes to therapy. Some people are smart enough to see a psychologist while still in the "splinter" stage. Others wait until there is a serious infection—and they have disturbed major portions of their life.

What a pity to suffer needlessly, to continue in old, self-destructive patterns, and to miss out on a wonderful and fulfilling life, just because you were afraid to go to therapy.[6]

Different Kinds of Therapy

There is a great deal of confusion regarding the different kinds of therapy, but this puzzlement can be quickly resolved. The kind of therapy practiced by Sigmund Freud was psychoanalysis. In this type of therapy, the patient usually lies on a couch and attends therapy two or three times a week. The therapist says little, because his goal is to get his patient to reveal things about himself or herself from the past—as far back as possible. This kind of therapy is expensive, it takes many years, and in my opinion, is not usually very effective.

Psychotherapy is different. Its goal is to deal with the problems the patient is having in the present—problems in coping with specific life situations. Psychotherapy includes many types of therapy within itself, and to get into the branches would require a book in itself. Suffice it to say that the goal of a psychotherapist is to help you to deal with the present, and to go into past experiences only as they help to achieve that goal.

Finally, there are psychiatrists, who are medical doctors and have specialized in psychology in addition to medicine. They are the only practitioners in the field of psychology who can prescribe drugs. For this reason, psychiatrists often deal with patients such as schizophrenics, the severely depressed, and those needing medication in order to function in daily life

Patients not needing prescription drugs also see psychiatrists. However, since it is their training to think in terms of possible medication as a way of coping with mental problems, I fear that psychiatrists may be too quick to prescribe tranquilizing drugs to patients who might be able to cope quite well without them. Since, in my opinion, medication is an extreme last resort, if I were interviewing a psychiatrist with the view of possibly becoming his patient, I would be sure of his view on prescription drugs. Unless I felt that he was extremely conservative in that area, I would not choose him as my doctor. In fact, out of all three branches, psychoanalysis à la Freud, psychotherapy, or psychiatry—I would take the middle ground and choose a psychotherapist.

Choosing the Right Therapist

First, check your psychotherapist's credentials. Ask where he or she went to school and what hospital and organization affiliations he or she has. If it checks out, you can begin. It should be obvious to you, after one session you have been helped. A good therapist is dedicated to helping people—and is not just doing a job with clinical expertise. In addition, you should feel that your therapist likes you, and that you like him or her (in fact, studies show that success in psychotherapy is closely connected to strong and growing mutual respect and liking between the psychologist and the patient).

The right therapist is the one who makes you feel "heard," one who seems compassionate and understanding. It will not take more than one session to determine this. If, by the time you walk out that door, you sense that something is not right, trust your instincts. Try another therapist.

After a few sessions, a good therapist will make you feel that you are okay—just the way you are, with all your imperfections. It is only in this atmosphere that growth and change are possible.

In addition, you should usually feel as if you have gained

something when you leave the therapist's office. If your therapist just sits there with a blank stare and lets you do all the talking, giving an occasional grunt or "uh huh," you are wasting your money. Your therapist should actively guide you along the path of mental health—and help you to challenge your own self-destructive tendencies.

Finally, therapy should not last twenty years. Such endless psychoanalysis is a luxury that most of us cannot afford; and in the bargain, I don't think it's helpful. The goal of therapy should be to help you cope with life without a therapist—or, to put it another way, to help you function as your own therapist. This can usually be accomplished in anywhere from a few months to a few years.

Where Do You Start Looking?

One of the best ways to find a good therapist is to go on the recommendation of a person who has been to him or her, and who has obviously been helped.

Another idea is, if you are a member of a health plan that covers therapy, or a portion of it, you can start by looking in the health plan directory of doctors for psychologists who are within the plan. You can speak with several over the telephone and limit it to the ones who make you feel most comfortable. Then, all other things being equal, make an appointment with the one who is located most conveniently. If that doesn't work out, go for the next one, and so on.

It may seem like a time-consuming proposition, but in perspective, it is worth the effort. The direction of the rest of your life can be positively influenced to a great extent by the right therapist.

NOTES

1. Susan Forward and Susan Torres, *Men Who Hate Women and the Women Who Love Them* (New York: Bantam, 1986), p. 73.

2. Stanton Peele, *Diseasing of America* (Lexington, Mass.: Lexington Books, 1989), p. 174.

3. Rick Suarez, Roger C. Mills, and Darlene Stewart, *Sanity, Insanity, and Common Sense* (New York: Ballantine Books, 1987). The authors discuss these ideas and give further information about them on pp. 29–77.

4. Daniel Coleman, *New York Times*, 2 May 1992.

5. Leston Havens, *A Safe Place* (New York: Ballantine Books, 1989), p. 4. These words are paraphrased from Dr. Havens's description of the function of a good therapist.

6. Carl R. Rogers, *On Becoming a Person* (Boston: Houghton Mifflin, 1961), p. 44. This excellent, most readable classic contains such simply expressed wisdom that anyone either contemplating therapy or in therapy will gain comfort and insight—and will be encouraged to make the most of therapy.

16

Try a Simple Prayer of Faith!

I've saved this one for last, because it is the most simple, yet perhaps the most effective method of all: a simple prayer of faith.

You don't have to be a religious person; you can even have doubts that God even exists. It doesn't matter. All you have to do is ask God, in your mind, to have his will in your relationship situation. Tell him how you feel exactly—that you are feeling trapped in a relationship that you believe is hurting you. Tell him that you don't know how to get out—and that it would take a miracle to get out. Ask him to have his will in your life—and to deliver you from this negative relationship.

Then relax and see what happens. Miraculously, something will happen that will facilitate the ending of your negative relationship. The event, when it occurs, may at first appear to be a coincidence, and may seem to have nothing to do with your prayer, but in the end, you will be out of your relationship.

Once you are out of the trap, whenever you are feeling lonely and discouraged, or whenever you are feeling tempted to crawl back, shoot up a quick prayer (your thoughts are prayers when directed to God), and ask God to help you. Once again, ask him to have his will in your life. Ask him to prevent you from making a mistake—from going back into the mire. Ask him to fill your life with love and with positive relationships, so that you are no longer lonely and depressed.

Don't worry that you may feel foolish praying—especially if you're not really sure that God exists, or that he is interested in your personal problems. Just talk to Him by a simple act of faith. You may be amazed to see how much it helps.

A FINAL NOTE

It takes courage to make a change. But making a change is the only way you can hope to have a better life. Making a change is like deciding to bet on yourself. It's like saying, "I believe I'm worth it. I believe I have the right to be."

The fact that you picked up this book indicates that you love yourself at least a little, because even if you merely skimmed it, you've taken a first step.

To be completely honest with yourself is one of the most difficult yet most valuable things you can do for yourself: difficult, because the truth hurts—valuable, because it is only after the truth is faced that change can take place.

But once you face that truth, and take that action, you will have an inner strength that cannot be shaken—a power that will come from the fact that you knew what you had to do and you did it—and this will hold true whether you've done it by yourself or with the help of a professional.

I'd love to hear from you. Tell me your story. Tell me if this book has helped you or a friend. Tell me what you wish I would write for you next. If you enclose a stamped, self-addressed envelope, I promise to personally reply.

Joyce L. Vedral
P. O. Box A 433
Wantagh, NY 11793-0433

BIBLIOGRAPHY

Books Cited in the Text

Adler, Alfred. *What Life Should Mean to You.* New York: Putnam, Perigree Books, 1958.

Alexander, Franz G. *Fundamentals of Psychoanalysis.* New York: Norton, 1963.

Alexander, Franz G., and Hugo Staub. *The Criminal, the Judge, and the Public.* Glencoe, Ill.: Falcon Wing Press, 1956.

Anderson, Walter. *The Greatest Risk of All.* Boston: Houghton Mifflin, 1988.

Bateson, Mary Catherine. *Composing a Life.* New York: Penguin, 1990.

Boschung, Herbert T., Jr., James D. Williams, Daniel W. Gotshall, David K. Cadwell, and Melba C. Cadwell. *The Audubon Society Field Guide to North American Fishes, Whales and Dolphins.* New York: Knopf, 1983.

Branden, Nathaniel. *The Psychology of Self-Esteem.* New York: Bantam, 1969.

———. *The Psychology of Romantic Love.* New York: Bantam, 1980.

———. *How to Raise Your Self-Esteem.* New York: Bantam, 1987.

———. *Honoring the Self.* New York: Bantam, 1983.

Campbell, Joseph, with Bill Moyers. *The Power of the Myth.* Edited by Betty Sue Flowers. New York: Doubleday, 1988.

Cowen, Connel, and Melvyn Kinder. *Smart Women, Foolish Choices.* New York: Crown, 1985.

Eisenhower, Dwight D. *At Ease.* New York: Doubleday, 1967.

Ellis, Albert, and Robert A. Harper. *A New Guide to Rational Living.* No. Hollywood, Calif.: Wilshire Book Company, 1961.

Forward, Susan, and Susan Torres. *Men Who Hate Women and the Women Who Love Them.* New York: Bantam, 1986.

Forward, Susan, and Craig Buck. *Obsessive Love.* New York: Bantam, 1991.

Friedman, Sonia. *Men Are Just Desserts.* New York: Warner Books, 1983.

Hauk, Paul A. *Overcoming Worry and Fear.* Philadelphia: Westminster Press, 1975.

Havens, Leston. *A Safe Place.* New York: Ballantine Books, 1989.

Hazleton, Lesley. *The Right to Feel Bad.* New York: Ballantine Books, 1984.

Hindy, Carl G., J. Conrad Schwartz, and Archie Brodsky. *If This Is Love, Why Do I Feel So Insecure?* New York: Ballantine Books, 1989.

Hite, Shere, with Kate Colleran. *Good Guys, Bad Guys.* New York: Caroll & Graf, 1991.

Horney, Karen. *New Ways in Psychoanalysis.* New York: Norton, 1966.

Jeffers, Susan. *Opening Our Hearts to Men.* New York: Ballantine Books, 1989.

Jung, Carl G. *Memories, Dreams, Reflections.* Edited by Aniela Jaffé. New York: Vintage Books, 1965.

———. *Sychronicity.* Princeton, N.J.: Princeton University Press, 1973.

Kafka, Franz. *The Metamorphosis.* New York: Schocken Books, 1968.

Keen, Sam. *Fire in the Belly: On Being a Man.* New York: Bantam, 1991.

Maslow, Abraham. *Toward a Psychology of Being.* 2d ed. New York: Van Nostrand, 1968.

May, Rollo. *The Courage to Create.* New York: Bantam, 1975.

McGinnis, Alan Loy. *The Power of Optimism.* New York: Harper & Row, 1990.

McGraw, Ali. *Moving Pictures.* New York: Bantam, 1991.

Nir, Yahuda, and Bonnie Maslin. *Loving Men for All the Right Reasons.* New York: Dell, 1982.

Patterson, James, and Peter Kim. *The Day America Told the Truth.* Englewood Cliffs, N.J.: Prentice-Hall, 1991.

Peck, M. Scott. *People of the Lie.* New York: Simon & Schuster, 1983.

Peele, Stanton. *Diseasing of America.* Lexington, Mass.: Lexington Books, 1989.

Penney, Alexandra. *Why Men Stray and Why Men Stay.* New York: Bantam, 1989.

Rogers, Carl R. *On Becoming a Person.* Boston: Houghton Mifflin, 1961.

Sarnoff, Pam Martin. *The Ultimate Spa Book.* New York: Warner Books, 1989.

Schwartz, David J. *The Magic of Self-Direction.* New York: Simon and Schuster, 1965.

Shah, Idries. *The Pleasantries of the Incredible Mulla Nasrudin.* New York: Dutton, 1971.

Siegel, Bernie S. *Love, Medicine & Miracles.* New York: Harper & Row, 1988.

Suarez, Rick, Roger C. Mills, and Darlene Stewart. *Sanity, Insanity, and Common Sense.* New York: Ballantine Books, 1987.

Turner, Tina, with Kurt Loder. *I Tina.* New York: Morrow, 1986.

Vedral, Joyce L. *I Dare You.* New York: Holt, 1983.

————. *Now or Never.* New York: Warner Books, 1986.

————. *The Twelve-Minute Total-Body Workout.* New York: Warner Books, 1989.

————. *The Fat-Burning Workout.* New York: Warner Books, 1991.

————. *Bottoms Up.* New York: Warner Books, 1993.

Walker, Lenore E. *The Battered Woman.* New York: Harper & Row, 1979.

ANNOTATED BIBLIOGRAPHY OF JOYCE VEDRAL BOOKS

Fitness Books

The Fat-Burning Workout (Warner Books, 1991) is a twenty-minute weight-training program that reshapes the body and burns body fat; thirty- and forty-minute plans are provided for those who want to get in shape in record time. A low-fat eating plan is also provided. The workout is done at home with the minimum of equipment (three sets of dumbbells and a bench, or on the edge of a bed or sofa). Gym alternatives are suggested. The book is a *New York Times, Publisher's Weekly,* and *Washington Post* bestseller and has appeared on other bestseller lists as well. For video information, call 1-800-621-7026. Monday through Friday, 9–5, eastern standard time.

The Twelve-Minute Total-Body Workout is an intense exercise program for the busy woman or the beginner. Only twelve minutes a day (very intense minutes) and a pair of three-pound dumbbells are required. The book also provides clear instructions on what to eat in restaurants and hotels, and how to keep in shape while vacationing. It includes a nutritious diet that helps exercisers lose excess body fat without sacrificing good nutrition.

Now or Never (Warner Books, 1986) is a workout that shows women how to replace fat with muscle by working with weights the right way—either at home or in the gym. The exerciser will use slightly heavier weights than in the above books and will need an hour and fifteen minutes, four days a week, to use this program. The results are dramatic.

COMING SOON

Bottoms Up (Warner Books, May 1993) provides a routine that places the emphasis where it's needed: from the bottom up. It provides a routine of seven exercises for the thighs (especially the inner thigh) and hip/buttocks area, five exercises for the abdominal area, and three exercises for the upper body area—with special "wild woman" and "terminator" workouts for those who wish to go the extra mile. The workout combines the exercising of compatible body parts in "intersets," so that the highest muscle quality is achieved without exhaustion, while at the same time, maximum fat is burned. The workout takes 20–35 minutes. New and revolutionary diet information is given, and low-fat eating plans are provided. A special chapter, "It's not a stupid question," is included—where confusions of every sort are cleared up once and for all.

These fitness books can be purchased in major bookstores.

BOOKS FOR TEENS

My Teacher Is Driving Me Crazy (Ballantine Books, 1991). Attention: high-school and junior-high-school students who want to find out how to pass the course and get the best grade possible, no matter what the teacher is like. This book deals with teachers of every kind, including boring, unfair, burned out, out-of-control, and rigid; it talks about wonderful teachers and shows why dedicated teachers remain, despite the difficulties; it gives you insight into why teachers behave the way they do and instruction on how to get fair treatment from them. Joyce Vedral, teaching veteran of twenty-five years, gives away secrets. Learn what goes on behind the scenes; learn how your teachers are treated by *their* superiors!

Boyfriends: Getting Them, Keeping Them, Living without Them (Ballantine Books, 1990) shows the teenage girl how to attract and keep the attention of the guy she has in mind; it suggests ways to make the first move without seeming obvious; it looks into the insecurities of guys and shows girls what is really behind some of their angry words and deeds; it talks about how sex changes the relationship and about why guys sometimes break up with girls shortly after sex enters the picture; it gives advice on what to do in such a situation, and helps girls not only to get over a broken heart, but to find ways to enjoy life even more after the breakup. It helps to build self-confidence and self-esteem.

The Opposite Sex Is Driving Me Crazy (Ballantine Books, 1988) helps you understand why teens of the opposite sex behave the way they do. The book is divided into halves: Girls answer favorite questions posed by boys; boys answer typical questions asked by girls. Covered are such topics as jealousy and cheating, sex, spending time and money, turn-ons and turn-offs, and favorite lectures mothers and fathers give sons and daughters. Teens are helped to realize that they are not "weird"; they are not "rejects"—and they are given ways to deal with even the most cruel behavior of the opposite sex. The tone is humorous, with generous sprinklings of love, wisdom, and common sense.

My Parents Are Driving Me Crazy (Ballantine Books, 1986) gives you, the teenager, insight into the workings of the adult—specifically, the parent mind. It helps you to become more loving, compassionate, and understanding of your parents. Teens who have read the book often report that it has totally changed their relationship with their parents.

I Can't Take It Anymore (Ballantine Books, 1987). In its deepest intent, this is a suicide-prevention guide; this book aims to help all teens learn how to deal with anger, rage, hate, fear, the anguish of rejection, and other negative emotions that otherwise could blight, if not destroy, lives. This guide shows you how to channel such powerful emotions toward affirmative goals you can achieve instead of turning them inward against the self. Many young adults have written that the words from this book have come back to them and helped them to go on when they were feeling down or even having suicidal thoughts.

I Dare You (Ballantine Books, 1983). Here is a *How to Win Friends and Influence People* for teenagers. It motivates you to overcome obstacles and achieve goals, and shows you how to use psychology in dealing with teachers, bosses, and other authorities and friends in order to help make things run more smoothly.

COMING SOON

Teens Are Talking: The Question Game for Young Adults (Ballantine Books, 1992). The book provides thought-provoking, conversation-stimulating questions for teens to ask peers, the opposite sex, parents (and for parents to ask teens), grandparents (and for grandparents to ask teens), and also general questions to ask anybody. The goal of the book is to help teens to gain insight into the thinking and lives of others, and to become more tolerant of others' ideas.

BOOK FOR PARENTS OF TEENS

My Teenager Is Driving Me Crazy (Ballantine Books, 1989) will help you to understand why your teen does and says the things he or she does and says. You will laugh as you read direct quotes from parents and teens, and rejoice in the fact that you are not alone. Topics such as the "wrong crowd," dress, curfews, neglecting responsibilities, sex, drugs, and more are discussed. Encouraging information is given as to what really happens after you deliver all those lectures: Countless teens admit that the very words parents have spoken have come to mind just when they were about to do the wrong thing, and those words stopped them! Advice is given on how to listen first, and then speak; how, when, and why to apologize to your teen; as well as a host of other valuable information.

My Teenager Is Driving Me Crazy and any of the teen books can be ordered by calling the toll-free number at Ballantine Books: 1–800–733–3000.